LIFE TO THE FULLEST IN A TROUBLED WORLD

By Lulu Tira

D1603831

LIFE TO THE FULLEST IN A TROUBLED WORLD

Pictures owned by the author Unless it is indicated, all illustrations by Nikita Sushma, Henrick Vasquez and Lourdes Tira with the assistance of Elizabeth Leonardo

Cover design by Gerry Baclagon Book design by Gerry and Damples Baclagon

Published by Lourdes M. Tira Edmonton, Alberta, Canada

ISBN. Book 978-1-77354 -368-0
eBook 978 -1-77354-369-7

Publication assistance Canada by

PUBLISHING
PageMaster.ca

ENDORSEMENTS

Life to the Fullest in a Troubled World is a great book. I have the privilege of knowing Joy and Lulu since they first joined O.M. Ships but never really felt I knew Lulu until I read this unusual unique book. As I walked with her through the pages and especially saw the photos I felt I was really getting to know this special woman. Her story is such a great testimony to the power and grace of God and the reality of the HOLY Spirit. I hope you will not only read this book but become a proactive distributor.

Dr. George Verwer,
Author, Founder of Operation Mobilization
and OM Ships International Ministry

This book is a courageous presentation of the author's faith journey, living her "ordinary" life in the presence of her extraordinary God. This reflective recollection of her experience with God reveals the robust engagement of both parties: God with his audacious love and power and the author's unrelenting trust in her gracious and miracle-working God, defying human reasoning. The book would not only encourage and inspire readers but also challenge them to know and trust a much bigger God than our understanding would allow.

Dr. Wonsuk Ma, Author,
Dean- College of Theology and Ministry,
Oral. Roberts University, Oklahoma, USA

This book is an account of God's works in saving and transforming lives and in building and developing mission in action. Lulu Tira tells stories bounded by her own personal testimony with biblical reflection along the way as she recounts the dramatic and descriptive way in which God helped her through in her life. This is a testimony of God's intricate way in weaving His plan together including my own salvation in Lulu and Joy's home in Manila in 1979.

Dr.Chris. Wigram, Former OMer,
Ex OMF Director, UK, International Director of the
European Christian Mission, Visiting Lecturer at London
School of Theology and All Nations College

Lulu Tira in her book Life to the Fullest has demonstrated what happens when one's life is fully committed to God and His Word, attentive and obedient to the voice of the Spirit, and displays an unwavering faith in the power of the Gospel to transform lives. I admire her vulnerability and am inspired by her transformation from a girl who battled low self-esteem to a victorious, confident and beautiful royal child of God. Our "kababayan" around the globe (Fillipino Diaspora) will especially appreciate her immigrant story and God's favor and power in her life and ministry.

Lisa Espineli Chinn,
Leadership Mentor, InterVarsity, USA

The sweet presence of the Lord shines through Lulu Tira no matter what continent she steps down on. In the Middle East she has worked beside her husband to share the good news of Jesus, to strengthen and disciple believers, and to help churches for diaspora people put down roots. In Japan with great compassion she has pioneered a ministry to lonely Southeast Asian wives and their families. In the Philippines and in her adopted homeland, Canada, she has calmed up a storm, exhorted congregations from the pulpit, prayed and cried out to the Lord, supported her powerhouse husband--and through it all Lulu has channeled the sweet presence of the Lord.

Dr. Miriam Adeney, Author, Professor,
Seattle Pacific University, USA

Lulu's testimony is passionate, raw, and urgent -- the memoir of a woman who "God set ... on fire to share about Jesus." As she tells us the story of her life, from her childhood in the Philippines to her diasporic missionary work, she overflows with gratitude for God's grace and mercy, as well as showing us her deep faith and "kapwa" (sense of shared inner self). We can see the patterns God has set forth for her, and Lulu graciously shares the Good News of how seekers can find their own path -- one without fear, one with certainty of "who I am", and one that points to a rich and meaningful life in God. I feel strengthened after reading it.

Amanda L. Andrei; Playwright, Los Angeles, California

There are many books about how to draw closer to God or how to pray effectively give you a set of principles without showing how you go about following them. Life to the Fullest pulls back the curtain and invites you to see how Lulu has become an intimate friend of the Lord and a prayer warrior. As she shares her inspiring life story, she shares adventure, heartache, laughter and -- through it all -- God's faithfulness. She does not shy away from recounting mistakes or humbling situations; Lulu's authenticity will be a comfort to those learning to journey and partner with the Lord. Get ready to be blessed!

Katherine Lorance, Lausanne Committee for World Evangelization Young Leaders Group (Praying)

Lulu's unwavering devotion to prayer and her ability to see God's hand in everything is a common thread through this book. Discover Lulu's ability to take a chance meeting and turn it into a spiritual encounter. Her passion for reaching the lost is evident throughout. Her story will bring laughter, tears and joy as the pages unfold. You will be blessed.

Del and Carol Dyck, Elders, Spruce Groove Alliance Church

This book shows the unfolding of God's wonderful plan in a person's life as she relates with Him personally and intimately. Lulu shares her personal testimony in how she is overcoming life's challenges. How do you respond to the goodness of God? How do you react when facing trials and difficulties? How do you deal with your negative emotions like fear and anger or even suicidal tendencies? As you read Lulu's stories, may they give you hope and encouragement in your own life's journey.

Mrs. Bunny Tiangson, Pastor's Wife, Toronto

v

"Lulu", greets us with the challenge to bloom where we are planted. Don't blame circumstances but look to God and overcome in His strength whatever life throws at you. But how do you do that? Lulu shares of her personal experience of being set on fire by God, and it is clear that flame still burns brightly in her. The teaching on leading this transformed life is not simply dry theory but rather more a description of the life Lulu has known. As you read, you will be encouraged by the many stories of God's faithfulness and challenged for your own life to find a way to be fruitful in Christ despite the weeds that grow around you. Her testimony is not that there are no challenges to overcome but rather that God can see us through, no matter what. We can rest in the goodness of God. An important reminder from Lulu as we make our way through the chaos of Covid-19 at present.

Roberto Bolivar,
Executive Director, PALM Ministry Association

I enjoy reading LIFE to the Fullest, a memoir on Lulu's miraculous life journey. Lulu was a timid village girl and was transformed to become "a handmaiden to the nations". Lulu, aka Mrs. Praise the Lord, shares how she found LIFE and experiences the Truth, Love, Joy, and Peace. This book challenges readers, me included, to rekindle their intimate relationship with LIFE and the Holy Spirit.

Dr. Jacky Lau,
International Worker, C&MA, Canada

This book is a collection of inspiring narratives that enable us to reflect on God's faithfulness, goodness, and love. Narratives are powerful mode of instruction and communication. Lulu beautifully weaves her faith journey with the many lessons she learned along the way. I personally am blessed and encouraged by her stories. I believe many of us will identify with her stories as fellow pilgrims in this world.

Dr. Juliet Uytanlet, Professor, Biblical Seminary of
the Philippines and Asia Graduate School of Theology

This book enlightens, encourages, enkindles and empowers. It shows Faith in the Almighty God and experiencing Him even in mysterious ways that intellect cannot reason out. It presents principles, illustrations and insights to every reader. I recom-mend it to everyone young or old even to those searching meaning of life. It is a must to those in ministry. It is a good source for evangelism, spiritual warfare and deeper spiritual life.I was blessed reading it. I put it into practice at once.

Nene Legson Gima,
Tentmaker, Japan

Singular words flood my memory after reading this up-to-date journey. Vision! Capacity! Availability! Here is servant waiting for the next jet... reaching... occupying. Cutting edge mission employing every strategy. These snippets represent the motion and impact of Lulu Tira...non stop. This autobiography is her story...no holds barred. Be prepared for take off. Fasten your seat belt. These years Joy and Lulu served with Advancing Indigenous Missions were wonderful and incredible!

Rev. Dr. David L. Robbins, Founder and
President of Advancing Indigenous Mission

Lulu's book is such a joy to read. It is particularly inspiring because of the personal testimonies that she shares. This book clearly portrays that we are living in a troubled world, yet we can find hope and victory in the Lord Jesus Christ. This is a must-read for those looking for answers to their mani-fold questions about God as they face challenges in life. The truth revealed in this book is that the thief (Satan) does not come but to steal, kill and destroy—but Jesus said, "I have come that you may have life and have it to the full." Rejoicing in the Lord!

Teck Uy, Pastor,
Friends of Jesus Christ, Toronto

"Life to the Fullest", is a powerful testimonial of God's story in Lulu's life and ministry. From fear to being freed, from hunger to diving deep in walking intimately with God, Lulu emerged both blessed and a blessing agent in multiple ways and in many countries. Lulu's lifelong journey of being trained in God's school of faith and endurance has empowered her to share her insights loaded with authentic joys, tears, and Spirit-filled encounters. This book is inspiring in ways that not only it's full of interesting stories, it's packed with sound theology and practical guidance — a must read for anyone who cares about living out faith to the fullest, all the way."

**Philip Yan and Amy Cheung, Directors,
GenesisXD, Board Members of Move-In**

I am so glad Lulu has written a book on "Life to the fullest in a troubled world". She has raised some very valid questions... Why is there such a paradox of life? What is life to the fullest? What is the key to enjoy life to the fullest in a fallen troubled world? Am I enjoying life to the fullest? Do I have the power to live and to face challenges in a difficult world? Is this my goal? Or do I even have a goal in my existence? These questions leave us pondering. She shares answers to these questions through her own amazing journey to freedom, her amazing journey of prayer and faith and God answering her during her troubled times, journey to overcoming the negatives of life, journey in learning to enjoy the positives of life empowering her to bloom where she is planted to be a channel of love, peace, encouragement and faith. I would like to see this book going out to every continent people so it can inspire those who are seeking meaning to life to the fullest in these hard days. Even people like us who are in HIS work, are shaken time to time in our faith, will be enlightened to move forward in these trouble times.

**Pramila Rajendran, Director, Miila Consulting
[Membercare & Counseling] India**

This book, Life to the Fullest, is filled with inspiring personal stories on God's miraculous healing, protection and provision. Above all, Lulu's testimonies declare the tender loving care of the Heavenly Father to His beloved children - thus He listens and understands their cries, fears and prayers. It's a must read to those who would like to see God still performs miracles today.

Myrna Cuevas, CPA, Bible Study Leader

This book provides a wonderful chance to see where and how God took them and used them in many parts of the world in amazing ways. The book was is thought provoking and prayer enhancing.

Dr. Linda Cook,
Retired Professor of Nursing, Canada

Life To the Fullest, reads like the continuation of the Acts of the Apostles. This book is a testimony of Lulu Tira and her husband Joy's ministry lifestyle, a ministry of discipleship and spiritual multiplication. Their credibility as hum-ble servants of Jesus Christ is substantiated through the networks built among Christian leaders of many denominations. Their hope is for the world's billion to embrace God's loving gospel.

Lulu believe each ordinary Christian is called to this ministry. If God will use Lulu, a daughter, friend, nurse, wife, mother, teacher to minister across the world, why not you! Me! How? Lulu, shares how. She tells us how she learned to walk by faith and proved to herself that God is faithful.

In Life to the Fullest, Lulu shares real life difficulties and encounters with spiritual opposition. She speaks of her glorious Saviour who not only brought light to this dark world 2000 years ago but who continues today to pour His Holy Spirit into people so that we too may also have life to the fullest.

Do you need to be encouraged and challenged? Do you want to be part of the ministry of spiritual multiplication? This book provides encouraging testimony and guidelines how to partner with God the Father, God the Son and God the Holy Spirit and experience life to the fullest. Read it and pass it on.

Right Rev. David W. Parsons, Bishop
of The Arctic, Yellowknife, NT

~ DEDICATION ~

This book is dedicated:

- *to my loving family – my dear husband, children and grandchildren.*
- *to my supportive parents, siblings and in-laws.*
- *to my faithful friends.*
- *to my Godly mentors.*
- *to my spiritual family.*
- *to my co-laborers in the Royal Kingdom.*
- *to the faithful intercessors who had overcome trials in their lives and still @ The Upper Room.*
- *to my spiritual family in Japan who adopted me as their "ate" (big sister), their "tita" (aunt) and ministry partner.*
- *to The Dark Chocolate Ladies & Tanauan Bible Church—my Gilgal/ Refuge in the Philippines.*
- *to our faithful partners and supporters in the ministry.*

You have been part of my journey in life and are still continuing to be a part of our lives with my family and ministry. May God encourage you.

~ FOREWORD ~

I have known the author "Lulu" and her family for decades and am glad that this long-awaited volume finally is available to many readers. Out of her rich life-experience as a supportive wife to Joy (her life-time ministry partner), a godly parent to her children Lorajoy & Tonyvic, a pious lady of deep devotion and a faithful servant of our Lord with strong commitment.

In simple English and readable style, "Lulu" shares with readers her struggles and victories amidst hardship/trial and her journey towards "life to the fullest" first hand. It is uplifting and edifying to read her testimony, learn of her secret to success, and journeying with her from the valley of agony and pain towards the mountain-top excitement and joy.

This book is helpful to fellow homeward-bound Christian sojourners, discouraged Christian workers and frustrated Kingdom laborers because it is readable, edifying and practical. It is a choice for light reading at home or on the road. It can be used as an option for a reading club or a study guide for a small group. There is deep truth hidden by the simple writing style and valuable nuggets of insights buried in testimonies. By reading this book, the reader will journey with "Lulu" from the mundane Christian walk towards a fulfilled "life to the fullest."

ENOCH WAN, Ph.D. Author, Editor Professor,
Western Seminary- Portland, Oregon, USA

~ ACKNOWLEDGEMENTS ~

I thank God for enabling me to write this book in the midst of the Covid-19 pandemic and in the midst of family trial where we are tasting and seeing more of the loving kindness of God and His power. This book has come into fruition through the help and encouragement of Pastor Bob Matthew whom God used to remind me of His desire for me to write a book of remembrance of His work in my life and my family.

I am thankful:

- *For Beth Leonardo who patiently typed the manuscript and gave life to most of my illustrations.*

- *For Alma Briones who initiated typing my writing.*

- *For Linda Cook who did the first editing.*

- *For Damples and Gerry Baclagon who finally did the finishing touches of the book.*

- *For Nikita Sushma and Henrick Vasques who put work into drawing some of my illustrations.*

- *For the first readers of the book who became the endorsers of the book.*

- *For Carol and Del Dyck who gave me a ticket to Hawaii so at least I could work on the book. (That was my last international travel before the pandemic, which gave me a chance to be with my siblings).*

- *For my sister Leonie who hosted me in her condo at the Country Club Village in Honolulu and my siblings Leandro and Vangie, Lydia and Celo, Lilia and Floro who took turns in inviting me and taking me around.*

- *To Operation Mobilization (OM) Christian And Missionary Alliance of Canada. (C&MA), Advancing Indigenous Missions (AIM), PALM Ministry Association, Campus Crusade for Christ Canada (CCCC), Lausanne Committee for World Evangelization (LCWE), Move In, and*

SIM (particularly for Joy) who gave us the chance to serve God in their field of ministries.

- *To humble and kind giants who encouraged us especially Joy to fly and soar like a baby eagle to the sky of opportunities: George Verwer, Jack Klemke, Dough Birdsall, Ted Yamamori, David Bennett, Doug Nichols, Enoch Wan and Michael Oh.*

I am indebted to all those who introduced me to a personal relationship with God and those who discipled me; my Sunday School teachers, my Bible study leaders, seminary professors, and co-laborers in the vineyard. Some names are written in the pages of this book.

I am also thankful for those who mentored me through their sermons, teachings, writings and exemplified life to the fullest:

- *Kay Arthur*

- *Bill Johnson*

- *Heidi Baker*

- *Charles Spurgeon*

- *Charles Finney*

- *Oswald Chambers*

- *Madame Guyon*

- *Bill & Vonette Bright*

- *Paul King*

- *Billy & Ruth Graham*

- *Kathryn Kuhlman*

Lastly, I thank my husband Joy, my children Lorajoy & Dennis and Tonyvic & Zen, and my grandchildren: S. James, Isabel, Sophie and Bishop for their love and support.

To God be the glory!

~CONTENTS~

~ INTRODUCTION ~

This book is my journey to living LIFE TO THE FULLEST in a troubled world– my journey to freedom, journey in overcoming the negatives of life, journey in learning to enjoy the positives of life empowering me to bloom where I am planted. It is a journey encountering God in so many events in life. I have not attained all that God would have for me, but I trust and pray that in these pages you will find inspiration to seek God deeper and personally, that you will find the courage and strength to press on towards Life to the fullest (God's plan for your life). This book discusses how I found LIFE and how I navigated in both the earthly realm and spiritual realm. This book is my testimony of God's dealing in my life. It contains His revelations to me with the centrality of the Bible – the Scriptures, the Living Word and my personal experiences with Him.

This book has two parts. It includes testimonies from chapter to chapter with illustrations or diagrams of what I am sharing. These illustrations are revelations and instructions that the Lord revealed to me, unless otherwise quoted. It also contains some truths and principles that I have learned from the Bible and through my studies under mentors who exemplified life that become an "eye opener" in my journey to living life to the fullest.

With the book cover, the Lord showed me a vision of pink flowers and green leaves then directed me to the picture of pink blooms in the middle of weeds. This symbolizes a man/woman empowered to bloom in the world even in the midst of challenges or difficulties. The pink flower symbolizes life. The world we live in is a beautiful world. We marvel at the creation of God. But why are there negative things that man faces almost every day like confusion, worry, fear, sickness, trials, sufferings, hopelessness, etc.? I hope this book will let you understand why and how you can overcome them and live life to the fullest.

It is my prayer that God will use this book for His glory. It was 1996 when He first prompted me to write a book. I began to write but after a while stopped. Then in 2015, while I was hurting and in a very difficult situation, my faith and relationship with God was questioned because of some manifestation of His working power in my life, He prompted me to write about my encounter with Him. But then I failed again. Until in April 2019, God used somebody, a pastor who didn't know me prayed and prophesied over me – to be writing in such simple language that each person young and old, learned and unlearned can understand.

This is my story, the story of my family and of some people that I met in my journey; this is not fiction. I trust you will see God working in my life for Him to be known and glorified. Knowing my abilities, I could not have done this, but God assured me of His help. He assured me that He would reveal things for me to write. This is the reason why this book was written.

Thank you, Lord, for directing and inspiring me to write this book. Please release Your Presence and Power in this book through our wonderful experiences with You. "Be glorified oh God. May you be known through these pages. May the TRUTH be revealed. Many will be guided; many will come to your saving grace and live LIFE TO THE FULLEST."

For God's glory
Lulu M. Tira

WHAT IS LIFE?

Some questions you need to ponder as you read this book.

- *What is LIFE?*
- *Do I have LIFE?*
- *Why is there such a paradox of LIFE?*
- *How can I attain LIFE?*
- *What is LIFE TO THE FULLEST?*
- *What is the key to enjoy LIFE TO THE FULLEST in a fallen troubled world?*
- *Am I enjoying LIFE TO THE FULLEST?*
- *Do I have the power to live and to face challenges in a difficult world?*
- *Is this my goal? Or do I even have a goal in my existence?*
- *How can I overcome troubles in this world?*

~ CHAPTER 1 ~

INTROSPECTION ON THE MYSTERY OF LIFE

It was in the fourth month of the Covid-19 pandemic that I started writing the thoughts that would become this book. Known to some as World War C, this war was and continues to be unlike the previous World Wars during which citizens heard the sounds of bombs exploding, guns firing, and people crying. Death at the hands of other humans was visible on the streets.

In contrast, World War C is a war against the so-called Corona Virus, in short, Covid-19. Unlike wars past, the enemy in this war is invisible to the naked eye; the enemy is only visible under the microscope. Yet, the enemy is real causing suffering in all demographic categories. Death tolls climbed to more than 300 thousand in just three months. At one point the toll of the infected was at 8 million globally. In response, governments have kept their citizens at home. Almost two years in, thousands of people continue to be locked inside their homes. Often, Homes have been the only refuge and shelter in this viral war.

What is life like for someone who is locked in for days, weeks, and even months? In the early 2000s, I was invited to speak at the International Women's Aglow Conference in a region in which Christians had to be careful not to be seen or hear. The conference was held in a safe bunker—a bomb shelter located underground. It was so locked in that one could not hear the sounds outside. That was quite an experience for me though it was only for a few hours. It would be different for one who had to stay there for days, weeks, or months. What is the effect of being locked in? Left to seclusion by one's self or with people feeling equally isolated, would there be an increase in confusion and stir-craziness, clinical depression, suicidal ideation, or even domestic violence? Or, would there be for some, peace in the solitude, an ordering of life priorities, heightened family closeness, and rejoicing in the midst of sorrow and chaos? Why are there different reactions to this situation? What causes the different reactions? Is this life? What is life? Is it possible that there are what we call "the living dead"—living bodies that are dead inside?

Angie was a beautiful young woman who dreamed of becoming a celebrity in the entertainment world. From a barrio[1] Angie moved to Manila to fulfil her dream. There, she met a rising singing star and having had a "day relationship" with him, she was left pregnant and unmarried, and bore their child alone. And yet, Angie continued to dream, so when she met a Japanese man, she agreed to migrate to Japan with him, as his wife. Her marriage was difficult. Now and then, she suffered from her husband's physical abuse. With the events of her life, she was forced to work in a night club earning very low wages at $2.00 per customer. With two more children added to her first child, Angie's life had become incredibly difficult. She remembers that divorce and the fight in court about who would keep the children made her seek help.

Angie was introduced to the Giver of Life; she found a new life and she started walking in the Giver of Life's direction. Angie came to understand that she had not been living her life in its truest sense. We prayed with her, counselled and nurtured her towards spiritual transformation. In time, Angie won custody of her children.

Despite being a high-school graduate, Angie continued to study and improve her life. It was evident that the favour of the Lord was with her. Today, she counsels women, especially those who share experiences similar to hers. In her home, she operates a "Gilgal" – a refuge for women, and she founded an international school with her new husband who is also a follower of Jesus.

Angie has four children from three different men, but she does not live in the past. Angie, her new husband, and their young daughter live in the present, pointing many to the Giver of Life. If you could meet Angie, you would have a hard time believing some of her stories that are so full of suffering and shame. Today, Angie relates well with God, the

---

1   **Barrio is a Spanish word that means district. In the Philippines, it is used synonymously with "rural village."**

Creator and Giver of life. She is now full of life and an inspiration to many around her.

Then, there is Jade, a journalist working among entertainers and writing about their experiences. Jade came from a broken family. She says that she hated her father who had left them when she was young. While working in Japan, Jade heard a testimony from Coney Reyes, an artist who found Life in God. The moment Jade heard it, she responded to the invitation to receive Life. That changed her; she says that she forgave her dad. These days, she works among Indigenous Filipinos from the mountain tribes while she continues to write about entertainers. Jade has become a very happy person even in the midst of troubles around her.

Now let me tell you about Sue. She was a very talented high school student. She was very popular and pretty and her schoolmates wanted to be like her. But, one day, the school announced that she had jumped off of Edmonton's High Level Bridge and passed away. What happened? Why did she commit suicide? She had both beauty and intelligence.

Another one was Rissa. Like Sue, Rissa was so pretty and she wanted to be successful in life. Under the care of her relatives, Rissa had everything she needed, but there was one quest in her life. Rissa needed to know the answer to one question, "why did Tatay leave Nanay and me when I was young?" One day, Rissa told her relatives that she had found a friend and that friend knew where her father was. She told them that she wanted to go and see her father, but was warned not to go because it was too dangerous. Rissa went ahead anyway, without her relatives' knowledge. Upon meeting her father, she found the answer to her question. It was a painful answer. Not only that; her so-called friend was not a real friend at all. Rissa was sold into prostitution and trafficked. Though Rissa regretted her decision, it was too late. Rissa died an early death.

One of the children I am discipling is a young boy. He is gifted. One day as we were studying, he told me that sometimes he wants to die because he believes he is not important, and he feels useless. Nobody told him this—it was just in his thoughts. Why, even as young as that, does he already have this problem? Who is the unseen enemy who poisons many with all his lies?

How about the seven-year-old girl who was recently killed in our neighbourhood? As young as she was, this little girl was so vibrant, even involved in the community by selling lemonade to raise funds for needy children. One day, a man needing help was invited into their home so they could provide some of his needs. While her mother was busy in the kitchen, the man attacked the girl. The girl's mother heard it and she ran to them and pleaded with the man asking him to release her daughter, but it was too late; the girl had already died. I really believe that this was not God's plan for the little girl's life or for her killer. I believe God had a beautiful plan for that girl and the killer, a plan to prosper them and not to harm them.

Why is there such a paradox of life? Adolf Hitler, a German politician who became the leader of the Nazi Party, rose to power and started World War II (WWII) by invading and occupying Central and Eastern Europe. This world war resulted in 70-85 million reported deaths.2 Did Hitler find peace? Even before WW2 ended, he committed suicide. How about Judas Iscariot who was a disciple of Jesus? He saw the miracles of Jesus and was one of the disciples, but he betrayed Jesus for thirty shekels of silver, yet when he got the money, he was not happy, and he hanged himself.

How about the Covid-19 pandemic? It seems like the more we produce vaccines, the more people are confused and resistant to having it. People are confused whether to get vaccinated or not, and we even hear news of more unvaccinated people becoming infected. Why is there such confusion on solutions presented?

As I write, I remember that I was blessed while attending the memorial service of one of our friends. Because of the Covid-19 restrictions, the number of attendees was limited, social distancing observed, and no singing was allowed. But our friend Domie prepared a video before he died, so instead of us singing, he was the one singing on the video and at the end he was the one dancing, worshiping God, celebrating his life and his homegoing. Why was he celebrating on his last few days of physical life instead of grieving? Because, before he died, he and his wife Beng had come to know the Life. They knew that they would see each other again in heaven; that he was just going ahead of her. What a powerful hope—it made Domie's funeral remarkably different from some of the other funerals I have attended, in which there is much crying and grieving.

---

2   See https://www.nationalww2museum.org/students-teachers/student-resources/research-starters/research-starters-worldwide-deaths-world-war

I have encountered some of these people whose lives have been transformed by life, in fact a few of them became my friends. Who among these whose lives I write about in this chapter have found life? What is life? Just like some of them, I was living without understanding of what life is; I had many fears. I had low self-esteem. I was tempted many times to take my own life. My life was rocked by ups and downs—until I came to understand what life is and the mystery surrounding it, giving me wisdom to live in a troubled world—I too have been transformed. As of today, I am living my life to the fullest– even in the midst of the Covid-19 pandemic and locked-ins, with its negative effects of fear, chaos, and instability in our world.

QUESTIONS TO PONDER

1. *What is paradox of life?*
2. *What is common to the individuals mentioned?*
3. *Who among them challenge you?*
4. *Can you identify to one of them? Who among them should you emulate?*
5. *Evaluating your life, is there a decision you have to make to move forward in your life and not to lag behind.*

~ CHAPTER 2 ~

EARLY BEGINNING

A house surrounded by a vast expanse of farmland, and a winding river within a short distance--was the one in which I was born and where I lived for my first fifteen years. I was born about a decade after World War II, in which my father served as medical officer under one of the Infantry Divisions in Okinawa, Japan. My loving parents were Antonio and Fremia Manding—both children of "Hawayanos," Filipinos who worked and lived in Hawaii.

With the privilege of having Hawayano parents, my parents inherited lands which they farmed. I remember my parents teaching us the value of hard work, training us siblings how to work, even in the fields – planting and harvesting rice and other crops. We were twelve siblings but four died in their infancy:

- *Excellencia †*
- *Elinor †*
- *Lydia*
- *Leonila*
- *Francisco †*
- *Lourdes*
- *Lilia*

- *Emeterio †*
- *Lolito*
- *Leandro*
- *Luisito*
- *Lenigrace*

My parents gave us beautiful names, but there was a mystery to how we were named. The first two children died, but when they named their third child, Lydia, a name starting with the letter 'L,' the child did

not die as an infant. Similarly, with the fourth, who was named, Leonila. The fifth child was given a name that did not start with the letter 'L,' but with an 'F,' and he died in infancy.

My parents wondered about the circumstances surrounding the naming of their children, and why babies given non-L names perished soon after birth. When I was born, they wanted me to live and so, keeping with the discovered pattern, they named me "Lourdes." I lived beyond infancy, and so did Lilia, my sibling who followed me. After Lilia, our parents veered from the pattern, naming their eighth child, Emeterio (not a name starting with the letter 'L'), and he also died. After that, our parents figured out that they should name their children only with names starting with the letter 'L.' Four more children were born and they were all named beginning with the letter 'L,' and they all lived and did not die in their infancy. Why? Was this a coincidence or a mystery?

My brother Lolito lived, but then he got sick with Polio when he was an infant causing his muscles and bones to contract that made him an invalid (he could not feed himself nor put on his shoes or bathe himself or grasp onto something), but he lived. (Why did he not die? Is it because his name started with an 'L'?). He died when he was 21 years old. One time, I was asked to babysit him while the family worked. I was so tired that I slept. I was awakened and saw that his pyjamas were on fire. I had to wet a blanket and cover the flame. I am glad the flame was put out and my brother had burns on only some parts of his leg, even if they left big scars. Who woke me up? An angel?

There was another time that I was assigned to babysit him again. I left him in our balcony to get something. When I went back, I could not find him. I searched the house, but I could not find him. When

I looked outside toward the ground, I found him hanging from the balcony window, he was holding firmly to the window and so he did not fall down. We were on the second floor of the house so it made me think that there was an angel holding onto Lolito, because he could not grasp objects and he was certainly not strong enough to be able to hold on tightly to a windowsill. How could he hold onto the window for close to ten minutes—somebody must have been holding him, so he would not fall. Was there a ministering angel?

There was one thing that I often vividly remember. During my elementary days, my cousin and I were trying to pick a pomelo from the tree. Under the tree were two carabaos (water buffalo) eating. Suddenly, one of the carabaos hit me with its massive horn. I do not know what happened, but I found myself sitting on the caraboa's head and holding firmly to both of its horns. I was not even scared as it tried to shake me off its head. It was so angry, but I was so strong that the powerful carabao became so tired and finally lowered its head, calmly letting me go. Then, I ran. Generally, people who get into situations like this die because the horns of the carabao would hit and puncture them, especially their abdomens, causing them to burst, but I believe that there was an angel who ministered to me and protected me. Maybe the angel commanded the carabao to put me down. I believe it was an angel of God.

I was a sickly child–so one day my parents performed a ritual which they believed could heal me. They wove me through all the open risers of our house's staircase in the presence of two witnesses who my parents said became my godparents. But, this ritual did not help me—I continued to be sickly until I became an adult.

We, as a family, had close family ties. My parents were disciplinarians.

They taught us the importance of education and work that began at home.

We, the older children, were studious and became honour students.

My first friend was Manuela de la Cruz. We were like sisters through elementary and high school, until she left for Hawaii. In my school days, I found many good teachers, but there was one who particularly recognized my potential, and she became my friend and mentor— Miss Adeline Santos at the Dingras National Agricultural School. In university, I had a friend named Tessie, who died at a young age just after we completed our university programs. It made me wonder why such things happened. Tessie's parents worked so hard to earn money to send her to university, where she finished her degree, only to die in a car accident in America, on her first date.

What a paradox of life? If God, the Creator is loving, why do things such as this happen?

This book describes my journey to Life and life to the fullest. Most of it is written chronologically, but some of it relates to certain topical areas and will at times refer back to earlier writing in the book. Here you will find answers to questions I am writing about.

QUESTIONS TO PONDER

1. The way we were named was mysterious, do you have any mysterious experience in your life? What have you done about it?

2. Do you see the hands of God in protecting my brother and protecting me?

3. My parents did a ritual for me but it did not helped. Do you believe in rituals?

4. What does God say about it?

~ CHAPTER 3 ~

THE KEY TO LIFE

Growing up, I never tried to understand what LIFE was? To me, life was just living, breathing, and not being "dead." Life was waking, eating, drinking, sleeping, playing, working, etc. This was life to me, until I encountered the GIVER of LIFE, and I began experiencing LIVING LIFE in its true sense.

We are eight living siblings from a family of twelve. We were raised to be religiously devout. Every Sunday was a day for us to go to church. We came from an Aglipayan Church background, which is an offshoot of the Roman Catholic church in the Philippines. I knew about God. I knew Him as the Creator – the One who controls everything—the events of life, the weather, and the likes. But like other kids, I just lived every day without relating to Him. Sometimes I was mischievous, rebellious, and lazy. I was also timid and had lots of fear. When I was called on to help at home, I would run away and say bad words to my parents and siblings.

One day, my sister, Leonila, and I were invited to a Sunday school in our neighbourhood. This was my first time to study the Bible. The passage studied was Luke 16:19-31:

19. *"There was a rich man who was dressed in purple and fine linen and lived in luxury every day.*

20. *At his gate was laid a beggar named Lazarus, covered with sores*

21. *and longing to eat what fell from the rich man's table. Even the dogs came and licked his sores.*

22. *The time came when the beggar dies and the angels carried him to Abraham's side. The rich man also dies and was buried.*

23. *In hell, where he was in torment, he looked up and saw Abraham far away, with Lazarus by his side.*

24. *So he called to him, 'Father Abraham, have pity on me and send Lazarus to dip the tip of his finger in water and cool my tongue, because I am in agony in this fire.'*

25. *But Abraham replied, 'Son, remember that in your lifetime you received your good things, while Lazarus received bad things, but now he is comforted here and you are in agony.*

26. *And besides all this, between us and you a great chasm has been fixed, so that those who want to go from here to you cannot, nor can anyone cross over from there to us.'*

27. *He answered, 'Then I beg you, father, send Lazarus to my father's house,*

28. *for I have five brothers. Let him warn them, so that they will not also come to this place of torment.'*

29. *Abraham replied, 'They have Moses and the Prophets; let them listen to them.'*

30. *'No father Abraham,' he said, 'but if someone from the dead goes to them, they will repent.'*

31. *He said to him, 'If they do not listen to Moses and the Prophets, they will not be convinced even if someone rises from the dead.'"*

This parable talks about the afterlife of a rich man and Lazarus, a poor man. The rich man went to a burning lake called hell and Lazarus went to the "bosom of Abraham" called heaven. The rich man was suffering in the heat so he wanted Lazarus to dip his finger in water to cool his tongue. This parable made an impact in my life. It created fear in me – the FEAR of GOD.

I became conscious of the Creator – the God who created the universe, the heavens, and the earth; the God who created me and the One who holds every cell of my body; the One who will judge the living and the dead. I became conscious of the destiny of people when they die – heaven or hell; no purgatory, only heaven and hell. I did not want to go to hell. So, I decided to become a good girl, to obey God. He brought change in me. I became careful of what I said and what I did.

For example, I was afraid to tell a lie and to say bad words. I became obedient and kind. As a result, I became the God-fearing lass in our family. I have learned that the fear of God is the beginning of wisdom. Wisdom is knowledge applied at the right time and at the right place and in the right way. When we have wisdom, we are instructed to avoid evil, which is staying away from sin (sin is disobeying God). He knows if you are delighting in Him.

HEAVEN as illustrated by Nikita Sushma of MoveIn International, Toronto.

HELL purposely drawn for this book from the passage of Luke 16:19-31 by Miss Nikita Sushma of MoveIn International, Toronto.

The fear of the Lord is revering God and the things of the Lord. It is the consciousness of the Almighty Holy God who is watching over you – and He knows whether you are obeying or disobeying Him. Revering Him is obeying Him. This fear of the Lord continues to help me walk on the right path of life, avoiding doing bad things and wickedness, always obeying Him. I once heard a preacher say: "The more we honour and revere the Lord, the more we will experience His Presence and miracle-working power." Proverbs 9:10 "The fear of the Lord is the beginning of wisdom and knowledge of the Holy One is understanding." Proverbs 15:33 "Wisdom's instruction is to fear the Lord, and humility comes before honour."

Let me illustrate with the accompanying drawings of heaven and hell on the previous page, purposely drawn for this book, from the passage of Luke 16:1931.

Imagine heaven is a beautiful and joyful place and hell is an ugly place of torment.

Revelation 21:3 God's dwelling place is now among the people, and he will dwell with them. They will be his people, and God himself will be with them and be their God.

He will wipe every tear from their eyes. There will be no more death or mourning or crying or pain, for the old order of things has passed away.

Revelation 20:10 and the devil who had deceived them was thrown into the lake of fire and sulphur where the beast and the false prophet were, and they will be tormented day and night forever and ever.

Revelation 20:14 Then death and Hades were thrown into the lake of fire. The lake of fire is the second death.

Revelation 20:15 And if anyone's name was not found written in the book of life, he was thrown into the lake of fire

QUESTIONS TO PONDER

1. *What is Life to you?*

2. *In Luke 16:19-31, where did the rich man go when he died? How about Lazarus?*

3. *What are the only two destination of man when he dies? What does the Bible say about heaven and hell? Are you sure of where you are going when you die?*

4. *Do you warn others about the danger of going to hell? What is godly fear?*

~ CHAPTER 4 ~

FINDING LIFE

With the fear of God, I became so well-behaved in school and at home, but there was something that I always struggled with—it was the negative feelings. I felt that I was not loved enough by my parents especially when they got angry with me. I was so afraid when my parents disciplined me for my misbehaviour that I was very careful not to commit any mistake. I also had feelings of rejection. Frequently corrected and scolded, I developed a poor self-mage and low self-esteem. I wanted to run away from home and from our town, but my fear of God prevented me.

I then started to dream of serving God by becoming a nun. After completing secondary education, I told my parents about my plan to become a nun. They disapproved of it, rather they instructed me to take up nursing in Manila (capital city of the Philippines). My parents had chosen me to receive the government scholarship for the children of those Filipino soldiers who served with USA in World War II as long as I maintained the required grades. In obedience to my parents, I started the Bachelor of Science in nursing program at Far Eastern University (FEU), in Manila. I was very studious, burning the midnight oil every night until 2 o'clock in the morning. Besides studying, I also became a member of the FEU Student Catholic Action. Now and then, I would go to the Daughters of St. Paul Convent – where I continued to nourish my dream to become a nun without the knowledge of my parents.

One day while my friend, Norma, and I were riding in a jeep along Quezon Avenue, we were seated beside a seemingly respected man in his 40's. He was listening to our conversation about movie stars like Vilma

Santos and Nora Aunor. He then interrupted us by giving us an idea to go to Sampaguita Productions where these superstars are found. He told us he could bring us there. We said "yes, let us go." While walking along the way to catch a bus, we passed by Torino, a fashion store where these superstars get their clothes. I told Norma and the man to stop and look inside the store. We went inside while the man waited for us outside. Just as soon as we were inside, one sales lady approached us and asked us, "Do you know the man you are with?" We answered, "No." She then ushered us to the backdoor of the store and said, "That man is a pimp, he will make you prostitutes. Come I will get a taxi for you to go home." We were terrified; we did not show ourselves anymore to the man. We were saved from prostitution. Was the sales lady an angel of God to save us?

Then, in the midst of my studies, I got very sick. I was so afraid to die. I was reminded of the two destinations of man when one dies – heaven or hell. I did not know where I was going. I did not want to be like the rich man who went to the burning lake called hell. I wanted to go to heaven.

It was then that my classmate, Tessie Magadia, invited me to a Bible study among nurses. There they shared to me about Jesus – the Life, the Truth and the Way.

John 14:6 Jesus answered, "I am the way and the truth and the life. No one comes to the father except through me."

They told me that even though I was planning to become a nun and know who Jesus is, I was still going to hell, because I have not accepted Jesus as my Saviour in my life. They shared to me that only Jesus can save me from hell. He is the only way to heaven, and He is the Truth and the Life. No other way—not religion, not good behaviour, not even attendance or membership at church. I did not need further explanation. I did not want to go to hell, so I told them, "I do not want to go to hell, I want to be with Jesus when I die. What should I do to be saved from hell? How can I receive Jesus as my Saviour and Lord?" They responded to me "By prayer."

You should believe Jesus as the life, the way and the truth, then receive Him as your Saviour and Lord through faith. You have to recognize that you are a sinner, you are dead to sin and separated from God and that you are bound to go to hell. And so, you need Him to save you. So, you need to repent—you have to repent from

your sins and ask God to forgive you. Ask Jesus into your life and give your life to Him.

With this, they led me in prayer, and I followed after them. I repented from my sins and accepted Jesus as my Lord and Saviour. I prayed, **"Lord, thank you for loving me. I recognize that you came here on earth to save me. Please forgive me for all my sins. This moment, I accept You as my Lord and Saviour. I give my life to You. Please reign in me completely and help me to obey You. Now my life is in You."**

Ephesians 2:8 For it is by grace you have been saved, through faith – and this is not from yourselves, it is the gift of God

The Gift of God the Father is Jesus Christ, the only salvation. Grace is undeserved favour from God. Faith is believing and acting upon the Word of God – the Bible. In one of his messages Chris Oyakhilome said,

The Bible is the written words of God using men like the prophets, apostles and disciples. God inspired these men to put these words into writings. The Bible is a revelation, a compilation of God's authority; it is God's revelation given in written words. It is God's authentic declaration of Himself, of His works, of His plan and purposes and of His teachings. It contains poetry, prophecy, laws, history, parables, and teachings, but these are all through the inspirations of His Spirit and from His perspective. You'll see what God said, what the angel said, what Satan said, and demons said, what men and women said, but they are all God's testimony of what they said.

The Bible guides us even in details about our lives, our career, our decisions, and in everything present and future.

This means that the Holy Spirit did not only breathe God's word into the lives of these people, but He also actually moved them to write. His words lighten our path and guide our lives. For me, the Bible is the Blue Book of Instructions in life, like the things we used whether for food, medicine, tools, or technology. There is a manual of instruction that explains what it is and how to use it. God created human beings and the Bible tells us who we are and gives us direction on how to live our lives. We are all significant. I found in the Bible why God created me, what His purpose is in my life, how He loves me so much, instructions on how to use my time, talents, blessings, how to deal with my frustration, failure, sin, how to deal with problems, and many more.

March 16, 1972, I found Life in the person of Jesus by faith. Through prayer, I received the Gift of God the Father – Jesus, His Son, as my Saviour and Lord. That day I began to be assured of going to heaven when I die. I continue with this faith. It is not only hoping; it is real.

At that time, this was my basic knowledge of eternal life—it's life after death. I did not realize that there was more to eternal life – not only life after death, but a changed quality of life as one lives life with Jesus as Saviour and Lord. (Note: You will see more of this as you continue to read.)

Things changed. I was healed miraculously. I was no longer afraid of dying because I knew I was going to heaven when I die. I was taught through the Bible that something happened to me the moment I received Jesus, particularly in the spiritual realm. I was "born again." I became a new creation. The burden of sin was removed. I felt I had freedom. My sins were forgiven. Receiving Jesus–I felt, then, that the vacuum in my heart looking for love was already filled with the Spirit of Jesus living in me. Jesus—the life, the way, the truth is now living in me through His Spirit. Christ in me became my power to live. I am no longer alone. I am forgiven and my guilt of past sins has passed away. What a joy to become a free woman, no longer bound by guilt and sin. I also became a child of God, and He gave me a new life– an eternal life, a transformed quality of life. I began my personal relationship with Him. As I was before, many people know about God, but are not personally related to Him.

The Bible is fitted with wisdom and salvation to all who heed its words. It tells us an amazing story of the majesty of God and the desperate need of man for a Saviour.[3]

---

3   **Paraphrased from an email from Revelations Media, September 3, 2020.**

QUESTIONS TO PONDER

1. *What were my struggles in life especially when I was growing up? Can you identify with these struggles?*

2. *What drove me to seek God more? What decision did I make that brought change to my life?*

3. *How do you respond to the truth that Jesus is the ONLY Way, the Truth and the Life?*

4. *Have you ever find Life in Christ? Are you sure you have received the Life, the Way and the Truth? Share your testimony.*

~ CHAPTER 5 ~

GOING DEEPER

Prayer became a delight to me. I started communing with God often, wherever I was, and whenever I had problems or causes for happiness, I felt Him so near to me. I could tell Him anything at anytime.

The nurses who introduced Jesus to me encouraged me to look for a church where I could know more about God and where I could fellowship with others who had also accepted Jesus. My first church was pastored by Pastor Ed Banzuelo of FEBIAS College of Bible. I was nurtured spiritually at church, Inter-varsity Christian Fellowship (IVCF), and Nurses Christian Fellowship (NCF), but it was my NCF staff leader, Josie Quimba, who personally and patiently discipled me. She was strict with me; she told me to give up my unbelieving boyfriend and stop practices that were not of God's Word. I responded in obedience and broke up with my boyfriend. Initially, I was afraid to break up with him because he threatened to end his own life, but God assured me that he would be okay. I obeyed God. After two weeks

my ex-boyfriend found a new girlfriend (that was fast!). God kept His word to me.

I stopped believing in superstitions and many false beliefs. I also became actively involved in the youth group of the church and became one of its officers. Among the youth group officers, there was a marine engineering student named, Joy. This young man caught my attention because whenever it was his turn to pray, his prayer was always the same: "Lord teach me how to pray." That was his entire prayer. I thought this man wanted to be close to God because of his focused way of praying. Later, while working and serving in the youth group, we became close friends. One time, we went for a Bible study together in the park. After our study, he prayed a very long and earnest prayer. At the time, I did not know anything about "praying in the Holy Spirit." It brought joy to me as I listened to him pray, so I prayed "Lord, if that comes from you, please let me pray like this too." I did not realize that my times in prayer would lead me to **fall in love with Jesus**. You need to remember that I accepted Jesus as my Saviour and Lord because I was afraid of hell and did not want to go there. At the time, it was not because I loved Jesus. So, in prayer I was drawn to Him more. I would sing praises to Him again and again, thanking Him for His great love.

With these developments in my life, I stopped pursuing my dream to become a nun. IVCF played a great role in discipling me and training me in leadership. Joy Tira, who was like my brother, was also used by God to challenge me in my personal relationship with God. Every day, he would share his devotional lesson with me. We were close friends and helpful to each other, but we had our own crushes. He liked my dorm mate, and my crush was a church mate.

Then, at the first Asian Student Missionary Convention that was held in Baguio City (Philippines) in 1973, Joy and I joined numerous student leaders like us. Simultaneously, he and I responded to the altar call, by Rev. John Stott, to serve God. That drew us closer to God and to each other. After this momentous event, Joy asked me if he could pray for me, and I said "Yes!" Little did I know that God was already working in both of us for His plan. We became not only brother and sister in the Lord, but "friends" committed to each other, helping each other, especially in our growth in the Lord and in ministry. We were not only involved in the church but also with IVCF leadership in our own campuses where we were studying—Joy was in the marine engineering program at FEATI University and I was still at FEU, taking nursing.

After my graduation in 1974, I was assigned to Mindanao for my three-month long rural health training. Since Joy was continuing his education in Manila, his family in Cotabato was my host while I completed my rural health training. While preparing to go to Cotabato, I was warned by my friend, Ate Beth (Joy's older sister), "if a camel finds it hard to enter the eye of a needle, getting through our mother is harder." This, she said, was because I was Joy's girlfriend, and it might be difficult for me to gain their mother's acceptance. I was challenged and responded to her, "God will help me gain your parents approval."

With my daily duties at the Marbel Rural Health Clinic, I excitedly finished my work so I could go to the church I was attending, Marbel Alliance Church, and pray. I did that every day, except for on weekends, praying alone in the church until it was dark. One time, as I was praying, I started speaking in another language. I would utter names too. After each name it seemed a thorn or burden was lifted. I was praying so heavily and crying out to God while in my mind I was also asking God, "Lord is this from You? If this is not from You, please stop it, but if it comes from You then please continue it." The manifest presence of God was so evident. After each prayer and groaning in the Spirit, I started to sing. I knew the tune of the song, but it was in an unknown language as if I was singing a song with the melody of "What a Friend We Have in Jesus." I only understood one word, "Jesus," but it sounded like "Chesu." This was my first manifest encounter with God. I wished I could have stayed longer in the church, but it was already so late. I had to go home; my hosts would be looking for me. I took a tricycle, a common means of transportation in Mindanao. While on the way, I again started praying in another language, so I said to the Lord "Lord, please lower the volume so the driver will not hear me." I never did find out if he heard me.

After eating dinner with my host family (i.e., Joy's family) I went to bed. I was sharing room with Manang Bing (Joy's oldest sister), and two of the family's relatives, Tess and Cresie. Just as I lay down, I began to pray in another language, again. I tried to lower my voice, but I was not able to. There were utterance of words that I did not even think of; it went on until my roommates left for the living room.

Unity (Joy's younger brother), Dad Vic, and Mom Esther, also went to the living room, and I followed. We all hugged each other and worshiped God with tears. The Lord visited us that night. There was asking for forgiveness from God and from each other. I did not know much of the impact of that visitation of God that night, but Unity became a pastor. The family living above us also became actively involved in ministry. In fact, one of their sons is now pastoring one of the largest churches in the Philippines. I became involved with the Lord's work. Joy's parents showed their love for me as I stayed with them for three months. A few months later they moved from Mindanao to Manila where I had opportunities to visit them every week.

The next day, I shared what happened to our deaconess, Alice, and she told me it was called "glossolalia," and it comes from Satan. I was discouraged and stopped praying in tongues. I asked Dad Vic, though at that time he did not have that gift. He counselled me to go back to the Lord and ask Him if praying in tongues is of God or from Satan. God responded, assuring me that the gift of praying in an unknown language, whether a heavenly or earthly language, is from Him. The praying in tongues that comes from the evil one is when Satan tries to copy or fake it. We call it counterfeit. The gifts of the Spirit are from God—but the enemy can fake it. This is why we have to also ask for a gift of discernment and sensitivity to the Holy Spirit. The enemy lies about the gift of tongues to divide and confuse people and to discourage them from continuing to use the gift of God because God can use this gift to draw one closer to Him. After this "talk" with the Lord, I did come back to the gift of praying in another language.[4]

NOTE: On praying in tongues, some believe that it comes from the enemy because of the belief that it had already ceased or stopped. They believe it was only during the Pentecost, but this is not what the Word of God says. This gift, like other gifts, cannot be earned or learned. We can only practice it when the Holy Spirit moves us to do it. We cannot teach it or enforce on anyone either. This may upset people, confuse or offend others, but this should not be the reason to discount it. Like in Acts 2 where people present at the Pentecost were amazed and perplexed, others mocked the disciples who spoke in tongues, but this move of God saved thousands.[5]

We need to always examine if such acts bring us closer to God and if they come from God. When God moves in our lives, it can cause

---

4   While we were studying in Canada, Alice, the deaconess whom I had first consulted about my experience, wrote to me confirming that it is true—that it comes from God. She wrote to me saying that, she, too, had also been given this gift. She asked me for forgiveness because of her comments in the past, regarding the gift of tongues.

5   (See Acts 2:12-13—"Amazed and perplexed, they asked one another, 'What does this means?' Some, however, made fun of them and said, 'They have had too much wine'."

discomfort but always results in bringing people closer to God, and the person praying in such a way bears the fruit of the Holy Spirit, which is love, joy, peace, patience, kindness, goodness, faithfulness, gentleness and self-control (as we see described in Galatians 5:22-23). As you continue to read you will see how this gift has brought me closer to God as I commune with Him every day. I have been communing with Him daily now more than before. This communion gives me strength and hope every day.

1 Corinthians 12:1-11

1. *Now about spiritual gifts, brothers, I do not want you to be ignorant.*

2. *You know that when you were pagans, somehow or other you were influenced and led astray to mute idols.*

3. *Therefore I tell you that no one who is speaking by the Spirit of God says, "Jesus be cursed," and no one can say, "Jesus is Lord," except by the Holy Spirit.*

4. *There are different kinds of gifts, but the same Spirit.*

5. *There are different kinds of service, but the same Lord.*

6. *There are different kinds of working, but the same God works all of them in all men.*

7. *Now to each one the manifestation of the Spirit is given for the common good*

8. *To one there is given through the Spirit the message of wisdom, to another the message of knowledge by means of the same Spirit,*

9. *to another faith by the same Spirit, to another gifts of healing by that one Spirit,*

10. *to another miraculous powers, to another prophecy, to another distinguishing between spirits, to another speaking in different kinds of tongues, and to still another the interpretation of tongues.*

11. *All these are the work of one and the same Spirit, and he gives them to one, just as he determines.*

My first intimate encounter with God was that night at Marbel, South Cotabato. This was the point when I began to hunger and thirst for Him. Ezekiel 47 became so real to me.

Ezekiel 47:1-12

1. *The man brought me back to the entrance of the temple, and I saw water coming out from under the threshold of the temple toward the east (for the temple faced east). The water was coming down from under the south side of the temple, south of the altar.*

2. *He then brought me out through the north gate and led me around the outside to the outer gate facing east, and the water was flowing from the south side.*

3. *As the man went eastward with a measuring line in his hand, he measured off a thousand cubits and then led me through water that was ankle deep.*

4. *He measured off another thousand cubits and led me through water that was knee deep. He measured off another thousand and led me through water that was up to the waist.*

5. *He measured off another thousand, but now it was a river that I could not cross, because the water had risen and was deep enough to swim in — a river that no one could cross.*

6. *He asked me, "Son of man, do you see this?" Then he led me back to the bank of the river.*

7. *When I arrived there; I saw a great number of trees on each side of the river.*

8. *He said to me, "This water flows toward the eastern region and goes down into the Arabah, where it enters the Sea. When it empties into the Sea, the water there becomes fresh.*

9. *Swarms of living creatures will live wherever the river flows. There will be large numbers of fish, because this water flows there and makes the salt water fresh; so, where the river flows everything will live.*

10. *Fishermen will stand along the shore; from En Gedi to En Eglaim there will be places for spreading nets. The fish will be of many kinds — like the fish of the Great Sea.*

11. *But the swamps and marshes will not become fresh; they will be left for salt.*

12. *Fruit trees of all kinds will grow on both banks of the river. Their leaves will not wither, nor will their fruit fall. Every month they will bear,*

because the water from the sanctuary flows to them. Their fruit will serve for food and their leaves for healing."

Let me illustrate with this diagram given to me by the Lord in a vision:

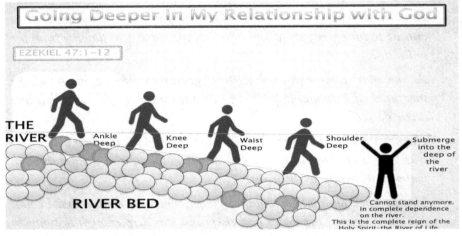

From an ankle-deep relationship with God, I wanted to go deeper and be intimate with God, becoming a blessing to others, and be submerged from knee-deep to waist-deep, to shoulder-deep. I wanted to swim in the living water. As I went deeper, I became aware of the spirit world. I began to see things and hear things that I had not seen or heard before.

I want to be immersed in the River of Life—Jesus Christ whose Spirit lives in me. I want Him to reign completely in my life. You noticed in the passage that Ezekiel measures how deep he is in the river. God measures how deep we are in our relationship with Him. Is our relationship with Him only ankle deep? Are we enjoying a deep relationship with him that will bring us into where the river flows so everything will live?

One day while my sweetheart was away, he wrote me a letter forgetting to write "I love you." Usually, he would write "I love you," whenever he wrote to me. But one day, I did not find "I love you" in his letter. I was so hurt that I cried and I told the Lord about it. The Lord responded, "Now you feel what I feel when you come to Me and do not tell me that you love Me. In the midst of your praises and thanksgiving, I want you to express your love to Me." But I reasoned out, "Lord, how can I tell you 'I love You' when I feel intimidated because I'm not really good? I feel short in obeying You." God answered, "just come to Me humbly and express your love and repentance. That will be a delight for Me." That improved my relationship with God. I was drawn to Him through prayers.

I just loved listening and talking to Him, singing in praises. The Bible became so alive to me! Like Ezekiel, I began to see things in the realm of the Spirit. When a problem would come to me, God would let me soar, flying over mountains and valleys through dreams. Flying over the problems, I would soar like an eagle. Oh, it was so relieving; it signifies victory. My growing relationship with God brought me to His Presence. The atmosphere produced by my relationship with Him ushered me to Jesus, to God's Presence. Like the song, "Your Presence is Heaven to Me," as I commune with Him, God's Presence became like heaven to me.

QUESTIONS TO PONDER

1. *How did I go deeper in my relationship with God?*

2. *Do you see the importance of studying and meditating His Words and prayer?*

3. *What do you understand in Corinthians 12: 1-11 ? Do the gifts of the Holy Spirit still exist today? How about tongue? What does the word of God say?*

4. *What do you understand in the passage - Ezekiel 47:1-12? What does the illustration shows? What happen when you go deeper in your relationship with God? Are you challenged to go deeper? What do you need to do more?*

CHAPTER 6

ADVENTURE

Upon finishing my rural health training in Mindanao, I worked at the University of Saint Thomas (UST) Hospital. Here, I saw the suffering of people, and much more when my first patient died. I was in pain seeing their sufferings. What could I do? I thank God for the Nurses Christian Fellowship (NCF) who taught me principles of life that helped me in alleviating pain. Walking in the ward was difficult, because everything was in a rush. I, too, developed fear of sickness and disease. I became afraid of patients, especially those with communicable diseases. With this fear, I learned to pray more—to pray for my patients and for me not to get sick.

One time, my patient was so troubled with her scheduled surgery. She had a bleeding ulcer. Without hesitation she asked me to pray for her. So, I prayed for her and encouraged her to have faith in God. That was on a Friday afternoon. When I got back to the hospital two days later, she was already discharged because she was no longer bleeding. She was healed, so they cancelled the operation and discharged her. God heard our prayer. He healed her.

With difficulty in bedside nursing, I transferred to St. Luke's Hospital and worked at the OPD (Outpatient Department) and emergency room. A few months later I was invited by the Dean of my alma mater to be one of their nursing instructors. I knew it was hard to teach in the Institute of Nursing of FEU. If the students did not like you, they would try their best to drive you out of your job. With this mindset, I refused the offer. But after refusing the offer, that night while I slept, I dreamt of God telling me: "Fear not, I will be with you. Meditate on my words and I will make you successful." I was awakened and opened the Bible at once, and I saw the following passage: Joshua 1:7-9

7. *Be strong and very courageous. Be careful to obey all the law my servant Moses gave you; do not turn from it to the right or to the left, that you may be successful wherever you go.*

8. *Do not let this Book of the Law depart from your mouth; meditate on it day and night, so that you may be careful to do everything written in it, then you will be prosperous and successful.*

9. *Have I not commanded you? Be strong and courageous. Do not be terrified; do not be discouraged, for the Lord your God will be with you wherever you go."*

The next morning, I went back to Dean Elegado at the Institute of Nursing, telling her that God wanted me to take the job and He would help me. I was then accepted for the job. With that job, I was assigned to be the adviser of FEU-NCF (Far Eastern University Nurses Christian Fellowship) which gave me opportunity to lead Bible studies to interested students and faculty. It was a great opportunity. Praise God for those who were exposed to the Gospel, and for those who responded to the salvation of God. God gave me compassion for those who were not born again, much more, when He gave me a vision of hell with so many people suffering there, including my family. I cried for them. I started praying for them and their salvation. One by one, I witnessed to them, I claimed God's promise of my family's salvation if I believe. Praise God, one-by-one they accepted Jesus as their Saviour and Lord.

The first one in my family who accepted Jesus as Lord and Saviour was my younger sister Lilia. Like me, she did not want to go to hell, so she responded at once to the love of God. Next was my mom, she thought she already received Jesus as Lord and Saviour because one time she was so much in pain that she hugged the altar at home, where a picture of Joseph, Mary and Jesus was hanging. She said, "Lord help me, I'm yours." With that belief she thought she had already accepted Jesus. I explained and told her about the love of God, the Gospel of Salvation and she realized she needed to ask forgiveness for her sins and give her life to Jesus, accepting Him as Saviour and Lord.

My sister, Leonie, who was residing in the US accepted the Lord while she was hurting in her marriage. Now she is actively involved in her church and is one of the leaders. My brother, Leandro, was next. He became a God-fearing man. Even as he served in his adopted country, the USA, in the US Navy, he walked in godliness.

Our eldest sister seemed not to be interested in what I was sharing as she was very active in the Aglipayan church. During one visit home, to our province, the Lord would regularly wake me up in the middle of the night for prayer. There I prayed in the spirit. I did not realize that my eldest sister was listening. Every night, she would listen as I prayed. Before I left for Manila, she found the verse in the Bible "If you know the truth, He will set you free." There she prayed, asking for forgiveness and prayed to receive Jesus as Lord. At present, she is one of the pastors in her church in Hawaii.

The two youngest siblings, Luis and Lenigrace, later on prayed to receive Jesus. My father, who was very kind, took nine years of my witnessing to him, on and on, until he responded. At first, he believed that because he was good, he would go to heaven. He even told me not to return home if I continued with my new-found faith. It took my father nine years to understand that only believing and accepting Jesus as Saviour and Lord would bring him to heaven.

God set me on fire to share about Jesus, to rescue the perishing, rescue them from going to the lake of fire called hell. I remember one of our brightest students at the Institute of Nursing. He wanted to be a priest after his nursing studies. I witnessed to him and told him about Jesus. When I asked him for his response, he told me, "I will respond by Monday." But Monday never came to him, because that weekend while walking on the street, he passed out and died. I wished that he had received the Lord Jesus before he died. That was an urgent reminder to me to rescue the perishing and care for the dying. "What does it profit a man, if he gains the whole world but loses his own soul?" (Matthew 16:26)

Whenever the Lord gives me an opportunity to talk about Him, whether in witnessing, leading Bible studies, teaching Sunday School or speaking in a gathering, I speak about His love and salvation, and always give opportunities for response to His love and salvation. I began an intimate relationship with God communing with Him as my Heavenly Dad, with Him as my Friend, as my King—my all. I also began the adventure of praying and receiving answers to my prayers; I also began communing with God as if He was always beside me.

QUESTIONS TO PONDER

1. *I began the adventure of trusting God and His words like obeying Him to take the job of being a nursing instructor and He helped me till I finished my contract. Does this encourage you to trust God?*

2. *Trusting God that if I believe my family will be saved. I reached out to my family and one by one they were saved. Are you challenged to continue reaching your family and friends and even co-workers?*

3. *Pray for compassion to tell God's love and salvation to the perishing?*

CHAPTER 7

MORE ADVENTURES WITH GOD

When Joy finished his marine engineering program, he joined Operation Mobilization (OM) aboard the MV Logos, OM's first ship, as one of their youngest crew. MV Logos is a missionary ship sailing around the world to bring Christ to the nations through Christian books, evangelistic and discipleship meetings on board, and speaking in churches and schools. Those years were not the years of computers and cell phones, so we communicated with letters daily. I received his prayer letter regularly and distributed them to his prayer partners.

At the end of my term teaching in FEU, Mom Esther (Joy's mother) became very ill. Joy had to go home to Manila, from the Logos docked in Germany, to see her. I remember what she said to Joy before he left as a missionary with OM. Bidding him goodbye, she said, "If I don't see you anymore, I will see you at suppertime in heaven." During the long flight from Europe to the Philippines, Mom Esther died before Joy arrived. He brought flowers from Europe to give to his mom. Upon his arrival at night, he passed through the church on his way to the house. The church was lit and full of people. So, he asked, "why is the church full of light?" What is happening there? And he was told, "it is the viewing night of your mother." He almost dropped the flowers he was carrying. Sure enough, they did not see each other again, but it is good to know that they will see each other in heaven.

The next months followed with uncertainty. Joy received a cheque for his plane ticket back to OM, but he was caught between a decision to go back to OM as missionary or to respond to the invitation of Caltex Philippines, an oil company, to join their commercial ship as one of their crew.

We had to wait on the Lord. During my prayer time, I asked the Lord, "What will I do? Shall I proceed with my plan to join my sister in America and apply as a nurse?" He spoke into my spirit saying, "You have to marry Joy and serve me together." I responded, "Why are you telling me first, before Joy?" Then He answered me, "I told Mary first, before I talked to Joseph." This was hard to tell Joy. In Filipino culture, it is always modest for the man to be the first to talk about marriage, not the woman. In the Philippines, if the woman talks first about marriage, it would be perceived negatively. Not thinking of what people would say, I told Joy what the Lord told me. His response was, "How come the Lord did not talk to me yet?" I responded, "Just be patient. Wait, He will talk to you."

Sure enough, after a few weeks, God spoke to him through Dad Vic. He said to Joy, "You have been seeing Lulu for about four years now; why don't you get married now and serve the Lord together?" We approached our pastor, Pastor Nene Ramientos, and he told us, "Joy if you work with Caltex and Lulu will go to USA then you will not go through with your relationship. You will find another, and Lulu will find another one. It is better for you to get married then serve the Lord together." That was the confirmation of God's voice. We got engaged, with our graduation rings serving as engagement rings.Preparing for the wedding, we asked ourselves, "Where will we get money for our wedding?" My

salary as an instructor was not enough. Joy did not have savings as he just came from OM. In the 1970s, OM workers did not have a salary, but together the crew trusts God for their support. The only thing we had was Joy's cheque for his plane ticket back to Germany. We prayed to the Lord, "What are we going to do?" We were then prompted to encash the cheque for his ticket to Germany and that would be enough for the wedding. With that direction we decided our wedding to be on May 5, 1977. We bought a very simple wedding gown for about 80 pesos, and wedding rings for 10 dollars (close to 300 pesos). Currency at the time was worth more than it is at present.

On April 1, 1977, Joy's brother, Bal, who was graduating from the Philippine Military Academy, and Angie, his girlfriend, approached us and asked us if they could join us on our wedding day. We told them that we were willing, and so a double wedding was planned. The cheque for Joy's return ticket to Germany was cashed. It was enough for two wedding gowns and a reception at the original Max's restaurant in the Philippines. The double wedding turned out to be a double blessing. Our brother, Bal, and sister, Angie, and Joy and I became closer to each other, especially in times of need. We became friends and ministry partners. Praise the Lord! It is always good to share our blessings. That improved my relationship with God and my relationship with them. It is always a joy to share our blessings.

The next day, on our honeymoon, God gave me Psalms 127:3 in my devotion, and I knew at once what it meant. Psalm 127:3 Sons are a heritage from the Lord, children a reward from him. I bargained with the Lord and told Him, "Not this time Lord. We're not ready to have children. We do not have the money yet." But, God is the God who knows everything, and He knew what is best for us. Sure enough, we had a "honeymoon baby" and we named her, Lorajoy. We gave her a nick name —Ianne. Lora means victory, and Ianne means God's precious gift. Lorajoy, or Ianne as I will continue calling her in this book, stands on her name. She has been a great encouragement and help to us, especially for Joy, as she has served as his assistant for many years, even up to now. God is using her tremendously.

In our first year of marriage, Joy started another engineering program, Industrial Engineering. He did this while serving with Christ for Greater Manila in their new jail ministry, and I continued teaching in different school of nursing – Northwestern College and de Ocampo School of Nursing. Our first ministry together as a couple was in the roles of foster parents of an orphanage composed mostly of street kids—beggars, drug addicts. Some were kids as young as nine years old who were victims of rape, and some who had been rescued from the garbage, etc. We cried for these children. The world for them was difficult, scary, dark, and dangerous.

While serving the Lord in the Philippines, I used to pray over the map of the world, telling the Lord where I wanted to go. I wanted to go to a snowy land, and I thought of Iceland. I also prayed to become a handmaiden to the nations. Sure enough, after a year of ministry in the Philippines, my prayer was answered. Joy was asked to return to OM, with me, and our baby, Ianne. Together, we served God through OM, on the MV Logos, sailing around the world.

Operation Mobilization, MV Logos - Lorajoy and I with some of our friends on board from the Netherlands, Papua New Guinea India, and Singapore

I was so happy and so excited. This was my dream—to serve God in full-time ministry. On the MV Logos, I learned what ministry is. I began a very humble job in the ship; that is, cleaning toilets, along with the foyer of the ship. I was so humbled. I thought of my previous job as a university instructor, where students call me "ma'am." It was hard to believe that I was cleaning toilets with my baby. What a humble beginning! But, this taught me humility. God blessed me in this job and soon I was promoted. The ship managers liked how I cleaned the toilets and so they assigned me more toilets to clean. Isn't that a promotion? We need to thank God for everything.

Prayer has always been a part of my life, but being with OM's MV Logos, with 120 crew and staff coming from diverse nationalities with different cultural backgrounds and languages, my prayer life was revolutionized. We were a mixture of cultures and backgrounds.

The extended prayer meetings, going from 6 p.m. to 2 a.m. were faith moving. We all prayed at the same time, but in different languages. Even by the next morning, we would see God answering prayers. One night we prayed for oil because the next day we would have to sail again, but there was not enough money to buy oil for the ship. We prayed for oil that night, and the next day, the government of that city gave us free oil.

MV Logos Moms and their kids, 1979

We asked God for our daily meals. The Asians would pray for rice and bananas, and the next day we would have rations of rice and bananas. It was with OM that I learned to ask God for everything I needed instead of asking people. At OM, we were taught to share our needs with those who ask, but to never ask them to give, because we believed that it would be God who would move them to give.

Joy tells the story of a time that he walked with an OM leader at the port. There, the leader saw a van, laid his hand on it, and prayed, "Lord we need a van. Would you please touch the owner of this van to give it to OM?" Later, when the ship prepared to leave the port, Joy saw the van being lifted into the ship. The prayer had been answered.

My first job in the ship was not just cleaning toilets and foyer, but primarily being a crew member's wife and taking care of my husband, who worked as junior engineer. Along with this, I was one of the nurses on board. I also was scheduled to do laundry for all. The highlight of being a missionary is doing all services for God. I did not feel lowly and despised, but privileged to be doing my jobs for God. The jobs we had were combined with many openings for sharing our testimonies with the guests who were invited to the ship for programs including "Opening Night," to which high-ranking leaders in the government, such as the president of the country would be invited. There was also "Nurses' Night," during which we would speak for the television. It was great training.

This was my first time to go overseas. First around Asia in major cities of Japan, South Korea, Taiwan, Hongkong, Singapore, Philippines, then the Pacific including: Fiji, Samoa, Solomon Island, New Hebrides, New Caledonia, Australia, New Zealand, Papua New Guinea, and Tonga. Sailing with a hundred and twenty saints from different parts of the world helped me to work with diverse groups.

I was once angry with one of my shipmates, but God quickly checked me, convicting me to ask for forgiveness and to forgive. After all, I could not hide, for I would see this shipmate once or twice on most days.

Nobody is above another, I learned. And, all are all equal in the eyes of God. We need each other. On the MV Logos, we were a big family and assigned to a smaller family groups. Even a princess of Tonga, who had joined us as a shipmate, became an equal with us even in work. The only difference was when she boarded the ship, she had a royal send off. The princess of Tonga was assigned to the pantry, to serve food and wash the dishes. Nobody, we were taught, was of "supreme" race, whether Black, white, brown, or yellow.

SIMPLICITY was another discipline that I learned from OM. Every week, each person in the ship, including children, received one dollar. There were three of us, Joy, Ianne, and I; so, our family received three dollars a week. What can one buy for $3.00? We used it for our tithe, and if we had extra, we would buy instant noodle soup. We learned to live without money. We learned to eat whatever was served in the ship kitchen, whether we liked it or not. Sometimes it was rabbit meat, other times it was Australian bread with salty spread. I learned not to complain and to just thank God for our meals. I also learned to ask God, sometimes, for Asian food and He answered this simple prayer. Sometimes, the kitchen would serve Asian food; or when we were in ports, Filipinos in the port would invite us for Filipino meals. We learned to use hand-me-down clothes from the "Charlie," where Christians from different ports donated new and hand-me-down clothes and accessories.

Thanking and praising God became a lifestyle for me, even in times of "sea sickness" and problems. There was one time that I vividly remember.

We were in Japan in 1979. It was a time when ESL (English as a Second Language) was not a trend yet, so people in non-English speaking countries did not understand or speak English. We were going to a Bible school for meetings and to sell Christian books and literature. We took the train, transferring from one train to another. In the middle of one journey, our team leader told us that he lost his diary with the money for our return train fare to the port. I thanked God and praised Him for that situation because I knew He would solve that situation. The team leader's wife, Pramila, told me, "How can you thank and praise God for the lost diary and money?" She was so upset, but by the end of our meeting, we had already raised enough money for our fare from the proceeds of our book sale, enabling us to return to the ship.

When we stepped out of the last train, we asked the train staff at the train station if they had found a lost diary. They answered in Japanese, so we did not understand, but I perceived that what they told us was how to get back to the ship. My spirit took that as from the Lord, meaning that when we get back to the ship, we would find what we were looking for. This turned out to be right.

As we walked back to the ship, a Japanese police officer called us to go to the police station. Sure enough the diary was there with all the money inside. In Japan it was the law to turn over to the police station any lost things that are found. The finder leaves their name and contact number so that they can be rewarded for turning it over. Who had brought the diary to the ship? Was it an angel of God? There was no name and contact information that was given. This experience changed Pramila, as she testified afterwards, "I learned to praise and thank God in every situation thereafter."

I also learned not to complain or grumble. This is how I learned: one time, I complained about the food that was served in the ship. So, instead of eating there, I told Joy, "Let us go out and spend our $5.00 in the restaurant" (food in 1979 was cheap) and that is what we did. But, on the way back to the ship, my stomach became painful, and I had suffered diarrhoea after. The Lord taught me a lesson about complaining. Complaining make us forget to thank God for His blessings. Other people do not even have food to eat. They just pick food out of the garbage.

LAUGHTER and FLEXIBILITY

We need to be serious about life, but then when situations come our way, that we did not intend, we just need to be flexible. Do not fret or stay angry over it, but give the "surprise" to God, then smile and laugh. Let me give you an example.

While our family called the MV Logos, "home" for two years, people would ask Ianne, who was a toddler at that time, "Where do you live?" She would, then, point to the ship and smile. One time we were in New Zealand attending a worship service. When it was time to celebrate the Lord's Supper (Communion), the pastor led the prayer of thanksgiving. Then, we opened our eyes and found the loaf of bread missing from the communion table. Who had taken it? We turned around to find, standing next to us, Ianne holding the loaf of bread. She was the one who taken it from the Communion table. Holding our tempers, we talked to her nicely and instructed her to return the bread to the table and she did obey. Joy and I were so ashamed, but at the end of the service, the people came to us and told us; "Your girl won our hearts." That was encouraging. They did not judge or criticise us. What if we had not held our tempers and had scolded her right there? That would have humiliated her and would have made her cry.

Travelling to different countries, we observed many cultures and sometimes we found ourselves perplexed. Just like one time when we were in Australia. Every Sunday when we were at port, we signed up to a church where we would like to go. At every church, they would indicate if there was a meal or teatime after the service. Naturally, we from the ship would like a break from eating in the ship so we signed up to a church where there is meal. Following the church service, we sat at the table, and they served us tea and biscuits. We thought that was just an introduction of the meal, so we waited for the meal but then each one started to leave; we realized that their mealtime is tea time, but that was it: tea and biscuits. The next Sunday, we signed to a church where teatime was included. We found the opposite. After the service, we sat at the table, and we were served with tea or coffee followed by a sumptuous meal. Wasn't this amazing! It made us smile!

When our plans are disrupted, we should not fret but give it to the Lord and we will experience good surprises in life.

SOWING SEED OF FAITH

One of the great discoveries that I learned in OM is the principle of Seed Faith, based on Galatians 6:7—"Do not be deceived: God cannot be mocked. A man reaps what he sows" According to Mike Murdock,6 "Seed Faith" is exchanging what you have been given for what God has promised you. Your seed is anything you have that will benefit another person—your smile, a word of encouragement, time invested, shared information, financial aid, etc. Your seed is any gift, skill, or talent that God has provided for you to sow into the lives of others. Do not hide it, use it, and enjoy it. Your seed is whatever you give to God, and your Harvest is whatever God gives to you. Your harvest is any person or anything that can bless or benefit you. It may be someone who can contribute something to what you need for the kingdom...information, favour, or finances. It can even be an explosive idea. Your seed is always your bridge out of trouble (pp. 5-10).

In the ship we had an allowance of $1.00 a week or $3.00 total for Joy, Ianne, and me. So, on Sundays, we would bring most or all of it to church and give it as our tithe. Most of the time, that $3.00 would return more to us through somebody else. For example, they would gift $10.00 to Ianne, telling her it was for her to buy ice cream. While we had prayer supporters in the Philippines and abroad, we never told them about "financial support" for us as missionaries, so whenever we checked

---

6   **Mike Murdock Seeds of Wisdom Vol. 4, On Seed Faith, Amazon Book Clubs,** pp.5-10.

our support levels on record with OM, we would find that nothing had come in. Still, we thanked God for the surprises.

One time, Eddie Blazey, in New Zealand, invited us for a meal, and we made friends with him and the family. When they took us back to the ship, Eddie spoke to Joy privately handing him cash for our support. Praise God! On one occasion, I was asked to speak to a ladies' meeting in a Chinese church in the Philippines. After speaking, one approached me and placed cash in my hand; another lady followed. I realised that one by one the ladies were coming until my hands were full. It was good I had a pocket to put all the cash into. I was so humbled by the love and provision of God and His people.

The most seeds that I can sow each day are my smile and words of praise and thanksgiving, even at times of physical or emotional pain, and weariness. Encouraging words are always seed faith. I found this seed faith produces good harvest, even with difficult persons to deal with. Almost every day, we see people who are sad or grumpy, but if we smile at them or commend them, for example, with a compliment like, "Oh, that's a great idea!" they may return that praise with a big smile.

QUESTIONS TO PONDER

1. *Adventure in knowing and obeying God's will, adventure in marriage, adventure in bearing children, adventure in dreaming, adventure in serving God together as a family, adventure around the world working with different nationalities and culture and adventure of experiencing God answering prayers - are you encouraged ?*

2. *Adventure with the Almighty and loving God are you encouraged to trust and obey Him always, to thank and praise Him always because He know what is best for us?*

3. *What did you learned about simplicity of life, a lifestyle of always thanking and praising God, Flexibility and Laughter? How about Seed Faith? What seed faith do you need to sow always and at this particular time?*

4. *Do you have a challenging situation today that you need to entrust to Him?*

~ CHAPTER 8 ~

SCHOOL OF FAITH
AND ENDURANCE

As we sailed to and fro, visiting port cities of different countries, I saw the need of people…I saw their pain, suffering, and deep longings. They needed hope, love, care…We, on the ship, were convinced that they needed JESUS. They needed LIFE to the fullest that only Jesus could give. But, they did not know Jesus, so they needed us, the children of God, to introduce Jesus to them, and to bring heaven to earth.

With this burden, Joy and I saw the need for Bible school training. We decided to go for training. We applied to Wycliff Training School (WEC) in Tasmania, Australia and they accepted us there, offering full scholarships. We also applied too New Zealand Bible College (NZBC), and they accepted there as well, offering partial scholarships. The third Bible school we applied to was Canadian Bible College and Canadian Theological Seminary (CBC/CTS) in Saskatchewan, Canada. It was recommended by one of Joy's co-crew in the MV Logos. We sought God's for God's direction. For WEC—we would have had to wait six months, because there was no vacancy at the couples' dorm. For NZBC—we also would have had to wait for three months for the same reason. CBC/CTS accepted us, and they had space, but CBC/CTS did not offer any scholarship. As we prayed, God showed me a vision of a city. I did not know what city or country that was, but when I woke up, I knew it was "CANADA." We would find out that CBC/CTS was located in a region much like the "Iceland" of Canada, meaning, it was a land of ice.

There was no scholarship. Where would we get the money to go and study there? Coming out of OM, we had no money as we had only been receiving an allowance of $1.00 a week, but we trusted the Lord for His leading. We were accepted to CBC/CTS, so the next step was to apply for a furnished apartment. We were told rent was $350 monthly. Where would we find money to pay the rent? We would be on student visas and, in the 1980s, foreign students were not permitted to work in Canada, so we changed our application to request a non-furnished apartment instead.

Next, was to apply for a student visa. When Joy went to the Canadian Embassy to apply, the consul asked him, "Do you already have tickets for Canada?" Joy answered, "We have no tickets yet, because you have not given us a visa. Give us our visa first." With that answer, the consul gave him a visa, including a visa for Ianne and for me. This experience was remarkable, because despite the usual requirements for family to be present to apply for the visas of separate family members, our family did not even have to go for that interview. We did not even have to present the customary "show money." All Joy brought in was a letter from Doug Nichols, the head of Christ for Greater Manila (CGM), a mission organization in the Philippines. In the letter, Doug had stated that they would help us whenever we need help. We got the visa, but where would we get the tickets for the three of us? Joy called His older sister, Ate Mercy, who was a diplomat and journalist in Europe. He told her that we got the visas for Canada, and Ate Mercy said, "Just wait for your tickets." Three days later, we received three business class tickets from Philippine Airlines (PAL), courtesy of the owner of the airline, Mr. Lucio Tan. God is so good; He knows and responds to the needs of His children.

We left for Canada with only $300 (USD) shared with us by the church of our friends, Manuel and Consuelo Wong. We had a stopover in Hawaii, where my parents and siblings lived. There, we attended a Bible study led by my former pastor in the Philippines, Pastor Jaime Manera, and the group there shared close to $200 (USD). So, by that point, we had around $500 (USD). My parents added $500 (USD) more, which brought us to $1,000 (USD) in all. That was the only money we had when we arrived at the Calgary International Airport. While we waited for our connecting flight to Regina, Joy suddenly threw down the $1,000 cash and exclaimed, "Is this all the money we have?

Where will we get our tuition fees? Our rent for the apartment? Money for food and other things we need?!"

Oh, it was good that it was already late and so the airport was not full of people. I immediately stood up and picked up the scattered paper bills on the ground. I picked them all up and said to Joy, "This is all the money we need for tomorrow. God will take care of the following days."

As it turned out on this journey, the connecting Canadian Airlines lost our luggage, and so, we arrived at the Regina Airport with none of our belongings, except for our small carry-on bags. Mrs. Thiessen, the nurse of the school met us at the airport, and when we told her that our other luggage had been lost, she sent a message to the school saying, "The Tiras arrived, but their luggage was lost." Sure enough, the Christian community of the Christian and Missionary Alliance (C&MA) of Regina was moved by our good Father to come to our assistance. One by one, people came and left something for us to use—blankets, comforters, bed, pillows, a living room suite, cooking pots and food, and even a little bit of cash. In one day, we arrived to an unfurnished apartment; and, the Lord moved the Christian community to furnish our apartment. Two weeks later our luggage arrived. To compensate us for the inconvenience, the Canadian Airlines also gave us a cheque for the delayed baggage.

What a comfort to stay on the trusting side as we are admonished to rejoice always and to thank God for everything. We did not grumble or complain about the missing luggage; instead, we thanked God and trusted Him. Because the Lord cares for even the "smaller" things in life, He brought back our things, and added more and more. He furnished our apartment in just one afternoon! Praise the Lord. He is surely the Great Jehovah Jireh our Provider. God has a sense of humour too. The enemy wanted to steal our luggage, but God provided more. Because our luggage was lost, He moved His children to share what they had, exercising the gifts of Christian community. Canadian Airlines compensated us too. Not only that, but God also spared us from paying for a furnished apartment for $350 monthly. Instead, we paid $49 monthly, because it was unfurnished, and because we were not permitted to apply for jobs.

MORE ON GOD'S PROVISIONS...

We were on a student visa and so we could not work. Where would we get our daily food, our tuition fee, other needs? Because of our OM experience we never asked people to help us. We did not tell them that we needed food for the next day. We just told God of our needs. Almost every day, God would move people to ask me for help. They would call me to babysit their kids while there were at ladies' meetings in the church. Some would also ask me to babysit in their homes, then they would feed us when Joy and Ianne would pick me up later. While eating I would be praying that there would be leftovers and they will pack it to send it with us—and God answered. Joy sometimes would ask me, "Did you ask for this?" I always responded, "Yes, I asked it from God, but I did not ask our host." God gave us friends in Regina who helped us. While in CTS, God's love and faithfulness was clearly seen.

The $1000 we brought to Canada plus the welcome cash for our food that week had been spent. Where would we get money to complete our tuition fees (Joy was a full-time student while I just picked up courses to take – I was a partial student)? Where would we get money for our food and clothing, and other needs like utility bills, etc., in the succeeding days, weeks, months, and years? We arrived in Canada in September 1981. We were attending a Baptist Church and studying in a Christian and Missionary Alliance Seminary. With desperation for the Lord and His enabling, we cried to the Lord in a nearby playground almost every day. We learned to lay hands on our bills. We did not have credit cards or cheques or savings. God, in His sovereignty, provided for all our needs, one day at a time.

Food was provided for us, one day at a time. We never told anyone that we didn't have any food for the next day. As the evening arrived, sometimes, a Filipino couple—R ograson and Cecille Euroba would invite us for supper. Eventually, they became our close friends and ministry partners. There was another couple, Rolf and Linda Sweitzer, who provided us with rice every month. Rev. Ray Matheson, the Dean of students in CTS, was a great help to us. There were more couples from CTS who gladly invited us for meals. One night, as we were preparing to sleep, not knowing where the next day's meal would come from, there was a knock at the door. When I opened it, it was Joy's classmate, a farmer bringing a big box of vegetables, milk, and two dozen eggs. TV Thomas, who became a Kuya (big brother) to us, helped us in those times by visiting and encouraging us, inviting us in for meals, and giving rides to us every weekend to go and buy day-old discounted bread at McGavin's costing 50 cents each. But where would we get money, even just a dollar? We did not tell TV that we did not have money; we just went with him. But before he arrived at our apartment, I would go to the closet and look for coins in the pockets of our outerwear. There I would find 75 cents, or exactly one dollar – good for two loaves of bread.

For tuition fees, the Lord did wonders in meeting our needs. One time, as we prepared for mid-term exams, we received a note from school reminding us to pay our tuition fee. Again, the Lord intervened. As I went to the office to let them know of our need (meaning, we didn't have money yet) the office told me, "It is paid already. Your professor paid for it." How did my professor ever come to know that my tuition fee was not yet paid? I did not tell him. It was the Spirit of God who revealed it to him.

For clothing and other needs at home, I thanked God for "NEW TO YOU" at the seminary, that was like the "CHARLIE" of OM. Students who would graduate and Christians who had more than enough would donate their stuff. They would be placed in a room called NEW TO YOU and we would go there to look for stuff we needed. Oh, there were lots of times that we experienced divine intervention. How did we live in Regina, Saskatchewan, Canada, where we studied for three years? We did not have a source of income for our daily needs. We could not work before because we were on student visas. We did not have savings. We did not have scholarships. Furthermore, with our OM training guiding us, we could only tell our needs to God, so we continued in that way. We lived one day at a time.

Some international students make their needs known, but not us. One time before Christmas, some international students were given free turkey. We did not know about it. But just a day before Christmas, one international student gave us their turkey because they were going to the USA. There, we found out that most of the international students were given turkey. Why did we not receive one? Because we never told our needs – the abundance of God was seen in us instead. Whenever we did not have food anymore, we would receive food in kind like potatoes, cabbage, carrots, eggs, etc. Surprisingly, somebody would hand us a cheque (just enough for our needs) from students. Every day we would be excited to open our mailbox, waiting for a surprise. Instant noodles and eggs were our staple food every day and we did not get sick. For birthdays and special occasions, we sometimes went to McDonalds to celebrate, if we had some cash from babysitting. For everything we received–whether it was something like food, cash or second-hand coats we wrote them in a notebook to remind us of God's faithfulness.

We were in the school of faith and endurance. Even with this situation we tried to give our tithes to the Lord. But after church, we received more than what we gave. For in kind, we also shared to other seminary students by giving to them or inviting them for a simple meal that we could afford. I was encouraged to learn to be a good cook. I learned to cook instant noodles in so many ways.

There was one thing that we learned while at the Canadian Theological Seminary. As church ladies meeting would call me to babysit, on rare occasions they forgot to give me money for babysitting. So, I would just be silent, not telling them but praying that they would remember to give it next time. And they did. I would also be planning already to buy milk and groceries for the $10 I earned for two hours and to take Ianne for McDonalds. But then if Joy needed to buy second-hand textbooks, the babysitting money was used for that. But daily we experienced God's provisions and one thing we learned is that God is always faithful. For those books we bought were so important, and we took care of them—but when we went for our summer ministry, our friends' basement where our books were stored, was flooded. Another lesson learned.

QUESTIONS TO PONDER

1. *Our life in getting to Canada at the Canadian Bible College and Theological Seminary and studying there for three years is unbelievable but experiences like these become a necessity to the development of faith and endurance. Through these experiences, we don't only know God through studying and meditating His Words, but experiencing who God is and experiencing the fulfillment of His Living Words. Declare who He is in your life and who you are to Him and claim His promises.*

2. *What is Faith?*

3. *What should be our attitude towards challenges of life?*

4. *Is there anything difficult or impossible with God ? Mark 10:27: "Matthew19:26: ......" with man, this is impossible but with God all things are possible........ ." and your faith in God will be rewarded. God can change impossible situations, so do what you can and God will successfully execute what you can't.*

CHAPTER 9

ON CHURCH PLANTING, PASTORING AND EXPANDING MINISTRY

In our first summer in Canada, we went to Seattle, Washington for our summer ministry. We started Bible study among the Filipino immigrants. There we saw our ninang (godmother) Josie, who discipled me again (She did not realise that it was us because the name submitted to them was Joy and Lulu Pira, not Tira.). It was funny and we laughed when she discovered it was us. She and her husband, Kuya Bert (former Philippine Nurses Christian Fellowship (NCF) staff), were great help while we were there. The Lord blessed the Bible Study group, and they grew in number. After summer ministry, we went back to CTS to continue our studies. That Bible study group called a pastor that became the Filipino Church of North Seattle Alliance Church.

During those summer months, I had a dream of my friend Ruth Chong. In my dream she became pregnant, and I, too, became pregnant after two weeks. After a few months, I found out that Ruth was pregnant with her second boy, Caleb. I also found out that I had become pregnant with our second child, Tonyvic. That dream was from God. It was not a coincidence. It was a revelation from God through a vision. It was a prophetic dream.

At the end of our second year at CTS, we needed to go for internship. We applied in California to intern in a Filipino church in Los Angeles, but the Lord closed it for us. Instead, God showed me a vision of us in Edmonton. The city of Edmonton was not familiar to us, but God showed me a vision of an elderly man helping us in Edmonton. Millbourne Alliance Church (MAC), which was in Edmonton had already accepted an intern that time but still accepted us as their second intern to work among Filipino immigrants. I found out later that the man in my vision was the chairman of the board of MAC named Horatio McCombs. He picked us up at the train station and brought us to one of the units in the apartment he and his wife owned at that time. There we lived for three months. They also bought us our first car – a very modest old yellow green Pinto. Horatio and Hope were so nice and kind to us. Sometimes they invited us to their home for a meal. The Lord used them greatly in our lives. They even provided the down payment for our first home in Canada. So, we gave them post-dated cheques to pay for it, only to receive them back later after five years with a note in bold letters saying **"FORGIVEN."**

Joy worked under the coaching of Rev. Vergil Schmidt, who became like a big brother to Joy. We started Bible study among Filipinos attending at Millbourne Alliance Church. Joy visited sports facilities where the Filipinos would play basketball. He would play with them and befriend them and invite them for coffee at Boston Pizza. From these basketball players were some youths, who joined our Bible study until they received Jesus as their Lord and Saviour. Some of them were baptized before we finished our summer internship and went back to Regina. The Lord is good, when we left Edmonton for Regina, they passed an offering to help us in our tuition fees. It was a generous offering–that paid all our tuition fees that last year of study. Joy finished the Masters in Missiology studies.

We were allowed to drive the old Pinto car back. In the middle of a Saskatoon Highway, the car gave up. We tried to ask for help but nobody was stopping. So, Joy stayed in the middle of the road until a tow truck came to help. Joy had to ask a passing truck driver to bring us to the city centre where we could rest. He trusted that man not to harm us. Praise God we were safe. Horatio called somebody to help us in Saskatoon. The car was fixed, and we managed to bring it to Regina.

After four years of waiting to have a playmate, Ianne asked us if she could have a baby brother or sister. We encouraged her to pray to God for a brother or a sister. And she did pray until I got pregnant after that dream I had (my friend Ruth and I simultaneously got pregnant). With this pregnancy I was found out to be diabetic. My obstetrician ordered insulin for me. I was not comfortable with it, and I studied about divine healing. The more I read about it the more I prayed, the Lord increased my faith that He will take care of me. With that faith, I decided not to have insulin injections and to trust God completely for the baby. God answered my prayers. On May 15, 1983, Tonyvic was born normal and healthy.

As we prepared for Joy's graduation, our thought was, "How can we go home to the Philippines? We do not have money for airfare. We cannot stay longer in Canada because we are just on student visa."

We prayed for God's direction. We wanted to go to Mauritius as missionaries, but the Lord did not allow us. Then in the middle of these questioning, Millbourne Alliance Church, where we interned, sent a message that they wanted us to go back and start a Filipino church as their daughter church. To be able to go to Edmonton and work there, we should go home to the Philippines and apply for a working permit. Rev. Vergil Schmidt used his credit card temporarily to buy us plane tickets. What a nice pastor, our big brother. From then on until now, he remains to be our family pastor, our big Kuya (big brother).

What a joy it was to be back home in the Philippines. That was a three month "treat" for us, in spite of a potentially dangerous situation that we encountered. This incident happened when we were busy preparing to go back to start pastoral ministry in Canada. One night as we were all sleeping, we were awakened by a loud barking of dogs. So, Joy stood up, turned on the light and opened our bedroom door which is adjacent to the house' back door. Something fell. It was a cobra on our bedroom door! It could not crawl because the floor was slippery but it moved towards Tonyvic and me. Praise God for His protection. This is one good aspect of having a life to the fullest, we have the divine protection of God.

We went back to Edmonton, Canada, and began our ministry with the goal to plant a Filipino church under Millbourne Alliance Church. We had Bible study groups, prayer meetings, camps, concerts, etc. God is so good; the Filipino Christian Alliance Fellowship (FCAF) was planted.

In my three pregnancies, I always prayed that I would deliver earlier than my expected date of delivery (and God answered it). When I delivered Tonyvic it was my first time to be hospitalized in a Canadian hospital. I was well taken care of. What amazed and made me cry with joy was when I was discharged with Tonyvic, we did not pay anything, even a single cent. We were not Canada's immigrants nor citizens that time, we were only aliens on a student visa but still the dominion of Canada took care of us.

After more than a year I wanted to buy a dress for mysef, but it seemed that the Lord was telling me that I did not need it. And I came to know the reason why – I was pregnant for the third time. The dress I wanted would not fit me later so, I did not need one. Then I had a series of dreams, one coming after the other. The dream was about me dying. Joy had a dream about me dying too. Ianne, in her young age, did not like the dream, so she started praying, "Lord, my brother and I are still young, will you please let my mom live longer." She prayed that constantly. Joy and I prayed too that the Lord would extend my years.

When I was already in my ninth month of pregnancy and was about to deliver our third child, the Lord visited me. As I was alone at home I went into deep prayer. I found myself pleading for my life praying, "Preserve me Lord," while on and on asking in my mind "why am I praying to God to preserve me?" Little did I know that something would happen the next day and God would preserve my life. The next day I was rejuvenated. I was singing with praises unto the Lord.

After the household chores, Tonyvic, Joy, and I went to church, and it was snowing. Just a few metres from the church we had a head on collision with a 1-ton truck. It was good that I was not wearing a seat belt–otherwise the baby should have been smashed and put more danger in my life. I was not thrown out of the little car, but I found myself sitting on the floor of the car in front of my seat. Somebody came and helped but then I did not recognize the person anymore, I just passed out. I was told later that it was our great helper - Horatio, the chairman of the board of Millbourne Alliance Church, our mother church. We were rushed to the hospital by an ambulance, but the emergency doctors said they could not find anything wrong in me, so in spite of great pain, they discharged me. They did not even call my obstetrician.

Thank God for Miriam Roque who took me into their house and nursed me. That night, the baby inside my womb did not move anymore. I called Joy who was in the hospital watching Tonyvic who was admitted in the hospital. Joy called my obstetrician who ordered my admission back in the hospital. The baby died that night and the next two days they found out that I had three ribs broken. My pelvic bone was broken and was told that I would not to be able to walk for a year. I had a haem-orrhage inside and carried a dead baby for nine days. The doctor could not do a Caesarean operation or induce delivery. My obstetrician waited until I laboured on the 9th day of my hospitalization.

It was so painful, even just to move. An eight-person moving team would change my position to prevent decubitus ulcers. But in the midst of pain, I vocally thanked God for it, and I praised Him for enabling me to live. The hospital staff saw and witnessed my positive attitude, and they were encouraged. With worship songs played in my room - I felt the Presence of God, I continued communing with Him, praising Him in my pain, thanking Him for His touch and healing. The anointed worship music played in my room by CD player brought by Liberty Tuazon indeed brought me into the presence of God. I was told by my doctor that I would not be able to walk for maybe a year because of my broken pelvis, and some of my ribs were broken. But God is the Jehovah Rapha, the Balm of Gilead, the Great Physician. He touched me and completely healed me after about three months.

This is what happened during the time of rehabilitation – learning to walk again, from wheelchair to crutches – it was easier for me to just crawl on the floor. Ianne would see that, and she pitied me. One day, after about three months of not being able to walk, Ianne declared to me "Mommy, you can walk now, you do not need these crutches anymore.

"Walk."

That was God speaking to me through my daughter. So, I put down my crutches and walked. And surely, I was able to walk within three months despite the doctor's declaration that I might not be able to walk within one year. That was a miracle. The doctor could not believe it. He literally let me stand on the table and saw me walk and jump to prove that I was healed. It's almost 36 years now and I am still alive, God answered our prayer for my life to be extended. He is Jehovah Rapha, the balm of Gilead. God completely healed me, there were no side effects of the accident.

TRAGEDY TO TRIUMPH

(This was my testimony of the accident written in our church bulletin at Millbourne Alliance Church)

"God causes all things to work together for good to those who love God..." (Romans 8:28)

In the afternoon of November 17, 1985, I was just led to pray. I was in tears as I praised the Lord and asked Him to spare my life.

It was a deep communion with God, and I enjoyed his presence. As I prayed, I wondered why I was asking the Lord to spare my life, but I knew of the elation I had in my spirit. I soon found myself singing and rejoicing in the Lord as I was doing my chores.

At 2:10 p.m. the next day, my son Tonyvic and I went out and as we were approaching the church, our car skidded and collided head-on with a truck. Our car was totally wrecked and the three of us were injured badly. We were rushed to the hospital by the ambulance. I was so helpless and in pain. However, the emergency staff found nothing wrong with me. Without further examining me or monitoring my baby who was due for about a week later, the emergency staff discharged me in the evening without consulting my obstetrician. That night was a difficult time for me especially when I noticed that my baby was not moving anymore. The following morning Joy called my obstetrician and he ordered me to be back in the hospital, I was rushed back to the hospital then only to find out that the baby was dead already. It was also diagnosed that I had pelvic fracture and three broken ribs. The dead baby was in my womb for nine days more before normal delivery came. Before my delivery, Joy and I prayed with our obstetrician. It was the hardest labour and delivery I ever had. The anaesthesiologist tried four to six times to put me to sleep but he failed. I cried to the Lord praising Him for His sovereignty over my situation. In His grace I delivered a beautiful dead baby girl weighing 7.8 pounds. We named her Charis Faith Jabez (meaning Grace delivered in grace and faith and in pain).

Through all my pains and sufferings, the Lord taught me many profound and beautiful things. My faith and forbearance increased. Indeed, this is the Christian's unique privilege. I'm so glad that I am His child, and He is all in my life. In that time of deep sorrow we felt His love, comfort and mercy. The sympathy and love of many brethren lightened our grief.

We cannot understand why we lost our baby, but we are sure of one thing: the Lord knows best, and He has a better plan. Because of Jesus, there is comfort in times of sorrow and hope for grieved hearts. As I lay in my hospital bed recuperating, I could sense God's daily presence and the peace, love, comfort and strength it brought. The hospital personnel were amazed as to why I could sing and praise God in spite of the crisis. They too, were surprised at the many visitors who came to encourage and pray with me. My room was soon flooded with flowers, food, and lots of letters from people who assured us of their love and prayers.

God's healing hands was upon me. The intense pain gradually subsided and after three weeks I was able to return home with crutches. Upon arriving home, I found a month-long schedule of ladies who would be bringing meals daily and cleaning the house. It was planned and organized by the ladies of Millbourne Alliance Church. They indeed helped me a lot in my recovery. Their assistance was God's provision to meet my need for some help at home.

God is so faithful. He turned that tragedy into a triumph. Out of that tragedy, I came to know Him more. Truly He is loving, merciful and compassionate. Indeed, He is a Great Physician and Comforter. Out of this tragedy, I came to know more of Christian love... how brothers and sisters in the Lord love sacrificially and truly.

Out of this tragedy, we saw the Lord sparing our lives. He prepared me for that accident by moving me to pray intimately to Him just the night before it happened. God never makes mistakes. He is great and all knowing. Someday we will understand why this tragedy occurred–this tragedy that was turned into a triumph... this tragedy that brought us closer to Him and to the brethren in the faith.

Ianne and Tonyvic grew up with the church family. The FCAF saints became their grandpas, grandmas, aunties, uncles, and cousins. One time, Tonyvic in his toddler years was enjoying eating a cob of corn. Later on, he used a silver fork to remove the kernels. He held it so hard that he poked his eye with the fork. He started crying. As for me, I closed my eyes so as not to see his eye that was poked and just prayed and praised the Lord. I thanked Him for healing Tonyvic. I did this for twenty minutes, just praying and thanking God. When I opened my eyes, I did not see any streak of blood, and he had stopped crying. This was the second miracle in Tony's life. The first was when I did not take insulin while I was pregnant with him. Like his sister, he prayed to receive Jesus as his Lord and Saviour when he was four years old.

When Tony turned six, he watched "Left Behind," one of the Second Coming series. The Rapture is one of the doctrines of Christianity prophesying that Jesus will come again to take His children to heaven. Those who accepted Him as Lord and Saviour will meet Him in the clouds. But those who were not raptured – those who have not received Jesus Christ as their Lord and Saviour will remain here on earth to suffer. He said to himself, "I do not want to be left here on earth to suffer, I want to be with Jesus in heaven." So, he prayed again and gave his life to God. I told him, "Tony, you already prayed to receive Jesus when you were four." He responded, "Mom, I just want to be sure that I belong to Jesus." That's Tonyvic. He grew up to be a fine man. He worked first with McDonald's restaurant, then in an accounting firm, Blue Cross, with Air Canada that brought him to many places, then at present as a pastor. I praise God for his life. His son Bishop accepted the Lord when he was four years old but later on as we studied the book of John through the Gospel of John movie, he said I want to receive Jesus. I told him you already received Jesus. And like his dad, he wanted to renew his relationship with the Lord and follow Him now that he understood more.

As a pastor's wife, I experienced being under constant scrutiny. I felt like a fish in an aquarium and so I needed to be careful of what I said and did. Sometimes, I was judged, and it discouraged me and gave me negative feelings like fear, and being suicidal, etc.–but as I spend time with God, He would speak to me in spirit and carry me through. He would comfort me and help me to soar like an eagle. He has always been a Healer to me even over my hurts. If not for my intimate relationship with God I don't know how I would have found and enjoyed life to the fullest. Jesus said, "If you abide in Me, you will bear fruits" (John 15:4) which means we will flourish or bloom. At the end of this book, you will read how I coped with discouragement, fear, low self-esteem, hurts, suicidal attempts, and others.

For Ianne, I told her since she was young, "I do not want to be just your mom, I want to be your friend and your confidante." Whatever problem you have, you have to tell me so I can help and pray for you.

And sure enough, we became best friends, even when sometimes her opinion differs from mine. When she has a problem, she would call and we would pray together. She became the right hand of Joy, as his administrative assistant. She studied Bachelor of Theology and went to Asia for internship (Philippines and South Korea) to teach in Christian School. Her family is also very involved at church.

I am happy God answered my prayers for my children. I vividly remember before, when they used to go to elementary school – I would

The Tira family

Our family's 1st Filipino ministry under Millbourne Alliance Church, 1983

watch them until they were out of my sight then entrust them to the Lord for their safety.

I thank God for the brethren in the church. I am away from my siblings–most of them are in the USA and one of them lives in the Philippines. But even though I am far away from my siblings, my church family became close to me. As we minister to them, they too minister to us in many ways like helping our kids, babysitting them, surprising us with gifts like food and many more. It is a joy to see them grow in maturity, loving God and becoming good citizens. Pastoring a church is challenging but fulfilling. It is a calling from God with a lifestyle of simplicity reminding us always not to want more of the world but want more of God, a lifestyle of dedication and sacrifice. It is always a joy when people would respond to the love of God.

EXPANDING MINISTRY

Life in the pastorate is challenging in a rich advanced area like North America. There are temptations around to have more treasures on earth, resulting to busyness, self-sufficiency, and pride; to others – frustration, discouragement, low self-esteem, fear, etc. But these did not discourage us. Joy and I felt that we both are called to ministry, not only him, but including me. So, I did not plan to work outside, rather I helped my husband in his church ministry. We lived a simple life. He opened opportunities for me to be involved in the ministry using the ministry gift the Lord gave me – teaching Bible studies, Sunday School, and evangelism. I made sure that in each class I teach, I present to them God's love and salvation and give them the chance to respond to it by praying in repentance and accepting Jesus, as their Lord and Saviour. I

2002, Expanding Ministry

enjoyed the ministry and feel fulfilled in spite of the trials and difficulties along the way.

In spite of our simple lifestyle, we taught our kids that we are rich because our God is rich, we told them "Our bank is in heaven. If we need something, we just ask our Father in heaven, in the name of Jesus. If you want toys you pray about it. If it is not good for you God will not give it." We also taught them to be sensitive to the needs of others and to be hospitable and generous always. Knowing that God provides our needs makes us unselfish, not holding on to what we have, but there must be willingness to share. "It is more rewarding to give or share than to receive."

God is the Great Shepherd. He will never leave us lacking. He always leads us to green pastures. We experienced living in a two-room mobile home. We grew a vegetable garden at the back yard. The first home that we owned was a three-story condo with four rooms. It was a favourite place of the young people since it was close to Millbourne Alliance Church, our mother church. One night, as I was with Ianne and Tonyvic in the room, fear gripped us. So, I told them that we will pray. While praying, I saw somebody at the door, so tall like the door, with a sword and dressed in white. With that vision I was comforted by the Lord – that He is watching over us and we do not have to be afraid. That was my first time to see an angel. We sometimes do Bible study at home, especially women's' Bible study and prayer time. I praise God for people coming over to pray and receive Jesus. For those who wanted to be prayed for, some received healing and deliverance, and some received more understanding of God and the Christian life.

While I grew in ministry, I also grew spiritually. I wanted to know more of God and his love. My prayer even, now, as I prepare this book, is to hunger and thirst for more of God and His words.

I learned my top priorities:

1st is God
2nd is my husband
3rd is my children
4th is the ministry

In spite of being a busy housewife and a busy pastor's wife, I made sure to have my quiet time with God and his words and prayer. Even if I only got a few hours of sleep, I have to rise up early to meet with God—worshiping Him, thanking Him and entrusting the day to Him. Worshiping Him, meditating on his words, soaking in his presence is a <u>must</u> and not to be set aside. This is where I find strength and courage.

My HUSBAND is my soul mate. He should be my next priority after God. He always wants me to be with him and help him in the ministry. I am his confidant, nurse, friend, home engineer, cook, home manager, etc. We mentor and teach each other. One time he told me, "Let's go out and have a date." I reasoned out, "I can't, I still have to wash the dishes." With that he rebuked me saying, "You know that I am a very busy person, so if I tell you that we go out, leave the dishes and come with me." That rebuke opened my eyes, after that incident we made sure that we have time for each other to kindle our love relationship, not only our role and ministry relationship. Marriage is not only EROS (romantic love) but also PHILEO (brotherly love) and AGAPE (love for God). In loving my spouse, there should be Eros, Phileo and Agape. If there's only eros, marriage is shaky. I need to love my husband as a brother too and love him with the love of God. Sometimes, our spouses have shortcomings and irritate us, that is the time we have to love them more, to be patient with them because they are our brothers and if they still come in their weakness and shortcomings, then loving them with God's love – help much to sustain our marriages.

That is one of the keys to have a successful marriage.

Our CHILDREN, as the <u>third priority,</u> are nurtured and disciplined. We taught them the importance of education – first from the Word of God, the Bible, so they will not depart from it when they grow older, and from the school and the local church. Personal Bible reading and meditation, attending Sunday School, going to school, and doing their homework is a must.

We taught them the importance of work while studying. Tonyvic first worked at McDonald's restaurant – and Joy would watch him with pity as he mopped the floor. Ianne first worked at a retail store. She first left us when she went to the Philippines for internship then to South Korea to be a tent maker, until she got sick after eleven months. So, we went to take her home. Tonyvic joined short term missions in Spain.

We tried to be balanced, but I know that we had shortcomings too. Sometimes in our busyness, we failed to pick them up at school on time. When we got angry, sometimes discipline became too much because of anger.

But we praise God for their lives. Now they have their own families, and they are walking with God and serving Him. At present, Tonyvic is the lead pastor of his church while Ianne is finishing her graduate studies. She continues to help her dad as his administrative assistant. In October 2021, she was in Ecuador as a workshop speaker at the Alliance World Fellowship (AWF) Quadrennial Convocation.

MINISTRY — For people serving in the ministry like us, there is a temptation to make ministry a top priority: starting when you wake up to a new day, even to the last minute at night before going to sleep. There is always a voice calling for our attention. And if we yield to the voice of ministry, we leave aside our top priority that is hosting the Presence of God who is the Holy Spirit. We ran at once to ministry. I see this temptation not only with me but to many others. So as much as possible, even with the problem of not being able to sleep well, I always try to stand up and spend time with God. I have learned through Bill Johnson's devotional book (Hosting the Presence Everyday) that having the Holy Spirit's indwelling in us is different from hosting the Holy Spirit. Hosting the Holy Spirit is taking action to host Him, action like praising Him, praying, enjoying Him, listening to Him, talking to Him, being still and know Him more.

We believers have the Holy Spirit indwelling in us but many of us may not be hosting Him. We just let Him be in us, but we are not enjoying His presence, no time to spend in the Word and in prayer; we just rush to accomplish our tasks. It is like a husband and wife so busy at work that there is no more time to be intimate with each another. No more time to encourage and speak words of love, words of appreciation, no more ears to listen, because either one or both are tired. There is no more time to listen to each other. That is what is happening to many of God's children. There is no more time to be still and know that He is God. We just put Him aside without intention to do it.

Hosting God's Presence is of utmost importance. He desires to move in our midst. The key here is us, stewarding His move accordingly. God's outpouring is nothing short of His indwelling. He is faithful to show us who He is and how He works. Again, Bill Johnson in his book, Hosting The Presence7 wrote: "When the Holy Spirit rests upon a person without withdrawing, it is because He has been made welcome in a most honourable way. To lose passion for God always affects our ability to allow the Holy Spirit to flow from us to change circumstances around us." Hosting His Presence through being still, through His words and communing with Him in prayer enables us to let Him work through us in His Power.

This is the power in ministry – the Holy Spirit in complete control. Not our status or high theological education. It is the presence of God – the Holy Spirit. Many believe in the Holy Spirit but reject His Presence, His works, and His Gifts to be manifested. They put timing into God's work or put God into a box. God's word says, "It's not by might nor by power but by My Spirit says the Lord" (Zachariah 4:6). Even I myself was an object of ridicule because of the gift of tongues the Lord gave me. I was branded a fanatic because I really believe the face value of the Scripture. The gift of praying in tongues has been a great help to me in my relationship with God. Whenever I pray in tongues, the Lord brings me to intimacy with Him and helps me navigate in the spiritual realm. I use this gift in prayer when I am alone praying. With this I ask God for the gift of interpretation.

---

7   Johnson, Bill Hosting the Presence Everyday: 365 Days to Unveiling Heaven's Agenda for Your Life, Destiny Image Publishers, Inc., Shippensburg, PA, 2014, Sept. 18 Reading.

QUESTIONS TO PONDER

1. *Without Joy's knowledge, I started praying for him to become a pastor while we were in OM with MV Logos. Sure enough, God started to work in his heart by giving him a desire to go for bible school training. After studying at Canadian Theological Seminary, God brought us back to where we interned and started planting a church . Inspite of the many challenges of being in just one pastorate, Joy was a pastor in this church from its inception in 1983 to 2008 for about 25 years until we left to become International Workers in our denomination partnering with CCCC and FIN.*

2. *What were the challenges we encountered especially for me as a wife, as a mother, as a minister's wife and worker? Did God gave us the victory ?*

3. *God is a healer, is there anything that you cannot trust Him? Do you believe that our tragedy can turn into triumph?*

4. *What should be our priorities? What were the principles God taught us to teach to our children?*

5. *For ministry and work, what principles do we learned from the Word of God. Can ministry become an "idol - one that take priority in our lives before God"*

~ CHAPTER 10 ~

GOD'S PROTECTION AND SURPRISES

While doing Joy's requirements for his ordination as minister, we would do long drives to a place where he would have enough time to write. And in all these drives, we always experienced the safekeeping of God. One time as we were driving back to Edmonton from Regina, we stopped at a hotel to spend the night in North Battleford so we could rest before we continued the drive back home to Edmonton. As Joy went to check in, he just changed his mind and said, "Let us continue driving, there is danger here, there's a witch." Another time, we found an inn in the middle of nowhere, we were so tired. We stopped and checked in. We told the receptionist that we are checking in for two days and two nights. But when we woke up the next day, he told me, "Let's get out of here before something bad happens to us." There were many times that God would alert us if there was danger and so we acted in obedience.

I cannot forget the time when we drove to Mexico from Edmonton. In one of our church celebrations, the FFAC board told us that they were disciplining somebody, and that is Pastor Joy. Joy was so nervous that he went in front and asked, "What am I being disciplined for, I cannot think of anything." They answered, "You have been working hard and you need to have a break." There, they gave an envelope of cash for our expenses and lent a van for us to drive where we wanted to go. We decided to go to Mexico via Utah. It was good that one of Joy's friends in the church, Robert Roque, accompanied us to help drive until San

Francisco, and then he flew back to Edmonton. That was the longest drive we have ever experienced, Edmonton to Mexico.

On our way back to Edmonton, we were fine until we were in Canada passing through Blue Water, etc. It was a bad weather, and the road was not visible, but we could not stop because we were in the middle of nowhere; it was all roads, mountains and snow without any house or building. With this danger, I was scared. But then God provided an elongated light like a fire in the sky. This light guided us until we reached a safe place. The light brought us courage to continue. We remembered the Israelites on their exodus to the Promised Land – a light by night to guide them, and cloud by day to shield them from the scorching sun (Exodus 13;21-22)   God is so good. Those who hide in the shelter of the Most High shall abide in the shadow of the Almighty (Psalm 91:1). God is still the same, yesterday, today, and tomorrow.

When you fully give yourself to the Lord to serve Him, He will equip you and provide all your needs, even clothes that you need to wear in the ministry. In Joy's early years of ministry with the elderly in the MAC church like Mr. Sinclair and Mr. Silver, they would surprise him by giving him a coat and tie, so he had something nice to wear when he preached. He used these give-away suits also to share to others who need it on special occasions like weddings. This reminds me of my wedding dress. I gave it to my eldest sister to wear in her wedding day. Then she passed it on, my wedding dress became a wedding gown of about 7 brides, Praise the Lord!

For trainings that equipped us more in the ministry, God also provided. Here is one of our experiences that God provides for our specific need. One day, a certain Dr. Holliday left a message in our answering machine that he needed to be called back. But Joy was hesitant to call back as he didn't know him. He thought it was just propaganda like a holiday promotion. Until the second and third attempt asking him to respond, Joy chose not to call back. With that response I told him, "Why don't you call him back? It must be so important that he called three times already." So, he responded and called Dr. Holliday. To his surprise Dr. Holliday told him, "It's good you called back, you are one of the chosen pastors of Canada to go for a study tour in Israel and Germany. And this is not for you alone, it is also for your wife." He could not believe what he heard and so he investigated Dr. Holliday; like who gave his name, etc., until he was sure that it is real. Thank God, he responded to the call, otherwise we would have missed it. That study

Pastor Joy Sadiri Tira and Lulu, left second row, with the participants of the _____ _____ _____ on the steps of the Dome or Rock in Jerusalem.

tour made an impact in our lives and ministry. It was an experience being in a special group hosted by the government. We were treated as VIPs, but the best experience was walking where Jesus walked and being in places that we read in the Bible. We had a preacher in the team and an Israel scholar who taught us. In going to Germany, we were able to visit where Martin Luther was born and grew up. It was an added bonus. This gift was a surprise from God. We could never have afforded such study of the Holy Land and Luther's place of ministry.

After taking some courses at Taylor Seminary, without intending to finish another degree, Joy finished another master's degree. With this he was given another surprise – a scholarship for PhD studies at Reformed Seminary, but he became ill and his health became a challenge. He was diagnosed with a liver disease and was told that his life expectancy would be short. But God touched him and healed him. As of today, he is still alive, and his specialist saw God's intervention upon his life. Through God's enabling, he finished instead two s – Doctor of Ministry from Reformed Seminary in Louisiana, USA, and Doctor of Missiology from Western Seminary in Oregon. These studies were given free to him through the help of people who have found the Life. Dr. Enoch Wan has been a great mentor and a fatherly coach to him. He and Aunt Mary became our mentors.

I thank God for the more than two decades in the pastoral ministry with humility, Joy depended on God to help him to become a good pastor. He had no experience in pastoring, but God enabled us to plant a church from a Bible study group to a daughter church of Millbourne Alliance Church. After about three years, we grew in number, and we became the Filipino Christian Alliance Fellowship. We got our first building with about a 100-person capacity with the help of the CMA district and generous and abled people. After a year we found the place to be small as people were saved and joined the church. We needed to look for a bigger place of worship. One time, Joy and another pastor passed through a United Church for sale. They stopped and Joy laid his hands on the building praying that if it is God's will for us to have the building, then they will sell it to us. They were selling it for one million dollars. We had no money, but we went there and prayed for his will and provisions. We offered to buy it for half a million. There were companies who offered more. But we persevered in prayer. We also had a 24-hour prayer. God is so good!

The church celebrates the final payment of the building. Now, it is debt free. The mortgage had been fully paid when Jay and I left the church for Toronto assignment. 2008

Miraculously, in spite of our lower offer the godly leaders of the United Church chose to sell it to us because they saw how we prayed, and God gave them the impression that we would use the building for the glory of God and not for business or other reasons. But where would we get the money for down payment? We had no building fund, most of our members were Overseas Contract Workers, Domestic Helpers and Students. Our helpers Horatio and Hope donated a cheque to be matched by CMA Western district. The FCAF had pledge and some gave their wedding and graduation rings.

Praise God we were able to give the down payment and returned the graduation and wedding rings that had been given. In about 10 years the building was paid off in 2008. This is a testimony of God's faithfulness. There is nothing impossible with God. If you believe Him, He will act on your behalf. By God's grace, our local church grew into more Filipino churches of the Christian Missionary Alliance, Canada. It became the CFAM (Conference of Filipino Alliance Ministries) where Joy became the first coordinator. We also helped other Filipino churches with different denominations to start churches in Edmonton.

There were so many surprises God has given to us like love gifts in cash or food or help. They came when we needed them, and we did not work for them or ask them. God used these people to bless us! I remember one time when we were in United Arab Emirates. Our van was stuck in the sand, and we cannot move on. We prayed, and you know what happened? A person of royalty passing by saw us and he came to offer help. He tried to pull our van with his sports car, but our van was still stuck. What he did, he left us and told us he would return. Sure, he did return with a truck to pull our van from being stuck in the sand. Can you imagine a person of royalty helping us? It is only God who can initiate such a response from middle eastern royalty!

We had two surprises at the time when FIN (Filipino International Network) was founded in Larnaca, Cyprus in the late 1990's. First was a surprise Wedding Anniversary get-away to a famous Mediterranean restaurant—while the leadership talked. We were in a hectic schedule to celebrate our wedding anniversary, but God prompted the Filipino leaders present in that gathering to give us a break by contributing for the gift so we could celebrate in the midst of busyness. Secondly, when we arrived, they told us that they voted Joy to be the coordinator of FIN, a position he held for many years.

One lasting surprise that the Lord gave me was an invitation to take a 400-hour biblical study program. At first, I did not accept it because I did not have the money and I felt I was already too old, but the instructors encouraged me and assured me that they would look for somebody to sponsor my studies. So, even though it was a long study, I accepted the offer. A few years ago, online study was not as popular as it is today in our pandemic times, but I still enjoyed the classes, because I could repeat them again and again, meditating and understanding them well. This surprise brought a breakthrough in my faith in God. The Bible became even more alive to me, and I better understood and practiced my identity in Christ; it's worth more than the degree itself. (Note: You will understand more of this in the chapter of My Identity)

Abundant life is a journey.

Abundant life doesn't come automatically, we have to go through the process- just like a newborn baby, he/she has to go through the process of growth - from baby to toddler, to a boy/girl, adolescent/youth, adult, senior. Like in the earthly realm, we also need to go through the process of growth in the spiritual realm to develop our spirit.

Life to the fullest is also growing spiritually- where our minds are renewed through the scriptures and we are being transformed by the Holy Spirit - creating in us the fruit of the Holy Spirit, which is love even in the midst of hatred, joy in the midst of problem, peace, goodness, kindness, patience, and self-control (Galatians 2:20). Life to the Fullest is freedom, soaring above the storms of life, in sickness and in health, over tragedy and problems of life.

My point is, we passed through trials, tragedy, insults, problems upon problems but through these, our **inner life** (our spirit) grew and was **empowered**. Being in the pastorate as a family - we became like fish in the aquarium, being looked at so that every decision made, words spoken or activities done, were scrutinized and judged either correctly or incorrectly. Misjudgements and negative talk brought me to my knees-there I would pray in the Spirit (this is the beauty of the prayer language, you do not think what you're praying, you just open your mouth and pray with your heart. At times you cannot stop, it is continuous). As I pray my head is lifted, I am comforted, and I am inspired again to love and serve God. I am drawn closer to Him. When I am in deep prayer - I realize God is also revealing something to me.

QUESTIONS TO PONDER

1. *Were there times in your life that you experienced the abiding shadow of the Almighty God protecting you? How about surprises?*

2. *To the child of God who trust and obey Him, the leading of His Spirit always follow. Do you believe it? Cite an example in your life.*

3. *Going deeper in my story, do you understand better now what is abundant life?*

4. *What is the key to abundant life?*

~ CHAPTER 11 ~

GOD IS GOOD ALL THE TIME

Expanding from the four walls of the local church at the height of pastoring the First Filipino Alliance Church in Canada, Joy got a surprise call on his birthday. The call was from the Chairman of the Board of Campus Crusade for Christ (CCC) Canada, inviting him to join the CCC International Leadership meeting in Jordan with paid travel expenses. Sensing this as an opportunity from the Lord, he accepted the invitation. In that meeting he was told that our countrymen, wherever they are, are bold witnesses for Christ. He was then challenged to take this "kairos," this opportunity to train disciples to become growing and multiplying disciples. He invited Christian Filipino leaders out of the Middle East (Oman, Kuwait, Jordan, Bahrain, UAE, Qatar) for a consultation in Cyprus, Europe in the late 1990s. There, the Filipino International Network (FIN) was conceived and formed, appointing Joy as the Chairman. This was the start of becoming a networker– challenging Christian leaders from different denominations, churches, Bible schools and seminaries, and mission organizations – local and international, to partner in reaching out to the lost and extending God's kingdom regardless of denomination.

At first, there seemed to be a feeling of "We are okay, we do not need to partner with others." Joy saw the need of Prayer Advance inviting Filipino pastors from different denominations in UAE. God moved the leaders who attended and recognized the importance of synergy or partnering together to bring God's love and salvation to the lost. The Filipino International Network started to do training then in different places, not only in Asia but in Europe and the Middle East as well. Joy and I and some of the leaders in our church were trained to be Family Life speakers. With FIN, we facilitated Prayer Advance, Family Life Seminar, NLTC (New Life Training Curriculum) training, Trainer's Training, etc. in different places, locally and internationally.

Taking the seminar on New Life Trainer's Training and the CGTC (Great Commission Trainer's Conference) had been such a great encouragement and help to me. We needed to become spiritual multipliers to reach out to billions of people who have not come to know Jesus personally. I have to train people who were won for Christ to also reach out and win others for Christ. This is what we call spiritual multiplication. God answered my prayers to be a handmaiden to the nations. I became a speaker, trainer, and found myself preaching – but only in the power of God, not by myself. I do not have anything to brag about. I was branded as "small but terrible." I do not know what they mean by that, but I hope they mean that I am small like David who killed the giant Goliath.

I like what some call me: "a friend of God." One day somebody asked my granddaughter Sophie, "What do you want to be when you grow older?" She answered, "I want to be like my Grandma Lulu – a friend of God." That's an inspiring answer. Others call me "Mrs. Praise the Lord" – because I praise the Lord both in good times and in difficult times. I am always reminded that we have to give thanks in everything because He reigns over good and difficult times. He is in control. I believe that He is the Almighty God, and He always operates in love and in power. We experience bad times, but He is always with us. His children overcome the bad times or the negative circumstances in life. God deserved to be worshiped at all times. Worshiping Him in praise and thanksgiving and trusting Him always because He loves us so much.

God is so good all the time. In different events or experiences in life He reveals who He is and allows you to experience who He is through His name.

JEHOVAH JIREH OUR PROVIDER

I have written already a lot of times where God revealed Himself as Jehovah Jireh, the God who provides. He not only provided for our personal and family needs, but He also provided for us to be equipped in the ministry. God provided us friends and foster parents. I remember the Silvers who became Papa and Mama to us. In Canada, every now and then they would invite us on special occasions like our birthdays and holidays, and especially Christmas. They would prepare a Christmas meal for us (Joy, Ianne, Tony, I, and them). After that, we sat down and worshiped, had a devotion, then they would distribute their Christmas gifts to us. Papa and Mama Silver became our adopted dad and mom in Canada. Even when it is not Christmas, they would give us clothing, food, etc.

I have told you about Hope and Horatio also, Jack and Carol, who had become uncle and auntie to us. They are also great ministry partners. They challenged us to dream big for God – not only for the local church ministry but also for extending the kingdom of God internationally. Jack and Carol challenged us to become spiritual multipliers. This led to the formation of the First Filipino International Network (FIN). First Filipino Alliance Church encouraged us to be involved with missions locally and globally.

CCC (now Power to Change), partnered with Joy and our church. They invited us to evangelistic and discipleship trainings. It was at that time that I was praying again, "Lord, please make me a handmaiden to the nations." With this, Joy challenged me to take the Trainer's Training and the Great Commission Training of CCC. At first, I hesitated because I thought I know much already but I yielded to God's prompting. After the Great Commission Training, we graduated during the CCC annual conference held at Whistler, B.C. There I was formally inducted as CCC staff. That brought me back to the different nations (first was when we were with MV Logos at OM). Telling others about God's love and salvation became urgent to me. Richard Wurmbrand said, "Souls won for Christ should also become soul winners."

GOD, THE UNSEEN GUEST

With FIN, we travelled to the different countries, training believers. As we travelled to the east from Canada we passed through Europe and did ministry there. Unlike my first exposure to missions in OM, this time was different. It is more on teaching and mentoring. It was a joy meeting and mentoring not only Filipinos, but other nationalities – like mentoring the wife of a high-ranking government leader of a certain country, etc. We usually had our training in different countries, but we did their final training in Cyprus.

At one time we decided to have the Trainer's Training in UAE and not in Cyprus. I was assigned to teach on the Holy Spirit. As I prepared, I was moved to pray that the trainees will not only understand the Holy Spirit but will experience the power of the Holy Spirit. Then in His gentle way He spoke to my spirit, saying, "Okay, I'm going to visit in your training." I reasoned out and said, "How can you visit us, we have a hectic schedule?" And He responded, "Wait and see." As I waited upon the Lord, something happened. Before the training, one of our trainers got into a "set-up problem" so we had to take out two sessions due to the problem. We prayed on what we would do for the two hours that had been cut off. Some suggested on a tour of the city, others spend time in prayers or group planning. What prevailed was to spend time in prayer. And I was assigned to do the first session on Prayer. This is after my session on the Holy Spirit. I realized God is really going to visit us as He arranged our schedule.

On that day, the morning of my session on the Holy Spirit, I had a prayer walk around the building where we were meeting. I thanked God that He is going to visit us. When it was my turn to teach, I just felt the presence of the Holy Spirit. I felt in my spirit His power. After the session, the trainees were supposed to have a coffee break before Prayer Time, but they did not move, they were just glued to their seats. I asked them "Are you not going for coffee break?" They responded, "We want to pray now." So, we started to pray but one of the staff came and told us, "It's coffee break, it is not prayer time yet." So, I responded, "They want to pray now." We were allowed to pray then. As the pianist started to play, without a plan to sing, my mouth opened, and I started singing a spontaneous song in another language. I have difficulty singing alone with music accompaniment, but this time I sang with the music. I just closed my eyes and sang for about twenty minutes, while most of the trainees (mostly men) knelt down, praying in different languages and raising their hands. I closed my eyes and concentrated on the Lord while singing. He encouraged me not to be afraid, but to go on.

Truly, God visited us. After that visitation there were testimonies of healing, and transformation that took place. The presence of God lingered in the entire training. In all of the trainings we had, this training event produced pastors, missionaries, and church workers/leaders. This was an encounter with the loving God. We all need to be visited and have encounter with the Holy Spirit. God is always with us, but experiencing His Manifest Presence is a show of His Glory. God provides faithful supporters in the ministry. They partner with us through prayers, encouragement and giving. We thank God for them and pray for all their needs and safety daily.

Note: Dawna De Silva in her book Prayer, Declarations and Strategies for Shifting Atmosphere states that the Gift of Tongues is sometimes frowned upon in Christian circle.3 Many see it as a time–specific gift reserved for the leaders of the early church. However way, you view the gift, speaking in tongues stands as an important aspect of prayer. Beware, these spiritual gifts can cause offense, because unfortunately they are outside the cultural norm.

GOD is an ENABLER and HELPER.

I remember before I became a trainer, one of the prerequisites for me to become a CCC staff was training on Speech Development. This is because I am a Filipino. They said I will not only be speaking to Filipinos but also to other nationalities, so I went for the training. The first day I had to read aloud from the English Bible. On the second day, I had to practise speaking again, but my mentor kept on saying, "You are not trying your best." Until he told me to stop, and he told me very discouraging words: "This is your last day of speech training. I give up." I left my mentor with a heavy heart, and I was so discouraged. I went home without telling anybody what had happened, except the Lord. I went to our basement and cried and cried to Him. I told Him, "How can I be a trainer then? You have to touch my tongue as you have touched Moses." Then in His still, small voice, He spoke to my spirit saying, "Do not worry when you speak for me, I will empower you. People will respond." What a promise. I was encouraged. Usually, those days I was so intimidated to speak. During conferences I just sat beside Joy and smiled. But after this conversation with God, I saw His promise to me being fulfilled. Dr. Henry Tan, the president of Campus Crusade Philippines, told Joy, "Lulu has potentials, why don't you give and allow opportunities for her to develop her potentials?"

As I prayed to become a handmaiden to the nations, God opened opportunities for me to be involved in training, locally and internationally. I was asked to speak and preach too in churches, not only in Asia but in the Middle East and European countries like Italy, U.K., U.S.A and Canada.

As I facilitated training, as I spoke and preached, people would respond.

Sometimes they were just so amused, even if I was not making them laugh. Or sometimes they would cry, even if I didn't make them cry purposely.

Just one time in one of our trainings in Japan, I was asked to coordinate that training. Part of the training was a Sunday worship service, in which I assigned one of the trainees, who was a pastor, to preach in that service. But before the training, he got sick so he could not travel anymore with us to Japan. In almost everything I do; I always inquire from the Lord. I asked Him, "Who then will preach?" And He told me, "You, and you will preach on Holiness." I could not reason out before the Lord, but I obeyed Him. But then one of the trainers who had a high position in Campus

Crusade told me (not knowing my previous conversation with God), "Ate Lulu, I will preach." So again, I went to the Lord and asked Him, "What will I do?" God responded, "What did I tell you earlier?" I answered, "I will preach." Then He said, "Do it and I will empower you." I told what God had spoken to me to my co-staff (the one who suggested to me that he will preach) and he understood. The night before the service, as I sat to write what I will preach, I could not write. I was just crying. I was not able to write anything. The next morning, I tried to write again but I couldn't because I was just crying again. I was so broken. Without notes, the Lord filled my mind with what to preach on Holiness.

Arriving at the worship service, one of the CCC staff came to me and said, "Ate Lulu, we have a Yakuza (Japanese Mafia) member attending the service." I asked the Lord, "Why did you allow him to come to our service? What if we are worshiping and he shoots us?" The Lord said in my spirit, "Do not be afraid. I am in charge." The moment we started singing the Spirit of God moved. He manifested His Presence. Even the songs we sang were in order.

Then I began preaching on Holiness. In the middle of the preaching, I saw the audience crying – church members, husbands and wives, dealing with their differences. So, I had to pause in my preaching. Later on, I just moved out from the front and my feet were led to Hiro San, the Yakuza member. I just told him, "Jesus loves you." And he nodded, I am amazed that he was not angry or irritated.

I went back to the front, but still the audience were settling their differences. So, I continued to pause, then I was led to Hiro San again and told him, "Even if you have killed many, God will forgive your sins if you repent and ask His forgiveness." He nodded again and tears started to fall down on his cheeks. I returned to the front and continued the message. Then I saw Hiro San raised his hands and he spoke, "I need

New Life Training by the FIN trainers in Japan hosted by FCMN, coordinated. by Hannah Galvez

Jesus." So, again, I paused and allowed the Holy Spirit to move. I asked Fel and our interpreter to go and witness to him. While waiting for Fel and Hiro San, the trainees took that opportunity to witness to five nightclub lady workers. Praise God, seven souls prayed to receive Jesus that morning: Hiro San, five ladies, and a child who had stomach pain. One of the trainers prayed for the child and he was healed.

This is the work of God. We need to be sensitive to his visitation through His Spirit. I wish I could write more stories like these, but the pages are limited. My point is that when God manifests His Presence, He is bringing heaven to earth, so people will come to know Him and worship Him. Being a Christian is not only living by faith; it is also experiencing the miraculous power of the Almighty God. In my daily conversations, I am intimidated to speak, but when the Holy Spirit moves, I become bold. Who led me to Hiro San? Who led me to speak those words to him? Was that a disorganized worship service that turned out to be evangelistic? This is the work of God. I did not plan for it. We just allowed the Holy Spirit to work in our midst. What if I did not stop and yield to His leading. We need to be sensitive to the Spirit of God.

One time there was an opportunity for me to speak to the student body of a college in Davao owned privately by a devoted Christian family. They invited the top graduating high school students to their college and give lots of scholarship support to deserving students. Their desire is for them to know Jesus and become successful in life. Before even travelling to the Philippines, I was really praying that the Lord will enable and help me to speak to them. I was praying that the Lord God will speak through me. The school gave me a topic on Challenges in the Family. On the day of my speaking engagement, the dean of the college would pick us up from where we were staying, but it was getting late, and he had not arrived yet to fetch us. Time was passing so fast; I was really praying. And when he arrived it was really late. He said the traffic was worst on that day because of some political activities. I was supposed to speak for about 40 minutes, I was losing time, but I just trusted everything to God. Praise God our ride arrived at the venue, and I was able to speak for twenty minutes. At the end, I invited them to respond to the love of God, to accept Him—the Life, the Way and the Truth who is Jesus. To my amazement, I saw many hands-about a quarter of the student body prayed to receive Jesus. God moved their hearts.

I do not have anything to brag about, only the Triune God: The Father - my heavenly dad, the Son Jesus - my Redeemer, and the Holy Spirit – my power and enabler. He is the <u>Master Mover</u> of evangelism and discipleship. He is the One transforming people. We are the vessels.

GOD OUR DIRECTOR in MINISTRY

He directs our moves as we rest on Him and allow Him to guide us. On one occasion while in Kuwait, I was asked to speak to about 300 Filipino women in the gathering at the Embassy. I was with some pastors from the Philippines and Kuwait who attended the celebration of the Filipino Church with whom we had series of training in evangelism and discipleship. They practiced what they were taught and so they have grown to more than twenty satellite churches in Kuwait and in the Philippines.

On our way to the embassy, I asked the Lord God, "What will I tell this group of women Lord?" He answered, "John 3:16, tell about my love and sing People Need the Lord." So that is what I did. First, I asked somebody to sing with me the song I was asked to sing then spoke on God's love. At the end of my message, I gave them a challenge: I encouraged them to thank God and repent for their sins and ask Jesus to be their Saviour and Lord. I told them not to receive Jesus only but give their life to Him. I asked them to close their eyes and if they decide to accept Him and give their life to Him, they should raise their hands. All of them raised their hands, so I thought they did not understand what I've said–because all of them raised their hands. I repeated the invitation and made it clear—in that moment I told them, instead of raising their hands they should kneel down if they made the decision to ask Jesus into their hearts as their Lord and Saviour and gave their lives to Him. All of them knelt down. So, I thought they still did not understand–but the Spirit of God spoke to my spirit, "This is not your work, this is My work. Just trust Me."

We always need to be prompted in hearing and obeying God. One time as I led our prayer time before the Sunday Service in Japan–the Lord instructed me to prophetically pray. I reasoned out that the people I am ministering are not used to that. So, I did not do it. When it was time for me to preach, I felt the loss of His presence. I did not have spiritual power, I struggled to speak so I asked the Lord, "Lord how come, I cannot feel anymore Your anointing?" And God said, "Because you did not obey me." That was a lesson for me that I always remember. When God tells you to do something do not reason out, just obey and He will take care of the rest. I asked God's forgiveness for my disobedience, so the next day I spoke, I felt God's anointing. As a result, a Japanese husband prayed to receive Jesus. Three others did the same after the service. That was a miracle, the work of the Holy Spirit.

God is the director and I learned to follow His direction. One thing I am learning in ministry is saturation with God in prayer and in His words. With this, He sharpens our spirits, our spiritual eyes, spiritual ears, spiritual sense of touch, spiritual sense of taste, and spiritual sense of smell. Through these, we are given a discerning spirit – being able to discern the voice of God, directing us in our ways. Even with spiritual gifts, I cannot depend on it. I depend on the direction of God, and this can only be attained through soaking with God in prayer – worshiping Him, telling Him our cares, our prayer requests, and our concerns.

Even as we have so much knowledge of the scriptures and have advanced academic degrees, this knowledge cannot become wisdom (applied knowledge at the right time, right place, right way) unless you allow the Holy Spirit to direct you through soaking in God. Prayer + prayer + prayer and His words + His words + SILENCE = Being Still.

GOD –Our JEHOVAH SHAMMAH–
The GOD Who is always with us, Our EMMANUEL.

Joy and I were attending the Filipino European Ministries Conference in Switzerland. In those times we used video tapes, not DVDs. We were travelling from Paris to Switzerland. We were carrying loads of Jesus video tapes to give to the delegates. So, Joy and was carrying one big piece of luggage each, plus our hand carry bags. We flew from Edmonton to Toronto, then to France. This was our first time to take a train from Paris to Switzerland. That time, ESL (English as a Second Language) was not popular yet, so everything was in French. Our train was in the higher level of the escalator. What did we do with our luggage? Joy put them on the escalator first, then stepped on the escalator in front of the luggage so he could pick them up when it reached the top. I stepped on the escalator behind the luggage. The escalator was high. Soon, when Joy was in the middle, one of the bags fell on me so I fell down and was left lying down on the escalator, I tried to stand but I could not. I called Joy but he did not hear me, so I shouted "Help!" Then, he came down to help me to stand, but it was difficult to stand on a moving escalator, until I caught his jacket and held on to it. Joy fell down on top of me. We wiggled and wiggled, trying to stand but we were not able to until we reached the top, the next level. There all our stuff was waiting for us, even my shoes were waiting for me. What an embarrassing moment! – This is one of the funny experiences in ministry that makes us laugh when we remember it especially when I recall the man who saw us and kept laughing while watching us. I think he could not figure out what we were doing on the escalator, ha ha ha.

Anyway, it was getting late. We needed to catch our train to Switzerland. We did not even know that there were assigned seats on the train like in the plane. As we walked through our train station with our heavy luggage, we realized we were getting late for our train, so we had to walk faster. Suddenly, a tall and elderly man came to help us. Without talking, he carried some of our luggage, and he directed us to the train and our seat. Soon, as we found our designated seats, we turned our heads to thank him, but he had disappeared. Without that man we would not have caught our train. That was a divine intervention – an angel of God?

Prayer is not only communicating with God - it's relating to Him. The more I pray, the more I get deeper in my relationship with Him. The more I know Him and even though I don't see Him, I experience his presence, I hear Him relating with me, speaking to my spirit, instructing me, encouraging me, comforting me. He answers prayers in his will and so many times I am amazed. He doesn't only show that He is powerful, that nothing is impossible to Him, that He is loving, but He also shows that He cares even for the smallest details of our lives. I will mention some of these:

One time, my favourite sweater was stained, I tried removing the stain, but I was not successful. I got so tired that I rinsed it and hung it and said to the Lord, "Lord, you know that I like this sweater so much. You see that I tried removing the stain but failed. Can You please remove it Lord?!." When the sweater was dried - I saw "no more stain," and I was so touched by His care. I praised Him for removing the stain.

Again, one time I had to do laundry. When I started the washing machine, it did not work. I tried and tried but I failed. So, then I laid my hands on the washing machine and said "Lord, I believe You don't only heal people but You can also touch appliances, I pray now that You will heal this washing machine. I declare that this machine will wash now. I tried to put on the washing machine and there it started to work until it was done. I shared this story in Japan. After a year I went back to the church where I shared about the washing machine. A young mother came to me and told me, "Ate Lulu, do you remember about the washing machine testimony you've shared? It happened to me, so I did what you did, and God answered my prayer. Wow, thank you Lord!

Even when my children were young when they had constipation - I usually told them while they sat on the "throne"- pray to Jesus to help you, so that's what they did, and it worked. I also would teach the nannies or governesses in our Bible study group to do the same with the children that they were taking care of, teach them to pray. They learned that God answers prayers.

When I shared to the ladies' care group (of which most of them were domestic helpers) about Joy's testimony on how God answers prayers (on the van I have mentioned in a previous chapter) they were so encouraged. Truly God is a prayer answering God. After that, one Nanny did the same over one of the cars of her employers. She prayed that her employer would be touched to give the car to her to use, and they did.

There was one time that we were doing an evangelistic training (NLTC- New Life Training Centre) in a very secluded place in the Philippines. I did not want to go there at first, because they said there was NPAs (New People's Army-leftist government people) there. But the one sending me from Japan is a very devoted Christian and even though she did not have much money, she already bought me a plane ticket instead of a bus ticket. So, I went there. We had the training in an open place but with a galvanized iron roof. The first day of the training, heavy rain fell down and it caused loud noise on the galvanized roof. The participants could not hear well anymore. What I did was to pray, "Lord, I know You want us to continue, so please stop the rain so the people can hear and understand the training." Then I commanded the rain," In the Name of Jesus, rain stop, rain go away, come again another day." Amazingly in just few seconds the rain stopped. The dark clouds moved away, and we were able to continue. As a result, the uncle of the one who sent me was so encouraged and he prayed to receive Jesus as his Lord and Saviour.

This next testimony is unbelievable but it's real. Tonyvic got a back problem after years of playing Rugby in his high school team. So, when he was working at Blue Cross, he started having back pains until he could not endure it anymore. He was prescribed a strong pain reliever, Oxycontin. At the end he just wanted to be lying on his tummy even as he ate. One sister told me, "The Lord will heal Tonyvic." I told about it to Tonyvic, and he said, "I believe mom, God will use surgery too." There was a long wait for his surgery, but we prayed that the Lord will fast track it. Sure enough, God fast tracked it, but that time they called him I was in Hawaii doing training and visiting my family. So, at the time of the surgery, I fasted and the Lord told me through a saint while we were in a prayer meeting. She said, "the Lord will lead the hand of the surgeon and those assisting him." This was the time when laser surgery was new.

They did a back operation, and it was successful. After an hour in the observation room after the surgery, Tonyvic woke up and he was able to move his feet without pain. Then he said, I want to go home now. When they tried to transfer him to the wheelchair to be pushed to the car, he said, "I do not need a wheelchair, I can walk." From there they went to the restaurant because he was so hungry as he was without food before the surgery. Oh, there are so many more stories, but I can only write what I am prompted to write.

My pastor's wife asked me to pray for her so they could have a child. I prayed that the Lord would open her womb and that she would become pregnant. After some months, she told me, "Lulu, thank you for praying for me, I am now pregnant." Praise the Lord! And soon after, I did pray for another pastor's wife. Their son was already five years old, and he was asking for a baby brother or sister, so I prayed for her. God answered, some months after, she got pregnant. God is a prayer answering God, He said "Call to Me and I will answer you and tell you great and unsearchable things you do not know. (Jeremiah 33:3). Ask and it will be given to you; seek and you will find; knock and the door will be opened to you. (Matthew 7:7)

There are many testimonies on how God answered prayers, but the pages are limited.

JEHOVAH SHALOM — OUR PEACE

Every day, our peace is tested especially when we feel something weird in our bodies or think about the economic condition of our nation or hear about the news nationally and globally. In one of my ministry travel schedules, I was just wondering why the training event was fast approaching but my materials had not arrived yet. So, with this, I planned to cancel the training but the pastor hosting the training in Japan told me "Just come, the Lord will work on His plan. So, I did proceed and planned back up topics for our training. Usually, we do "fasting and praying" a day before the training. On our day of fasting and prayer one of the trainees who have never spoken in another language–prayed in another language. So, I asked the Lord, "Lord, is that coming from You?" What does it mean? An interpretation came – a prayer of asking mercy, a cry for mercy. The next day as we were having our training, the building was shaken. At first, we hid under the tables then when it grew stronger, we went out the building, some had no shoes on–because if you enter a room in Japan you have to remove your shoes. The magnitude of the earthquake was 8.5 in the place we were. It was so strong that you could see the building and the electric wires outside were swaying. We did not return to the building anymore but went home watching what was happening. That was year 2011 when a tsunami struck in Japan. Tokyo became a "ghost city." The airport was closed, no trains and buses. We were warned for a stronger earthquake, so we needed to be ready anytime. I wondered if I would ever be home in Canada or vice versa. I wondered if I would ever come to Japan again.

This experience was so memorable that it taught me a lesson. My presence there at that time was appreciated–encouraging the believers in time of calamity. Then again, the Lord spoke to my spirit saying, "Do you remember why your materials did not come in time? Do you remember why Tess prayed in tongues and the interpretation was a prayer asking for My mercy? Because I knew this tragedy will come." The Lord prepared us for this during the fasting and prayer for mercy that reached God's throne. Did the prayer lessen a greater disaster? Did that prayer not only save us but others who are in the household of faith? I believe so.

The Lord shortened the days of lockdown after the tsunami, and I was able to go home but decided in my heart not to ever return to Japan. But the Lord is good. He always inspires me to go back. After just a few months the International Saints of Kuwait gave a sum of money for the victims and asked me to bring it to Japan. I could not say "No"- I went back and since then I continue to minister in Japan. Japan to me became my third home. I appreciate the believers who were working with me. They continue to do so–online.

JEHOVAH ROI — GOD SEES EVERYTHING
The Stolen Briefcase (taken from our Church Bulletin, 1984)

For the past eight years we travelled to more than 35 countries. We never lost our passports and money in rough cities as Naples and Sicily, Italy where the MAFIA are notorious. We were in Sydney, Arab lands, but the terrorists did not grab our bags. I was in Hongkong, Tokyo, Seoul, Frankfurt, Washington D.C and other capital cities but was never harassed. I took planes from big airports like Amsterdam, Bangkok, Los Angeles, Manila and Hawaii where thieves are famous to tourists–but we did not meet these criminals.

September 13, 1:30 pm–a thief took Joy's briefcase at Vancouver International Airport in Canada, while he was changing money in front of a kiosk. His briefcase contained our passports, Canadian visas, $150, camera and other important documents. What will you do if you are in our situation? It was good we already passed the immigration.

We as family did not panic–before reporting the incident to the police, we prayed and praised God and He assured us, "Be still and know that I am God!" That was enough for us to have peace and confidence much more when Ianne said, "Don't worry, the Lord will return it to us." The Lord's intervention was so timely, if not we could have had problems in re-entering Canada. We prayed specifically that the thief would not throw the bag in the garbage. After such waiting, the Lord gave us John 11:40 to claim. As a family, we agreed together that we're going to believe that the Lord will return it to us. Exactly one month after the incident, two days after we claimed the promise, the BC POLICE RECOVERED IT. What an answer to prayer–truly the Lord is sovereign, and He is in control even in the hearts of people. We praise Him for this experience.

As I write this book—we are also locked down because of the pandemic. It is hard to travel. I thank God for the technology. We now have a Zoom prayer meeting with some Filipino leaders in Japan. I also join them sometimes in their Sunday Service which is Saturday here in Canada; I still can talk to the saints, I have been ministering, encouraging and praying with them. I know God is directing my ways. I thank God for technology. We have an Almighty God to listen to who gives us peace in the time of unrest as it is happening this time: Covid-19 pandemic, political and people unrest, protest and riots due to racism, economic problems, disasters, etc.

God gives peace to his children. Living life to the fullest is having peace in spite of chaos and disorder. Even when the event seemed to be hopeless, there is always hope because Jesus the hope of glory dwells in his children.

(Filipino delegates. - Lota, Laurie, Myrna and I, International Women's Conference, Switzerland)

QUESTIONS TO PONDER

1. *Have you experienced a problem and you called upon the Lord God and He intervened? Have you experienced God, as your Provider? Your enabler and helper?*

2. *Do you see Him in the spirit as the "unseen guest" in your life, in your home or in any gathering? Are you allowing God to direct your moves?*

3. *In times of difficult situations do you experience peace and comfort from God by seeking Him?*

4. *God sees everything, there is nothing impossible to Him, whatever is bothering you today go to the Lord in prayer, He will hear you. He is good.*

---

3 de Silva, Dawna, Prayer, Declarations and Strategies for Shifting Atmosphere: 90 Days to Victorious Spiritual Warfare, The Presence Every Day: 365 Days to Unveiling Heaven's Agenda to Your Life, 2011 pp.57-60

~ CHAPTER 12 ~

DREAMS, OPPORTUNITIES AND CHALLENGES

God gave me compassion to those who are perishing—to those who have not heard his love and salvation through Jesus Christ alone. My heart cries for them. It is my desire that they will be like Lazarus who reached Heaven, his final destiny, unlike the rich man whose final destiny was Hell. So, I prayed, "Lord, I want some opportunities for me not only in the local church but make me a handmaiden to the nations also."

Telling others about God's love and salvation became a lifestyle to me–whether I am standing in line waiting for my turn or sitting beside somebody in a bus, taxi or plane. If I go out, I pray for opportunity to talk about Jesus–the life. Like one time, I was on the plane sitting beside a man. Oh, he was smelly (with cigarette and liquor smell). I wanted to transfer to another seat but then the Lord spoke to my spirit to witness to him. So, in obedience I told him, "Do you know that Jesus loves you, that is why you are seated beside me"? Instead of being irritated, he nodded. He told me his story, that he is a drug addict, womanizer and so on. At the end he heard about God's love and forgiveness, and he prayed to receive Jesus as his Saviour and Lord before we landed in our destination.

God answered my prayer to be a handmaiden. He opened the nations to me – to talk about his love and salvation, to challenge and train believers to be involved in winning people for Christ, to build them in the faith and sending them to do what they are trained and built for and vision casting. My involvement with Campus Crusade for Christ (CCC) and the Filipino International Network (FIN) and CMA opened opportunities to serve God in many nations. I travelled in many different countries in Europe, the Middle East, Asia, the Pacific, America, and including Egypt and Turkey. I found spiritual families there especially in Japan, Qatar, Kuwait and the Philippines. Their partnership in the Lord's work became so intense. Whenever I am in Japan, the home of Jojo and Butch Balona becomes my "home sweet home." So also, with the homes of my many wonderful hosts: Jose & Nene Gima, Pen & JoAn Hore, Herbert & Helen Rodriguez, Ferdie & Micha Barro. In Qatar, the friendship, partnership and love of Celso & Anabel and Jun & Mayette of Kuwait was so encouraging. They were all loving and kind. In the Philippines, the home of Mark & Susan Sosmena, Ate Bing & Manong

Maligayang pasko at manigong bagong taon to our kababayan and friends.
First Filipino Alliance Church · 10115-79 Street, Edmonton · (780) 468-1743 · www.ffaconline.org

FFAC with Pastor Jamal, Nabril, Ricky and PJ

Semy became our home, plus the different homes in Tanauan, where the dark chocolate ladies and Tanauan Bible Church is. I appreciate the privilege given to me by Josie Watanabe—one of the CEOs in their Zaika Construction Company giving me opportunities to minister to their office staff. What a privilege too being hosted by the Ang Family in their family home in Davao and the Ebenezer Bible College in Zamboanga whenever we went there for speaking and teaching.

Our church (FFAC) became a model for missions especially when Joy started to write. With a growing responsibility for global missions, we accepted the call to become international workers with unique responsibility in our denomination. With this new assignment we had to leave our spiritual family in Edmonton—our beloved First Filipino

Alliance Church. We had to leave our dear children and grandchildren to be based in Toronto. It was hard to say goodbye. Edmonton had been home for us for 36 years, but we obeyed knowing that God is with us.

I remember before we found a place for us in Toronto, our new mission base, we stayed for two weeks at Kathy Klassen's home. Kathy is one of the pastors who had been an encouragement to us. Her home is opened for pastors and missionaries who are in Toronto for some reasons like meetings and conferences. In her home is a room where you can go and pray with worship music on. One time as I sat there and waited for the Lord to speak to my spirit, I just saw white clouds just outside the window not up in the sky but adjacent to the windows surrounding me. I experienced once again God's visitation with peace and joy—telling me, "I am with you, do not be afraid, I will help you and provide all your needs. Be still and know that I am God." I never forgot that. Every moment when I need strength to go on, God reminds me of this.

God gave 80 Coe Hill Drive in Toronto for us to live in. It is situated in a very scenic place. On the left side is just a short distance to Ontario Lake where we walked daily seeing the beauty of Toronto. Just at the back of the condos in front of us is a small lake where ducks stay and lay their eggs–and the beautiful High Park. We walked there almost every day. I would sit and face the beautiful garden with a maple leaf design and there I would pray for Canada, the government and the people. In the High Park Garden is a restaurant called Grenadier Cafe where we usually met with our newfound friends and ministry partners — Kuya Mike & Ate Betty Harrison and Pastor Jun and Bev Lagud. We settled in this beautiful place. Thank God for Pastor Larry who helped us find this place. He and Magda, his wife had become close friends and ministry partners to us.

There were lots of challenges in our new assignment and new surroundings—there were lots of hurts and pains, but this drew me closer to God. I learned to soak in his Presence, especially if Joy was away for meetings. At night I would go in the living room–put on the worship music and there I always experience his Presence— speaking words of encouragement, words of joy and healing. It was in Toronto that I learned more to be still and remain in God's Presence. Being in his Presence is better than sleeping. There I received comfort, healing and words of love. There my head would be lifted up. It is in soaking that my spiritual eyes, spiritual ears, spiritual touch, taste, smell become so real–the flesh becomes inactive—the spirit becomes strong so that I do not feel the hurts and anxieties anymore. The Holy Spirit is completely in control.

We were in Toronto for three years. Halleluiah Fellowship Baptist Church (HFBC) adopted us. They have been supportive of us even now. Dr. Enoch Wan continued to mentor Joy and challenged him to study migration and people in the move (Diaspora). His wife, Auntie Mary was so helpful to us too. During that time, Joy had been given time to do a lot of networking locally and internationally, partnering with C&MA, CCC, LCWE and FIN. We did a lot of travelling especially for Joy.

In 2007, the LCWE, now the Lausanne Movement, appointed Joy as the Senior Associate for Diaspora (scattered people uprooted from their homeland. He held that position from 2007 to 2019. With this, he founded the Global Diaspora Network (GDN) and led it for more than a decade. He gathered practitioners and scholars who are leading different diasporas and challenged them to write about it—like how we can reach out to the scattered people around the world–the international students, the OCWs (overseas contract workers), the seamen working on cruise, and different migrants. He started writing and editing books distributed free–to raise awareness on Diaspora Mission. Diaspora–are those who moved out from their country as a result of war, work, education, political asylum, and many more.

Mission is not only from country to country, but to the cities, to urban places where migrants immigrate and workers work. We were challenged to give and minister through book publication, and writing. One time I was challenged to give my savings to somebody whom we travelled with in the Middle East for her airfare and other expenses. We have learned to give to the work of the Lord and not to hold back for ourselves. We believe God will provide our needs; He is Jehovah Jireh. Joy also gathered these practitioners for consultations (forums), the first ones were with fewer participants until he envisioned a global one. In one of the bigger consultations, our faith was so stretched. We believed that funds and logistics would come–but then funds had not come yet for the consultation. As the event came closer while praying at High Park, he saw a cent on the ground.

What would he do with a single cent? According to him, he hesitated to pick it up, but then it seemed that God spoke to his spirit saying, "Pick it up, there is no dollar without one cent." So, he picked it up, prayed and trusted the Lord to provide. A week after that, funds and logistics came in for the consultation.

The biggest conference Joy had organized was GDN 2015 (Global Diaspora Forum 2015) which involved more than 400 participants from all over the world. He needed to look for funds, logistics and teams to help determine the right place for the conference, hotels to place the delegates, sponsorship for the needy invited participants. My main job was to intercede to ease his pain and encourage him despite frustrations and stress. It was hard for me. I would wake up in the middle of the night and pray earnestly in tears. We did not realize that as we prepared for this conference, we would experience spiritual opposition that came through bad dreams, panic attacks, not being able to sleep, etc. There was one time that Ianne, Tonyvic and I were physically attacked with an unseen enemy at the same time as we were in our homes in different places. One prayer partner told me "You and your ministry are being attacked by unseen enemy." We hesitantly believed it and sure enough later on we found that it was true. But through it all—the God who came to destroy the work of the enemy, delivered us and gave us the victory.

Despite the setbacks we continued to pray and trusted God for his deliverance. He fought for us. Living Life to the Fullest is overcoming the enemy who came to steal, to kill and to destroy. The Lord also provided logistics, volunteers and enough funds for GDN 2015. God touched people to help. Greenhills Christian Fellowship hosted the forum free of charge. One of the most noted donations was the donation of fishermen of a small church in Zambales. They gave one night of their catch from fishing worth 5,000 pesos equivalent to US$120. Joy was so touched that he was hesitant to receive it—and he wanted to return it to them to help them in their needs, but their pastor (Pastor Bal Tira) told Joy, "This is their gift to God, you must receive it." So, Joy got it and it completed the amount needed for the forum.

God is awesome, Jesus said "I came to give you life, and have it to the fullest (John 10:10). Ask according to my will and you will be given. Truly, the Almighty God, the creator of heaven and earth is so powerful that nothing is impossible to Him. The result of the forum is synergy (partnership) in reaching out the scattered people around the world whether in the mountains or in the urban cities where different people group flocks for their livelihood, studies, and professions. We need to learn to discern the will of God. We discern the will of God as we intimately fellowship with Him.

Back to Edmonton as our Base.

Again, the Lord gave us a new assignment that is to work under a ministry among indigenous people with AIM (Advancing Indigenous Mission) as our main focus but continue with Diaspora mission–doing training, teaching in seminaries and Bible schools, writing, networking, etc. This opened new opportunities for us to be more involved in our home country-the Philippines. As Joy had teaching assignments, he started to involve me also in teaching. Teaching is one of my passions and one of my gifts. This brought me to different cities of the Philippines that I have never been before like Zamboanga City, Davao City, Jolo, etc. I enjoyed teaching Bible school students and sharing to graduate students. In my first time to go to Zamboanga at the Ebenezer Bible College, I had the opportunity to be their speaker at their Spiritual Emphasis Week. Before going there, I was instructed by the Lord to speak on Deeper Life. Before even going there some of the students had encountered the Spirit of God stirring them to prayer until 2:00 in the morning. What happened gave them a desire and hunger for more of God. This was a preparation for them to the Spiritual Emphasis Week–which theme was Deeper Life. The messages within that week opened many hearts for more of God. The ex-president of EBCS, Mrs. Adynne Lim became a close confidante of mine, and we did follow up of those students wanting more of God.

One time we were invited to join the President of EBCS to go to Jolo. I was scared to go there. It was at that time when two Canadians were kidnapped and beheaded. Our children told us not to go there but Joy really wanted to go there with the EBCS Team. With this I asked the Lord what his will on this is, for us to go there or not. He answered, "Declare your safety if you go there." So, I began declaring our safety. With such declaration my fear was gone.

So, we decided to go. It was about four hours boat ride. Jolo is near Sabah, Malaysia. When we were about to depart, somebody prayed, "Lord, thank you for this opportunity to go to Jolo. Please keep us safe. We pray that we will not be kidnapped and not be beheaded, but if it is your will for us to be kidnapped then let your will be done." With that prayer my spirit reacted so I stood up and prayed, "Thank you Lord for keeping us safe. I declare that we will not be kidnapped and that when we go back to Zamboanga, we still have our heads on." Sure enough, we enjoyed our visit in Jolo and when we went home, we still had our heads on.

As Joy travelled more, I became so desperate for God to draw me closer to Him and to open my eyes to know Him more, and to know more of the things in the spiritual realm. One day, I received a telephone call from the USA, offering me the opportunity to undergo an extensive 400-hour long biblical training program. I told them, "I am already old, and I do not have the money for this." They said, "It's okay, we will look for a scholarship for you. Our main textbook will be the Word of God and our main goal is not to produce a research paper or thesis, but to produce people of God who will become like Jesus in character and power in ministry. You and your life will be the thesis read by people everywhere you go." I was so excited so, my response was "Thank you Lord." I applied for it and took the study.

This theological study gave me a breakthrough. It opened my eyes more on the love of God, the width and heights, and the depths of God's love and my identity in Him. It encouraged me of my relationship with Him. It helped me understand more about the mystery of life and the paradox of life and opened my eyes to the "enemy" which helped me to overcome my fears and overcome the negative things of life. It increased my faith in God and to do action. What an encouragement to know and understand the power or dominion God has given to his children.

Some of my course topics were: God the Father, Jesus, The Holy Spirit; Heavenly Identity, Authority, Faith; The Supernatural; Healing in the Atonement; Ministry Gifts, Anointing, Miracles; Prophets and Prophecy; Demon and Demonology; Supernatural Encounters; The Power of Confession; End Time Dominion; The Indwelling; Prayer and

Graduation, 2014

Intercession; Biblical Economics; Growing in Grace and Abounding in Faith; Performing the Miraculous; Dominion Over Darkness; Ever Increasing Faith; The Activity of Angels; Purpose and Destiny; Prophetic Vision and Wisdom, and many more. It was a great study.

I also found out that the donor who gave my program scholarship was wife who had a broken marriage–but who in her heartbreak had found life in Jesus. Now she's involved in bringing ladies and children to Jesus, the Way, the Truth and the Life. She is enjoying life to the fullest in spite of what happened to her.

> *Note: You will see more about my breakthrough in Chapter 23. It is important for you to understand what I went through in my life so you will understand more the secret or the key to overcome the negatives of life. You also need to understand who the enemy is and his tactics (Chapter 21–The Enemy).*

QUESTIONS TO PONDER

1. *What are your dreams?*

2. *What is your priority? Do you pray for opportunities to share the love of God whether in person or in the cyber? Are you moved to rescue the perishing?*

3. *Are there challenges in your life? How have you been responding?*

4. *Do you see my dream how I went about it? I prayed for my dream and God answered it. Hope you are encouraged. We had challenges but God enabled us even to the present. He can do that for you. Dream big for God.*

~ CHAPTER 13 ~

NAVIGATING IN THE SPIRITUAL REALM

I have learned that as a child of God I live in two realms: the Physical or Earthly Realm and the Spiritual Realm. I have two identities: the Earthly identity and the Heavenly identity. My earthly identity is my earthly family, achievements, education, address on earth, Canadian citizen, cultural background and many others.

My heavenly identity is my spiritual identity. I belong to Jesus. I belong to the Royal kingdom of heaven. I am a royalty, a princess. I have a delegated authority from God (I Peter 2:9). I am empowered to be his child (John 1:12). I am raised up with Christ and seated with Him in the heavenly realms (Ephesians 2:6). Heaven is a realm of authority, a place of dominion. As a child of God, I am legally seated with Christ in the heaven lies having dominion over the enemy (Ephesians 2:6). We are commanded to subdue the earth (Genesis 1:28). We need to subdue the ungodly elements, the wicked spirits of darkness. The Spiritual realm is more powerful than the physical realm.

When a man is born, he goes through the process of growing to maturity. He navigates through the earthly realm. He learns to drink milk, to eat, to associate with his mom and family through smiling and cooing. As he grows, he learns to speak, to walk, and to navigate in this world–he becomes intellectual and sees things with understanding.

The man who finds life in Jesus becomes a child of God (John 1:12). He is born not physically when he receives Jesus, the Life, but born in the spirit meaning he is now in personal relationship with God.

He then should start navigating in the spiritual realm. We have read earlier that as I went deeper in my relationship with God, He started to meet me through manifesting Himself to me. The River of Life in Ezekiel 47 tells that after the prophet was submerged in the river, he then began to see things more than what he had not seen before. We begin to see things in the spirit through faith. We begin to see and experience the invisible. We also need to recognize that our relationship with God is measured–how deep our relationship is with Him.

The Child of God because he is born of the spirit and born of earthly parents lives in two realms: the earthly or physical realm and the heavenly or spiritual realm.

EARTHLY OR PHYSICAL REALM
VISIBLE
TEMPORARY
NATURAL **In the Flesh**

SPIRITUAL OR HEAVENLY REALM
INVISIBLE   **In the Spirit**
ETERNAL
SUPERNATURAL

SPIRIT

SOUL

SOUL

BODY

His spirit with his soul navigates in the spiritual realm

His soul and body Navigates in the Earthly realm.

As the soul and body learn to navigate in the earthly realm, his spirit should also learn to navigate in the spiritual realm through spending time in prayer and meditating God's words and obeying in faith.

Illustration: The Spiritual Realm and the Earthly Realms

Life is Spiritual.

Man is a spirit with a soul and a body. Our spirit is unseen but what is seen is our body, and our flesh. Surrounding us are spirits that we cannot see unless they manifest themselves, these are spirits in the spiritual realm– either the spirit of God's heavenly host like angels, archangels, seraphim, etc. or the spirit of darkness– rulers and principalities like demons, evil spirits, dwarfs, mermaids or marine spirits, and other evil creatures. to destroy God's plans and creation. Since life is spiritual and we are born again in the Spirit, we need to identify with Jesus– always choosing to trust and obey God. We need to be careful not to partner or identify ourselves with the enemy. For example, if we see that "anger is coming," we need to partner at once with God by choosing not to get angry and bind the spirit of anger and shift that feeling with love through the Holy Spirit. In navigating in the spiritual realm—we have to have intimacy with God and ask for a spirit of discernment.

Early in 2005, I attended a Breakthrough Canada Conference held in Red Deer, Alberta. Several of the speakers were revivalists from Latin America, like Claudio and Betty Freidzon, Carlos Annacondia, Sergio Scataglini. It was a very powerful conference. There were healing and deliverance, but most of all it fed our souls and stirred our spirits to know, love and serve God. Even when a speaker was not through yet, people were already lined up in the side to go in front when they call for prayer. There were about more than a thousand delegates so, I would run to go in front to be prayed for—but I never had a chance to be prayed for by one of the speakers.

As people would testify about their healing, I said to myself, "Lord, please heal me too." One specific prayer I asked was the healing of my eyesight. I have been wearing eyeglasses because I cannot read or see well for long distance vision. Anyway, on the last day of the conference, the speakers wanted to pray for God's touch to every delegate. They formed a "military line" just like in a military wedding, hands meeting together at the centre. Every participant was allowed to pass through it. We formed a line and each one was given a chance to go to the speakers' line which was about two meters long. When it was my turn, I entered, and I was blown to the end of the line without walking on the floor. That was mysterious! Who carried me to the end? Was that the wind of the Holy Spirit? – I believe so.

The next Sunday when I went to church, I was amazed to be able to see the songs we were singing. My eyesight was improved. Following that month, I went to Hawaii. I am usually given the opportunity to preach in some Hawaiian churches whenever I go there. After one of my preaching times, I initiated an altar call for the congregation. As the saints went forward, I was instructed by the Spirit to go down from the pulpit and lay my hands on each one of the people and they were slain in the Spirit. I did not understand that time what being slain in the spirit is, so in one of my preaching times again in which I did the same, I doubted if I ever pushed them, so I asked one of the persons that I prayed for, "Did I push you?" and she answered, "No." That was the work of God. In that doubting, I grieved the Holy Spirit—so I asked for his forgiveness.

Our relationship with God is measured as we go deeper, like a tree our roots grow deeper, and this deepness allows our spirit to rise. So, if we are rooted in Christ, our spirits also soar higher. It means our spiritual heights grow higher opening our spiritual eyes to many extraordinary things and events, because the power of the Holy Spirit is manifested. We began to have more encounters with God. An encounter with God is to come upon us unexpectedly. It is an unexpected meeting with God that changes and transforms you. It is an encounter that brings deeper intimacy with God. This encounter is a place of confrontation, meeting, wrestling, etc. with

God and his Word, yourself and his grace. The manifested presence of God, for example: Jacob as he slept, saw a stair from heaven to earth; Peter walking on the water; John in Patmos writing the last book of the Bible; the 120 believers at the Upper Room during the Pentecost (Acts 2).

I never knew about encounters with God. I have written in the earlier chapter that I heard a friend that did not know much how to pray, but when we had a Bible study together, I heard him pray a long prayer and it was in another tongue. It was just like words that even though I did not understand it brought joy and peace to my heart. So, I prayed, "Lord if that is coming from you, can I also, have it?" When I prayed that, I started to have a desire to pray, started to yearn to talk to God–until it became a longing to be always with God. When God answered my prayer for a prayer language, it was my first manifest encounter with God. Now I pray for more encounters with God. The objectives of encounter are to get real with God that may lead us to his will and direction–it may transform our thinking into the renewing of our minds; it may transform our attitudes that are not pleasing to God; it gives fresh revelation of God and his will; it may challenge our personal beliefs. Encounter with God may bring deliverance and healing.

When we had that head on collision accident, it was in my hospital bed that I had an encounter with God, and it brought fast healing to my broken body, bones and emotion. An encounter with God the Holy Spirit might bring a radical change in life like what happened to a brother dying from a disease on his deathbed. But he testified that a light passed through him and in that light was a voice of God telling him of his love for him. That night he encountered God and lived, he's now active in bringing people to the Light–Jesus who is the life.

Seeing In the Spirit Is the Working of God.

Each child of God should learn to navigate in the Spirit. Through getting deeper in my relationship with God, I am navigating in the Spirit, I have been learning the mystery of the Triune God, how to address Him, how to relate with Him, how to soak in his Presence, how to hear and discern the voice of God, and how to have peace in difficult times. We have to navigate in the spirit world by faith in Him and his Words. We allow our mind to be renewed by the Scripture–put it in our hearts then act on it. Let me cite an example: we navigate in the spiritual realm as we meditate and take to heart his Words. What does God want us to see in his Words?

For example, the Word of God says," By his stripes we are healed. (Isaiah 53:5 But He was pierced for our transgressions, he was crushed for our iniquities; the punishment that brought us peace was on him, and by his wounds we are healed." And I Peter 2:24 "He himself bore our sins" in his body on the cross, so that we might die to sins and live for righteousness; "by his wounds you have been healed."

Seeing through the eyes of faith–I see Jesus being beaten with blood coming out from the wounds, there I am stirred (imagine Him in his suffering), my emotion is touched–I feel his great love for me, and this will lead me to act on my will to love Him more. I see by faith the healing of my body and my emotion. This is how I live above sickness, pain and problems.

There is power in the blood of Jesus (Matthew 26:28 This is my blood of the covenant, which is poured out for many for the forgiveness of sins; Romans 5:9 Since we have now been justified by his blood, how much more shall we be saved from God's wrath through him!; Revelation 1:5b To him who loves us and has freed us from our sins by his blood) There I navigate with my soul and spirit–seeing in the eyes of faith the power of the blood, being poured out on me, washing my sins away.

One time I travelled to Hawaii to visit my parents and attend my sister's wedding. In the first few days, I could not sleep. Then one night, I went into deep prayer, God opened my spiritual eyes; as I laid down on my bed praying in the spirit - I saw a vision of multiple miniature black dogs (smaller than mice) coming from the house going to the door to exit - so I bound and rebuked the enemy in our unit, until all of them had gone out. The next morning, I did some cleaning in my parents and siblings' home. There I saw rock music CDs, a book on Hare Krishna, even a nude magazine hidden under the bed. I threw out all of them. After throwing them, I was able to sleep.

Again, a day before my sister's wedding, I was in a deep sleep then God woke me up. When God wakes you up, it means you need to pray. I did not know what to pray but the Holy Spirit led me to pray in tongues. So, I prayed, I am pleading and crying but I do not understand what I am praying. I prayed until peace came. The next day while on the way to the wedding, the minister and his wife who will officiate the wedding had an accident, but their lives were spared. God protected them from premature death. How did I know? The Lord spoke to my spirit saying, "This is the reason why you prayed intensely last night." God said, "My Spirit will help you what to pray." I see by faith, healing through the atonement–the power of God in the suffering, death and resurrection of Jesus.

After such time, as my dad witnessed the work of the Holy Spirit in my life, he began to understand what it means to become a child of God. For nine years I had been praying for his salvation, finally he understood that Jesus is the only way to salvation. He then received Jesus Christ as his Saviour and Lord after nine years of prayers and witnessing to him. The Holy Spirit opened his spiritual eyes and led him to repentance. Years after that, my mom got sick. I had to go back and forth to Hawaii to take care of her. Those times were also times of bonding with my dad- spending time studying the Bible.

In early 2004, the Lord spoke to my spirit- that the suffering of my mom will end, and she will be promoted to heaven. He gave me a vision of my mom dressed in white worshiping God in heaven. Then one Sunday morning as I was taking care of her, the Lord prompted me to worship with her and my dad, so we had a worship time. We felt God's presence as we worshipped through songs and prayers. After that I went to the room and changed, that was the time my mom was taken to glory– no pain, it was a peaceful death.

Two months after, while planning to go for a ministry in Japan, I decided to go through United Airlines so I can have a stop-over in Hawaii to be with my dad again to disciple him. But then my cardiologist advised me not to fly at that time, so I had to cancel my plan. September came, four months after my mom's death, we had a telephone conversation with my dad, and he concluded our phone call with a very intimate prayer to God. That was so sweet of him to pray like that. I was so blessed. Two weeks after that while he was attending a prayer service, he fell down on his chair, they say that he was fine after the fall but the next day he could not talk anymore. He lost consciousness until he was promoted to glory. Like my mom, he too was not in pain when he left us. He died peacefully. There is joy even in mourning. Joy because we know that both of them are with Jesus since they accepted Christ as their Lord and Saviour, and that we will see them again in heaven. Their sufferings are over. It is a joy to know that they are not in hell, but they are now with Jesus. Jesus said, "I had come to set you free." Abundant life is freedom, freedom from hell, which is freedom from the second death. This is LIFE - life in Jesus Christ. Living life to the fullest is belonging to Jesus.

One time in our ladies' Bible study, we watched a sermon on worship by Jim Cymbala of Brooklyn Tabernacle Church. While we were watching, the spirit of God moved in our midst and most of us were crying. Then the Lord spoke in my spirit asking me, "What did you do with the prayer language I gave you?" I was so convicted because I was afraid to talk about it. With humility, I asked for forgiveness. As I prayed, He allowed me to pray in tongues publicly. I was so afraid but then an interpretation came. The interpretation was, "I am calling you (including the ladies with me) to be intercessors. But you will receive oppositions and hindrances, etc." While the interpretation came, I was asking the Lord in my mind, "Lord, is this coming from You?" The Lord told me, "Have faith, wait for the fulfilment."

From that Bible study, we started the Upper Room – prayer time every Saturday morning. It is different from the usual prayer time which is structured. It is a time of worship, prayer and listening to God speaking in his Presence. Thereafter, there would be testimonies of emotional and relational healing, even physical healing, encountering God in an extraordinary way. But even from the start, we experienced oppositions and hindrances either as a group or individually.

One good result was, one of the ladies in our Bible study group was so convicted for the lie and deception she made. To be able to come to Canada she changed her name and status. When the Holy Spirit convicted her, she went voluntarily to the immigration office and told of her wrongdoing, and because of this she had to be tried in the court. When she was called at her trial, she told the truth that she had previously lied. The consequence of such lies is deportation. So even before her trial we prayed that she would not be deported. But one lady told her, "Just pack your luggage so you will be ready if you are deported."

Upon hearing that I told Ria, "Ria, we have been praying that you will not be deported, so why would you pack? Have faith." On the day of her trial, many of the church members took time to be in the courtroom. ---And by God's grace --- Ria was pardoned and she was not deported but was accepted as an immigrant. Now she is a Canadian citizen and walking with God.

The original ladies' Upper Room idea has spread to other churches and other parts of the world. The enemy has been trying to destroy the Upper Room through many problems but the strong, those overcomers, those who persevere still come to the Upper Room until now, in spite of setbacks and negative events in life.

I remember that sometimes when I explain an issue, I usually hear this comment: "Why do you always spiritualize things." And I did not know how to respond to their inquiry until I understand more the spirituality of man. MAN is more than a BODY, it is more than a SOUL, it is mainly a SPIRIT more than a material being. Man lives in two realms, the spiritual realm and the physical material realm. The unseen spiritual realm cannot be seen by the physical eyes or be felt by our body unless our spiritual senses become sensitive to it. The spiritual realm is above the physical realm. We need to learn that the spiritual realm is more powerful than the physical realm, that is why faith in God is powerful, prayer is powerful, worshipping God is powerful, thanking God is powerful. There are angelic forces in the spiritual realm always ready to obey God.

There are also demonic forces from the kingdom of darkness operating in hierarchy position. The angelic forces from the kingdom of God operate as they see our faith in our action and in our speech. I remember when I was hospitalized because of the accident we had in the beginning of our ministry in Edmonton. I was carrying a dead baby for nine days with a broken pelvis, some broken ribs and facial wounds. It was so painful that I needed an eight-moving team to turn me. But the physical pain was overruled by God's Presence in the room brought by worship music, thanksgiving and praising God every time that I felt the pain. The doctor told me that I will not be able to walk in a year. But praise God! He did a miracle. I was completely healed in less than three months, no trace of accident and there was no grieving over the death of our second daughter Charis Faith. This was also true to Stephen in the Bible in the book of Acts. As they stoned him to death, he was focusing on the sight of heaven and not the pain of being stoned to death. How about

Paul and Silas that was put into jail? Instead of complaining or being discouraged, they worshiped God. Then the jail was shaken opening the gate. Instead of running away, Paul and Silas just stayed there and talked to the jail keeper. What happened was; the jail keeper and his family came to know Jesus the Life, and Paul and Silas were freed. That is powerful! Who shook the jail? The ministering angels of God cooperate with us when they see our faith. It is important to confess our faith in God and his words and to act on it. Speaking God's words strengthen the angelic host.

If they do not see our faith they wait for us, they will move when they see our faith.

The demonic forces of darkness operates when they see that we do not have the faith through our actions and our speech like speaking negatively, for example: complaining of sickness or pain instead of thanking God for healing us and focusing on Him. The more you speak of sickness the more you delay your healing. because you are allowing the spirit of darkness to operate on you. The more you speak of your problems or trials the more you become discouraged and hopeless. We need to navigate in the spiritual realm. We are not only physical or material being. We are spiritual beings.

Here's another example of navigating in the spirit realm. I wrote in the earlier chapter about my first time going to an Islamic province of the Philippines. I had thoughts of discouraging myself to go and it was causing me fear. What I did is to navigate in the spiritual realm. I let my mind think of the protection of God, then I visualize myself being in a Muslim place befriending a princess, the daughter of the chieftain called Datu. That's all I did, and my fear was gone. But this is not the end of the story. When we arrived in Zamboanga at the school where we will be teaching, Joy and I had a student assigned to take care of our needs like food, accommodation and laundry. Her name is Joy. She was so kind and caring to us. She ministered well to us. She became our friend. At the end of our stay there, I had time with her and her boyfriend. They told me their story. There I realized that Joy is a daughter of a Datu, a Muslim leader, so Joy was the princess in my vision. Joy came to know Jesus Christ, the Life, and have been witnessing to her family. At the time of this writing Joy and his boyfriend got married and now serving the Lord together.

Navigating in the spiritual realm is letting our spirit soar using our spiritual senses—our spiritual eyes, ears, smell, taste & sense of touch with the back-up of who God is—his power, immutability, love, mercy, faithfulness, and many more, and the back-up of his Word allowing the Holy Spirit to take control whatever the physical situation is. We thank and praise God for healing us instead of grumbling over our pain and sickness. We see by faith that He is working, making a way for us. It is fighting the wicked elements through reigning with Christ in the heavenlies, binding the enemy and declaring his Words.

QUESTIONS TO PONDER

1. *What is the spiritual realm?*

2. *Navigating in the spiritual realm is allowing our spirit to be in the spiritual realm connecting with God - that is fellowshipping with the indwelling God - spirit to the Holy Spirit not by sight but by faith. Do you see the difference between navigating in the spiritual realm from the earthly realm? Which realm is more powerful? Which part of man - body, soul or spirit connect in the spiritual realm?*

3. *What are the two forces in the spiritual realm? What kingdom will not end and ultimately be the only reigning kingdom (Rev. 11:15-19)?*

4. *What are the two identities of a child of God? Which identify is more powerful?*

CHAPTER 14

ANGELIC INTERVENTION

Do I believe in angels? Yes, because the Bible talks about angels. I also have experienced their ministry for me and my family.

I have seen one angelic form (with wings and sword) some in human form and some unseen. I am talking about angels of the kingdom of God and not the fallen angels of Satan. Angels are benevolent celestial beings that mediate between God and man. They protect and guide humanity, minister to God's children. They are servants of God. There are thousands of angels of the kingdom of God that surround us. We call them heavenly host. When the servant of Elisha the prophet was so afraid because of the enemy's army, Elisha prayed to open his servant's spiritual eyes and there he saw chariots of fire protecting them (2 Kings 6:8-17).

I have written of some earlier instances where I have experienced angels. One time in my trip to the Philippines, my ticket included two luggage pieces paid in my domestic flight to Davao. So, going back to Manila, my hosts–Mrs. Rosario Ang, Sid and Joanne filled up the second bag with mangoes and cacao chocolates. Upon arrival at the domestic airport, a porter assisted me to the line for check-in. After he left me, a white uniformed young man came to assist me. I told him that I am alright, and I do not need assistance anymore, but he insisted. When we got into the check-in counter, I was told that I can only bring one piece of luggage. So, what would I do with the 2nd bag? The white uniformed man told me "Ma'am, I will just put your bag in the plane" but I reasoned out and refused. The supervisor told me later that I can have two carry-on bags. So that is what I did. The uniformed young man was with me, passing through the security up to the departure gate. I was just wondering why he was with me even through the security carrying my two hand carry bags. Before leaving, I tried to give him a tip, but he refused it. When it was time for boarding, the attendant announced that we can only bring one carry-on luggage. So now, what would I do with the second carry-on that I have? I whispered a prayer "Lord, help me please, what will I do?" After uttering that prayer, the uniformed young man who was with me assisting me all the way to the gate appeared again from nowhere. He said, "Ma'am I will help you; I will go inside the plane now. I will bring your bag." I just entrusted my 2nd bag to him. When I got closer to the plane, I saw him again and he told me "Ma'am, God bless you." Who was that white uniformed young man who assisted me, and he could enter the security and the plane? He was a great help to me. I believe he was an angel.

On another time, the bus we were riding in Manila lost its brakes. It just kept on running. Approaching a four-way traffic, meaning we could crash into any of the vehicles on the road. I stood up and prayed "Praise the Lord, thank you for delivering us from crashing into anybody." God intervened; the bus turned to the side crashing just in front of an electrical post where nobody was hurt. What if we had crashed into the four-way traffic? I believe there were angels who helped us.

One time I lost my cell phone after coming from the grocery. I prayed that I would find it. One week passed but still no cell phone appeared so I started to think I will not be able to find it but there's a voice in my spirit saying, "don't give in, trust me." So, I continued to thank God for it. After about 3 weeks, as I prepared to attend a Bible study group gathering, Cecille, my "inaanak" (I am one of the principal sponsors of their wedding) called me. "Ninang," I have somebody in the phone, he said he has your cell phone. Praise God, this somebody said, he is visiting from the U.S.A. We went to meet a young East Indian fellow. How did things connect? Who was that young man?

January 2019–I had been scheduled for my Asia Mission trip, first to the Philippines then to Japan. I praise God for every opportunity He gives me to extend his kingdom through training believers in the faith, preaching and doing evangelistic outreaches. As soon as we touched-down at the Manila (Ninoy Aquino) International Airport, my dear sisters–some of the "Dark Chocolate Ladies" of Tanauan Bible Church (TBC) came and met me to bring me in Tanauan for a two-day rest before proceeding to Dipolog City in Zamboanga del Norte for our healing and deliverance crusade. Who are the "Dark Chocolate Ladies" of Tanauan Bible Church? These are the lady leaders of TBC. They give me "missionary care package" whenever I visit the Philippines. They take care of me, check my health and bring me for detoxification and take me around town. The ladies take a "day off" from their busy schedules and we go for a day relaxation like swimming in Laguna hot spring pools, or a gathering to hear the Word and have fellowship over a meal. Tanauan Bible Church in Batangas had become my refuge whenever I go to the Philippines. The pastors and the leaders had adopted me as their own. They also involved me in ministry like speaking to the ladies, seniors, their mission committee and other church activities. It is always a joy to be with saints sharing to them the goodness of God.

Picture of the tire that burst.

It was already late at night when we left the airport and Tanauan is more than an hour drive from the airport. As we were driving on the highway, the front wheel exploded, and our van skidded and almost hit the centre divider of the highway. We prayed fervently for God to protect us, and the van from its speeding mode slowly moved to the side of the highway, as if somebody was directing our van. Even in a busy highway we managed to reach the safe side and stopped. Our wheel and all the rubber around it were gone up to the rim. God had protected us. As Elmer, the driver, and others changed the tire, a vehicle came, put on the light of his vehicle so, they can see what they are doing as they changed the tire. We did not have any flashlight that time, we were just using cell phone lights before the help came. I remember the man who gave light did not really talk. With his help we were able to change the tire. Who was that man? Was he an angel of God?

Going to Dipolog, a town in North Zamboanga, Philippines, whose government head is a believer was such an additional blessed experience in the Lord. Our host is a government leader and a strong believer in the Lord. We noticed that his province had peace unlike the other nearby provinces. He also had weekly evangelistic outreach especially among students. We were invited to this outreach but some of us were taken to another place to encourage the believers there, so we were not able to attend. I was frustrated for missing the opportunity to be at the governor's student reach out. I grumbled, but I repented.

The next morning, I was not feeling well but that day I was informed that I am personally invited by the governor in his home. What a privilege! Who arranged it? When I was frustrated not to be able to see his outreach, I felt so down but the Lord spoke to me and so I repented. But now God is giving me a privilege to be in a private session with the head of the province. It was a special time; my goal was just to present him some tools of introducing our Lord to others, but God gave me a chance to explain and teach him how to use those tools and he listened attentively. After that, I was invited to join him and his family for a very sumptuous meal of sea foods, vegetables and tropical fruits. It was like sitting with the king. Again, I took it as an angelic intervention. God must have arranged a human to coordinate my special meeting with him when He saw me frustrated but then came to my senses and I repented. So, He made a divine intervention that I can have a special time with the governor and his family.

What a joy to be involved in healing and deliverance crusade. We saw healing, people repenting from witchcraft, receiving the Lord, crying out to God, etc. The angels of God were intervening. Angels are servants of God always ready to obey Him.

In August of the same year, it was already four months since I was prophesied to be writing a book and had not started yet. I had been so busy unpacking our stuff–as we had just moved to the apartment to minister with new immigrants especially East Indians. That was the time that Joy was preparing to convene an international forum for Sikhs–to create global ministry for them to be reached and helped. God opened the door for me to rest in Hawaii so I could start the book. Almost all my siblings live in Hawaii, so I have family there to stay with.

Praise God, that in Hawaii, I was able to start this book that I was writing in spite of the enemy's distraction, like insomnia attack, etc. But after three weeks I needed to go home even if the book was not yet finished. Joy picked me up at the Edmonton International Airport. As we drove home on the highway, something happened to our car, like what happened on our way to Tanauan from the airport last January in the Philippines. The front tire that was new just burst. Again, an unseen hand slowly moved us to the side of the road. God also used a driver–Dustin and his friend, Ayril, with a tow truck to come and help Joy bringing him and the car to the machine shop. Was that a coincidence? No, the enemy was trying to destroy me/us, but God is always there with his unseen hand and his angels.

How about in the ministry? In speaking, in preaching? When the prophet Elijah had to prove that God is the true God and not the pagan gods–Elijah called upon the Lord to prove that He is the true God by consuming the sacrifice on the altar and God did it (1 Kings 18:21-39). I believe there were angelic hosts. One more example is Elisha and his servant (2 Kings 6:17 NIV – And Elisha prayed, "Open his eyes, Lord, so that he may see." Then the Lord opened the servant's eyes, and he looked and saw the hills full of horses and chariots of fire all around Elisha). I believe, on a daily basis, we are surrounded by angelic hosts to minister to us, protect us and to fight for us against the fallen angels of the diabolical kingdom. That is why we children of God should not be intimidated or be afraid or anxious.

God is always with us.

I believe when I preach or speak–there are angelic hosts working behind the scenes. The angelic hosts do what God tells them to do. They also see our faith. If they see that we trust God then they do what needs to be done, but if we doubt, they will not be moved to do what we pray because we are lacking faith.

I love teaching the Word of God. I once taught the Seven Steps to Freedom Series by Neil Anderson to the Adult Sunday School. As I taught it, I have observed the opposition of the enemy – some minor and others are major attacks. There are two major attacks I remember. One was during our church's couple retreat. Part of the activities was horseback riding. Horses in Canada are big, unlike the horses in the Philippines. I needed steps to climb the horse. At first, we went to the woods, then to an open field. As soon as we reached the open field, my horse acted weird. He became uncontrollable and ran wildly and far from the others. I prayed, "Lord please help me." I was so afraid. Then you know what happened? The horse slowed down and stopped, knelt down and lay on his side to let me down. As soon as I was down, the horse stood up and ran like crazy. I really believe an angel of God stopped the horse on the way and told the horse to put me down like Balaam and the donkey in the Bible. The donkey saw the angel stopping him to go through, but he cannot see the angel. Balaam was asked to curse Israel, but God sent an angel to stop him. With what happened he blessed Israel instead of cursing it.

Secondly, was when one time I went to the grocery store. When I went out afterwards, I saw a jeep that was parked just in front and the engine was not running, but the moment I stepped outside, passing at the back of the jeep, the driver suddenly turned on the engine and moved backwards like it would hit me. Praise God I was one step ahead, so the jeep did not hit me. Maybe an angel pushed me one step ahead so I would not be hit. Truly God protects his children. Psalms 91 and John 10:10 confirm this. The enemy wants to destroy, to kill us, to steal from us. He doesn't want me to teach Freedom in Christ, so he attacked me. I will tell more of these experiences in the topic of Spiritual Warfare and Angelic Intervention.

There are two Spiritual Kingdoms, but God's dominion is over all.

1. The Kingdom of Light–where God rules and reigns
2. The Kingdom of Darkness–where Satan, the enemy rules, just a small kingdom.

As we navigate in the spiritual realm, God will open our eyes in both kingdoms, so we know how to reign with Christ on high and become effective in spiritual warfare.

QUESTIONS TO PONDER

1. *What are the two spiritual kingdom?*
2. *What is the highest kingdom? Read 2 Kings 6:17. Whose kingdom reigns forevermore (Revelation11:15-19).*
3. *What are the two kinds of angels?*
4. *What motivates the angels of God to mobilized. How about the fallen angels?*

~ CHAPTER 15 ~

DEALING WITH SICKNESS

Whatdo you do when your loved one had a brain aneurysm (bleeding in the brain)? No intervention like surgery and drugs are possible because of his pre-existing condition. Then the doctor tells you if he goes into coma – "that's it, we will not resuscitate." Shall I look at it the natural way, like the doctor said or will I look at the Creator God and trust Him for his powerful acts to intervene. He created the world, the heavenly bodies and all that is into being even humanity. (I will tell more of this at the end of the chapter).

One difficulty in life that I struggled with is sickness. Even as a baby, I was sickly. That moved my parents to do a ritual but that was in vain, I was still sickly. I grew up with frequent visits to the doctors and quack doctors (did not graduate as medical doctors but use herbs and spiritual means to treat their patients). I did not realize at that time that even such quack doctors receive their power to heal by spirits of darkness (I had to repent and ask for forgiveness from God when I realized it).

In my high school year, my sister and I got sick of Hepatitis A (inflammation of the liver) due to what we ate. I became skin and bone, so yellowish. It was so painful to move, even just a slight move or just smiling and I almost died but God spared my life. It was in sickness that I sought God. I was interning as a nurse when I got sick again. I was so afraid that I would die. The thought of "hell" disturbed me. I remember the story of the rich man and Lazarus in Luke 9. If I died at that time, it would be the worst scenario of my life because I had not accepted Jesus yet as my Lord and Saviour. I was so afraid to die because I did not know where to go—heaven or hell. Yes, I was God fearing, I was a churchgoer, but these could not bring me to heaven. So, it was because of sickness that I looked for God through the Bible, through attending Bible study and praying.

There He revealed Himself to me through a Bible Study of the Nurses Christian Fellowship. That was the time that I received Him as my Saviour and Lord. Since then, in spite of the pain and difficulties that sickness brings, God gave me the power to overcome it. Like in our accident in 1984 when I was broken physically (pelvic bones and three ribs broken, face wounded), and emotionally (our third child–Charis Faith Jabez, had died). With a fractured pelvis and with a dead baby inside the womb for less than two weeks, can you imagine a baby absorbing the bleeding inside and putting pressure on my broken pelvis? It was so painful I am small, but 8 nurses would move me so as not to cause more pain and I would cry "Praise the Lord." God gave me a contrite heart, offering a sacrifice of praise to Him. The doctor said it will take a year for me to be able to walk again but by God's grace I was able to walk in three months. Isn't that a miracle? One of God's names is Jehovah Raphah–Great Healer and Balm of Gilead. He is merciful to heal when you call upon Him--Triumph Over Tragedy.

Diabetes had been a chronic illness for me but again the Lord empowered me to live above it—lots of medications 4 to 5 times a day insulin injection, 6 times pricking of fingers a day to check blood sugar, fasting from delicious, sweet foods and drinks. But I can still bloom and live to the fullest without suffering from complications. I was diagnosed with diabetes since 1984, thank God I am still alive and blooming in this difficult world—like the blooming flowers in the cover of this book.

One way I dealt with sickness was through inner healing. I went into a process where I was led to list all the people that have hurt me, and the first one was my mom. Don't get me wrong. My mom loved me so much. I saw her care for me but when I was growing up, she would always correct me and scold me like one time my cousin and I tasted what she was cooking for a birthday party and she scolded me and made me kneel for twenty minutes, but she did not do that to my cousin. With her scolding and corrections, I felt I was not loved and felt dumb. I then began to be afraid of angry people, even for just a high tone of voice I would get nervous.

Parents think that always scolding and correcting a child will help them but in the process of growing this would develop low self-esteem in a child and a feeling of rejection and not being loved. Children

Richard, Cecille, and Ricel

should receive a balanced dose of correction and affirmation. Everybody needs to be encouraged not discouraged. As a mom and a grandmother, with all the counselling I have done, I believe that correcting a child every time will result to low self-esteem that would paralyze a child to act and excel even when they get older. He thinks he will always be wrong. This also causes a loss of affection from the child to the parents which happened to me. As a result, I had more affection to my dad who only corrected me a few times. So, when I received the Lord, it was my mom whom I forgave first.

In inner healing, it is not only forgiving those who hurt you but also putting those hurts at the foot of the cross and putting them to the grave and not digging them up again. So, at the process of inner healing, I listed those who hurt me by their judgmental attitudes, gossiping, and verbally and physically hurt me. I released forgiveness to them one by one and put the hurts at the foot of the cross and put them to the grave. Oh, that brought healing and freedom to me. Today, if ever I remember the hurt feelings, I have tears of joy because of God's victory in my life.

I remember Cecille, our "inaanak." She was 23 weeks pregnant. She called us one day that she had delivered already a 470 grams baby girl. When we went to see her in the hospital, she and Richard told us that the medical staff asked them what to do with their baby that could hardly be seen as a "formed baby." This precious baby girl was so small— she was supposed to be almost 11 inches in length for a twenty-three-week foetus, but she was born as small as a fist. She had no defined form. The medical team asked Cecille and Richard if they would allow them to take the baby into a research study (like a guinea pig). Joy told them to tell the doctors "Please do whatever is best for our baby"–meaning do not make her a research study but do what you can to save her. They've done their best; they did not make her a "guinea pig." Their faith was tested, her BP went down only the heartbeat showed life. The social worker told them that she would be cremated, but they prayed for God's intervention and said, "Praise the Lord for healing our baby." God did a miraculous thing–doing what the hospital team cannot do. Cecille's baby Ricel developed and grew in an incubator for months. Richard and Cecille trusted God for their baby. They wanted Ricel to grow and develop, trusted God for all the management the doctors did, even when the teeth came out and they were green in colour. This test in their lives stretched their faith in God. They have learned to be strong in the midst of difficulties. Ricel today is a beautiful girl, and excelling in school. What if Cecille and Richard gave up their baby as a "guinea pig" for research? Is there anything that God cannot do?

One time I had a dream about Tonyvic in a difficult situation. When dreams are bad, renounce, and cancel the plan of the enemy to destroy. Some dreams are prophesy looking for its fulfilment. There are good dreams & bad dreams. When dreams are good claim it but when it's bad rebuke it. Bad dreams come from the enemy that seek to destroy us. So, I renounced the bad dream about Tonyvic. After a few months he asked us to drop him at the emergency for abdominal pain, that was 4pm–but it was already late in the ER and he had not yet been attended to. Instead, he was told to go home and be back the next day. So, after some tests the next day, he was found out to have appendicitis and was scheduled for appendectomy. The medical team waited for another 5 hours. At the time of laser surgery, they found out that the appendix had ruptured but still did not clean him. The result was a tummy getting distended with a reddish colour–that it became purplish then blackish, yet they just gave him oral antibiotics and discharged him. Waiting for 3 days, fever developed and so we rushed him to another hospital–the largest research hospital in Alberta. When they saw him, they took him at once at the emergency and did paracentesis (removing about 3 litres of dead blood and pus). They opened and cleaned up the abdomen. Thank God there was no peritonitis–that can cause blood poisoning, but they had to cut out 1/3 of his larger intestine and put a colostomy tube. He almost died, but we prayed, and God intervened. The enemy wanted to destroy Tonyvic but praying for him even before the surgery worked. God created a miracle, a natural way of healing so the colostomy tube was not permanent but removed. Tony still serves full time in the ministry today. He loves young people. May God call many young people to ministry.

We read in the Bible, about Jesus ministering to the sick in different ways like the case of different blind people. Jesus spit on one, in the other one He used mud, the other one He spoke to, the other one He touched him and the other one He cast out demon. It was always done with mercy and love. Sickness has many root causes. It may be from unhealthy lifestyle like eating junk food that is not good to our body, lack of exercise, exposure to chemicals at work, generational sickness, or work of the enemy. Root causes have been known by pathologists and the medical industry. There are also spiritual root causes like generational sin, curses, negative emotions causing stress both physical and emotional; bitterness, anger, unforgiveness, hatred, fear, worry and anxiety, discouragement, guilt, shame, rejection from self and others, a spirit of infirmities (like deaf & dumb spirits), sexual sins, weird thoughts, direct attacks from the enemy, etc. Praise God—He is the Greatest Healer.

On Joy's first 1-2 weeks of confinement in the hospital, sometimes he did not recognize us, half part of his body (hemiplegia) had been affected, he had no sensory response, continuous bleeding in the brain and medicine and surgery was not possible because of his pre-existing condition. Completely in bed, he could not even raise his head and neck. The doctor told me, if he gets into a coma—that's it, we will let him go. I thought of a funeral—but my eyes were drawn to God the Giver of life—reaching to Him. I declared that God's will be done and if it is his will to extend Joy's life then He will let him live. In spite of not being able to do anything against the bleeding, Joy still progressed from his slurring to better speech.

After two weeks he was discharged from Critical ICU and moved to a unit where they continued to monitor his vital signs and care for him. He was just lying down for 50 days and on NGT (Naso Gastric Tube) feeding. He could not lift his head; he was turned every two hours. According to the poster in his hospital room, ten days of just lying is equivalent to ten years of muscle wasting or atrophy. Joy was in bed for about fifty days, with nasal tube feeding, half of his extremities restrained. What do you think would be the muscle wasted? Fifty days of lying down is equal to fifty years of muscle wasting, but Joy only lost about thirty pounds.

In the fifth week, some sensation had developed in the paralyzed half of the body, although it was still not recognizing hot or cold, praise

God there is some sensation and he started to move better and better. I knew he would come into full rehabilitation and healing. As he entered the fourth month–he was being rehabilitated at a dedicated rehabilitation hospital. He could then stand longer with assistance.

It is my prayer that as God extended his life, He will grant him the needed healing for Joy to be able to walk again like me and God will be glorified. I believe healing is a part of salvation that Jesus finished at the Cross. The salvation through Jesus is not only salvation from sin, from hell, from destruction of the enemy; not only a salvation of spirit but also salvation of the soul (our mind, emotion and will) and salvation of our bodies from sickness. We are healed through the stripes of Jesus so, we can live above sickness, we do not let sickness control us, but we have to be victorious above it. Isaiah 53:5 "But He was pierced for our transgressions, he was crushed for our iniquities; the punishment that brought us peace was on him, and BY HIS WOUNDS WE ARE HEALED." As one who has a heavenly identity, I see the Almighty God who is working, and nothing is impossible to Him. With his power in his children–we can live victoriously over sickness. Sickness cannot put us down. We have to overcome its power.

In concluding this chapter, I am reminded by the Lord to write the following testimony of his healing and faithfulness to his children particularly his workers in the kingdom.

In the early part of the 20th century when the Filipino International Network was in full swing; Joy had started to have stomach pain on his flight back home. He then consulted his family doctor, who in turn referred him to Dr. Ma, a well-known Chinese specialist at the University of Alberta Hospital (UAH). It was then found out that he had a serious liver problem, and the prognosis was Joy had only about five years to live.

Joy was so down then. Ianne and Dennis had decided to have their wedding in Manila, Philippines. Joy was so sad that he could not attend their wedding anymore, because it was overseas. But he was encouraged to move on as God would undertake for him. He trusted God to touch him for healing. His ministry partners and friends around the world prayed for him. In one of the seminars, he organized in Singapore all the delegates prayed for him. Praise God, he was able to attend Ianne's and Dennis' wedding. With his work globally, God gave him grace to go on.

When we moved to Toronto, he was given a good liver specialist there, an Egyptian. He was like Dr. Ma who was kind and caring and sympathetic to him. When we were based again in Edmonton, Joy visited his specialist, Dr. Ma. He exclaimed, "You are still alive?" Yes, it is almost twenty years now from when Joy was diagnosed, his kind doctor still follows him up even in the midst of Covid-19 asking how he is.

Two years ago, while attending a conference as one of the speakers in Bali, Indonesia, Joy was rushed to the hospital after speaking. It was found out that he had three blood clots in the stomach, and they restrained him so the blood clots would not travel to more dangerous sites. They planned to do exploratory surgery on his abdomen, but he was scared and called me, "Come and get me here, I do not want to die here." In spite of tiredness, as I just arrived from a transpacific flight from Japan, I got a ticket going back to Asia from Canada. At the Manila airport I waited for our surgeon nephew Dr. Bonilla to join me in bringing Joy to Manila for further management and to give us a signal to fly to Canada if possible. We had not cancelled our flight back to Manila from Indonesia and our flight back to Canada from Manila the same day, trusting the Lord for his intervention. Can you just imagine the hectic schedule? Dr. Bonilla and I arrived in Indonesia in the middle of the night. We had a short sleep then went early to the hospital. Steve talked with the doctors in charge, and we were allowed to take him home that same day. They have to take the IVs, catheter, NGT (nasogastric tube) for food feedings then went to the airport. Arriving at Manila International Airport our nephew Pastor Rollyvic picked us up and brought us to the hospital where Steve works. It was a stormy day and there was flooding but praise God, we arrived at St. Luke's Hospital where a medical team was waiting to check on Joy whether he could travel or not. They did MRI. God is so good. The two blood clots had disappeared, while the one remaining blood clot had shrunk, so we were given a green light to fly home to Canada.

It was a 13-hour long haul to Canada, and it would not be good for Joy just to be sitting down in a narrow plane seat to prevent blood clotting. So, we prayed for God's favour and that PAL staff will provide a better seat for Joy. While the check in lady went to ask her supervisor if they can upgrade us, I was there, declaring God's help and love, and declaring favour for our request. I was there, praising and thanking God. Sure enough, our request was granted without additional fee. We were put into the first class. There Joy was able to eat solid food and lie down and sleep. For me, crisscrossing the pacific four times in a row was tiring, but on the fourth time he gave me a bed to rest and sleep in the plane. God is so good. That morning we arrived in Edmonton; Joy was admitted at the UAH for further management. Our good and loving God intervened to deliver him from premature death three times already so that his plan for Joy will be fulfilled giving glory to Him. This is living life to the fullest—overcoming sickness and trouble.

QUESTIONS TO PONDER

1. *Have you experienced healing in a miraculous. way?*

2. *One covenant name of God is Jehovah Rapha meaning Healer. What is the promise in Exodus 15:26 and in Isaiah 53:5 ?*

3. *From my stories how have I been dealing with sickness? How about Richard and Cecille, how did they dealt with Ricel's condition? What was the outcome?*

4. *God is a miracle worker, a way maker a promise keeper - will this encourage you to seek him?*

~ CHAPTER 16 ~

THE LOVE OF GOD

Ephesians 2:4-10 (NIV) v4-5 But because of his great love for us, God, who is rich in mercy, made us alive with Christ even when we were dead in transgressions—it is by grace you have been saved. The love of God is so deep, so wide, and so high. Nobody can fathom it–but as one goes deeper in his relationship with God, he begins to understand more the width, the height and the depth of God's love and who He is. He is present even as you read this book to set your heart ablaze with his love and his glory. Do you desire to go into that glorious realm beyond the veil? Do you want to know the depth, the height, and the width of his great love?

As of the writing of this book, it's been 48 years since Jesus came into my heart–the year I accepted Him as my Lord and Saviour. The book I am writing is not enough to tell you about Him. I can only briefly say "WOW, Amazing God, Amazing Love, Amazing Grace, Amazing Power. Knowing

Jesus Christ <u>personally</u> is knowing God–the Great I Am. As Isaiah 9:6 says "For to us a child is born, to us a son is given, and the government will be on his shoulders. And he will be called <u>Wonderful Counsellor</u> (The 3rd person of the Triune God–the Holy Spirit), <u>Mighty God,</u> <u>Everlasting Father</u> (The 1st person of the Triune God–God the Father, The Great Jehovah), <u>Prince of Peace</u> (The 2nd person of the Trinity– Jesus, The Son of God.) He is the image of the invisible God. For by him all things were created; things in heaven and on earth, visible and invisible whether thrones or powers or rulers or authorities; all things were created by him and for him. He is before all things, and in him all things hold together (Colossians 1:15-17). Jesus is supreme. I am glad I am walking with Him. Even the name of Jesus carries authority.

The love of God did not only save us but gave us dominion, a delegated authority to shift the atmosphere of a troubled world to an atmosphere of peace, courage and freedom. Let me cite an example: there was one time as I walked in the park that I saw a man with three bulldogs coming towards me. The three dogs were angry and coming to hurt me. Their owner was calling them, but they went ahead coming closer to me. As soon as they were in front of me, with authority I said, "In the name of Jesus, you stop." They stopped and became like statues. When the owner called them again, they turned their back on me and went to their master. Wow, that's the power of God, I remember Kay Arthur testifying, "There was a lady trying on something inside a fitting room in one of the department stores in the U.S. As she tried the dress, a man came at gunpoint to rob her. The lady said, "In the name of Jesus get behind me Satan." Upon hearing that, the man rushed to come out of the fitting room. The God I have known personally is powerful. He is so loving and so faithful. He gave us authority to use his name. That is a privilege in having Jesus–the Life.

I remember when I was a child, our neighbour was bullying me, and I was crying. Then, my father arrived and castigated our neighbour. He defended me. He told our neighbour not to do it again. I appreciated my dad for doing that. From that time, my dad became my friend and confidant. My dad loved me so much and because of him, I came to better understand the great love of God. I have experienced trials, hurts, and pain in life, but God has been and is my defender, my shield, my deliverer, and the lifter of my head.

You have read lots of my testimonies. I have been broken physically and emotionally in experiences including the head-on-collision vehicle accident we had during which we lost our third child, Charis Faith Jabez. In the emergency department of a Canadian hospital, I experienced racial discrimination. In spite of the horrible pain, the hospital staff forced me to go home even though I noticed that they could no longer find the foetal heartbeat. The attending emergency room staff did not even call my obstetrician, who is also a friend of Jesus. But, the physical pain of broken bones (i.e., pelvic and some ribs), wounded face, and emotional pain from, most of all, losing our full-term Charis Faith, did not wound my spirit. I was there rejoicing in the love of God—his presence was felt instead of hurt and pain. Some friends suggested to us to complain and take the head of the emergency department to court because of discrimination and malpractice; but God spoke to Joy and asked him "What do you want, for Lulu to be healed [I had been told that I would not to be able to walk for a year] or money?" I am glad Joy chose what is more important—my healing. God gave us justice—the head of the emergency department resigned as head. God is also our defending lawyer. He fought for us. Usually, even the effects of accidents reoccur through pain or other problems—but to me I was completely healed.

I felt that I was put down and discriminated against because of my relationship with God, including the gift of tongues and my other spiritual gifts, as well as my studies in an apostolic tradition; but my life, my strong belief in the power of the Word of God and the works of the Holy Spirit remained even in times that I was judged as a fanatic and with wrong beliefs. I stayed strong to glorify God and to delight in Him became my goal—not the educational status or the diploma which I tore. I am stripped of SELF, but I thank God, JESUS CHRIST, the Hope of glory remains in me. It is no longer I who live but Christ lives in me. God's love is so powerful, it became my strength and pride.

The love of God — nobody can fathom, that is why the letter of Paul to the saints of Ephesus states: "16I pray that out of his glorious riches he may strengthen you with power through his Spirit in your inner being. 17 so that Christ may dwell in your hearts through faith. And I pray that you, being rooted and established in love, 18 may have power, together with all the saints, to grasp how wide and long and high and deep is the love of Christ, 19 and to know this love that surpasses knowledge—that you may be filled to the measure of all the fullness of God. 20 Now to him who is able to do immeasurably more than all we ask or imagine, according to his power that is at work within us, 21 to him be glory in the church and in Christ Jesus throughout all generations, forever and ever! Amen. (Ephesians 3:16-21)

The love of God cannot only be known through knowledge. Why did God the Father send Himself to the earth—by sending his only son Jesus? Why was Jesus willing to go through the suffering on the cross? Why did the Father promise the Holy Spirit? Why did Jesus give his Spirit to us? Theology is not enough to learn the answers to our WHYs. You need the Triune God to speak to you and to encounter you. God speaks through his Words, through godly counsel, through the peace that He gives you, which transcends all understanding.

Yes, I have known the love of God — but not as deeply as today. As I write this portion of the book, this is the 7th week of Joy's time in the hospital since he had a brain aneurysm. As I saw Joy pass through the valley of the shadow of death in my spirit, I saw Jesus walking, bearing the cross, being tortured as he was beaten and wounded for our sins. I felt the pain of the disciples, it must have been a struggle to see Jesus –their teacher suffering and thinking of what they did deserting Him especially Peter who denied Him three times. As I remember my shortcomings and transgressions, I felt the pain of the disciples when they deserted Jesus, when Peter denied Jesus–but at the end, Jesus showed Himself to them and after his ascension He gave his Spirit to them at Pentecost. That is the love of God. In spite of the disciples' sin of denying Him, He showed Himself to them and forgave them. Again, that is the love of God. Suffering here on earth is fellowshipping with Jesus' suffering–knowing the fullness of his love with promise and thanksgiving in spite of pain, my cup overflows–this is living life to the fullest. Always hoping, trusting of his great love and mercy.

We can never compare God to others. He is above all. God has covenant names in which we can approach Him.

Our God—his name is Yahweh

- *his name is Elohim- God, Judge, Creator*
- *El Elyon – the Most High God*
- *El Olam – the Everlasting/Eternal God*
- *The Great I Am, El Shaddai*

Jehovah

- *Jehovah Jireh–our Provider*
- *Jehovah Nissi–our Banner*
- *Jehovah Rapha¬–our Healer*
- *Jehovah Shalom–our Peace*
- *Jehovah Shammah–the God who is always with us*
- *Jehovah Sabaoth–the Lord of Host/Captain of the Host of heaven*
- *Jehovah Tsidkenu–our Righteousness*

Alpha and Omega, his Name is Jesus

- *Great Shepherd, Light of the world, Master Saviour, The Truth, The Way, The Life*
- *Emmanuel, Prince of Peace, Eternal God, Almighty God, Wonderful Counsellor,*
- *Our Passover Lamb, King of kings, Lord of lords, Holy Spirit, Advocate, Author of*
- *Life, the Door, and many more.*

God is our covenant God. We can call Him on his covenant name in line with our need. We should believe that He loves us so much that is why He made a way to redeem us back to Him by sending Jesus. That is why Jesus went willingly on the cross for us to have Him and live life to the fullest. I could not express more in words how great the love of God is. I thank Him for revealing Himself to me. As I was growing up, I was looking for love. I know my dad and mom loved me and my siblings loved me, but there was a vacuum to be filled in my life–there I found Jesus the lover of my life. He filled the vacuum of my life.

Jesus is the Emmanuel, Almighty God, Eternal Father, Prince of Peace, Wonderful Counsellor. The fullness of the Godhead dwells in Him. Jesus is the incarnate God, the God who came as flesh, died, was buried and rose again, is seated now on the throne and will come again to take us to Heaven with Him–where there is no more crying or pain.

(Revelation 21:1-4) I saw a new heaven and a new earth: for the first heaven and the first earth were passed away; and there was no more sea. 2 And I John saw the holy city, new Jerusalem, coming down from God out of heaven, prepared as a bride adorned for her husband. 3 And I heard a great voice out of heaven saying, Behold, the tabernacle of God is with men, and he will dwell with them, and they shall be his people, and God himself shall be with them and be their God. 4 And God shall wipe away all tears from their eyes; and there shall be no more death, neither sorrow, nor crying, neither shall there be any more pain; for the former things are passed away.

The following is an excerpt of my testimony: September 2021

I am sharing this to testify of God's Love in providing our needs whether how small or big they are. Last week, I got a KFC

(Kentucky Fried Chicken) coupon from the mail. There I started to desire for KFC meal. Every day I wanted to have it, but I just could not have it on my hand. I have been so busy going to and fro in the hospital, packing our stuff making ready to move again and finishing the book I am writing which is entitled LIFE TO THE FULLEST IN A TROUBLED WORLD. On the 7th day, Beth, the kind sister who had been helping me type the book came with a bag of KFC. My eyes widened and I asked her, "Who told you to bring KFC?" because I never told anyone about my cravings for KFC. Beth answered, "Nobody told me." Wow, it made me cry not because of the KFC but the love of God who prompted Beth to get it for me to meet my small desire for KFC.

Here's another testimony on God's love. As we had been on the crossroad waiting on God's direction to where Joy and I would stay after his discharge, I felt like I was in the middle of the Stop Sign not knowing where to cross: there was a STOP Sign on red light but no green light or direction where to cross—as if I am forced to cross already, but where? The train or other vehicles might hit me if I went in the wrong direction. Will it be in our home? Or will it be at Glenrose Rehab Centre? My children favoured Glenrose Rehab Centre. They said, "Mom, you cannot help daddy alone, you need help." I cried to the Lord again and again! Then one day, Mike and Nen who always volunteer to give me a ride to and from the hospital asked me, "How can we help you"? I answered, "You have been already helping me by giving rides to and from the hospital." But early in the morning the next day, they phoned me and invited me in their house. They prepared a meal and after eating together, Nen told me; "The Lord woke me up at 3am and gave me compassion for you. He used Pastor Joy and you to help us in coming to Canada, and helping us in our walk with God, so now it is time for us to also help you. Mike and I have decided to invite you to stay with us as Pastor Joy recuperates, so we can help you in assisting him. If our house will pass Glenrose Rehab staff recommendations, then we will do necessary renovation." Thank God, that was a relief!

This couple was touched by God to sacrifice even doing renovation in their home for us. Wow, this is God's love. I did not ask them; I was surprised, and I was in tears. I want the comfort of my own home, but now God is asking us to move to another place like Abraham, "Move and I will be with you. Cross over, do not be afraid. This is my work in

Joy and you and the family. This is to continue my work of Renovation, Releasing you of all the impediments that have been weakening you, to Restore you, to Reconnect you and to widen your Relationships." Wow. Thank you, God. I have many more to testify. I hope I can write all the people God has been using in our lives in the last pages of the book I am writing. These testimonies are like hugs and kisses from God. What can I say—they are all hugs and kisses from God. I salute them. May God reward them for their ministry to us. I always talk to God about them praying for them daily for his protection, blessing and enabling in life. Truly, God is loving, He hugs and give us kisses. God is here to embrace you, to put order in your life, to still your storms of life, to help you.

More Hugs and Kisses:

This book is also a memorial to those the Lord God used in my life, and in our lives—mine and Joy's—to testify to God's great love, bringing hugs and kisses to us through people who have walked with us, who helped us, and who continue to partner with us until now. There are already names listed in this book in testimony of God's love. We thank God for all of them.

With Joy's recent trial with a stroke, I thank God for the medical team of the University of Alberta Hospital; particularly the stroke units, especially 5G2, and the health team of Glenrose Rehabilitation particularly in 3A unit.

- *For those friends who volunteered to regularly give me a ride to and from the hospital to visit Joy—Richard & Cecille, Rajan & Lydia, Lota, Mike & Nen, Jacky & Anne. They also brought food with them for us to enjoy. Thanks, Ruth & Rene, for the sumptuous dinner that you brought into the University Hospital for one of Joy's first solid meals!*

- *For those who helped us by providing food, some of Joy's needs, and helping us in some of our expenses: ZAMIE Filipino Bible Study Group, Filipino Church in Kuwait, FCF in Japan, TGCGM in Qatar, Toronto Filipino Ministerial, Dante and Myrna, Myden and Mike, Tom and Cheryl, Joel and Lolet, Brian and Margie, Teg Chin and Deanne, Lilia and Floro, Bal and Angie, Ka Nellie, Leandro and Vangie, Rajan and Lydia, Rob and Judith, Mama Auring, Sam and Bopeep, Sally, Ro and Cecille, Togade Family, Bryce and Jen, Kit and Dorothy, Mesina family, Bill and Linda, Stanley and Eunice, Rick and Pat, Rey and Dee, Pat and*

Ardyce, TV and Mary, Jacky and Anne, Pastor Richard, Ana Aquino, Tina de Castro, and the Realon family.

- *And, for those who surprised Joy on his 65th birthday even while he was still in much pain and suffering. Thank you so much FFAC, CEAC, and Supper Club family for organising a birthday parade. You brought Joy to tears, because of your visible love that touched his heart.*

- *For those who faithfully prayed with me again and*

Again, during our crisis: Iris & her prayer team, Pastor Marcelo & Beth, Ate Leonie, my sister Leonie & Lydia, Judy, Pastor Bayne and Elenor, Helen, Raul & Donna and all ministry partners around the world who prayed and are still praying for us—LCWE, SIM, MoveIn, PALM, FIN, C&MA, AIM, FCF in Japan, ZAMIE, TGCGM, KNECK and many more— so many international partners and friends in the ministry.

- *For all those who helped me while Joy was in the hospital: Pastor Owen and Denny and his boys who mowed the lawn. I appreciate Pastor Anison Samuel who visited the UAH to pray with us during a difficult time of spiritual warfare.*

- *For our good neighbours who helped us: Don and Renee, Adam, Patrick, Doug and their families, Dave and Donna*

- *Praise the Lord for Mike and Nen who generously prepared and shared their home with us, by renting out (for a very modest monthly fee) an handicap accessible suite.*

To all our "destiny helpers ", Thank you for being sensitive to God's prompting in helping us. Thank you Horatio and Hope, Dr. Beck, Jack and Carol, Denny and Jenny, and Phil and family, for giving vehicles for us to use as we serve the Lord.

We praise God for those who initially supported us as ministry took us across the globe.

- *For Rebecca B. who helped much in our FIN projects*

- *For David Chung who encouraged Joy and helped with global projects*

- *For Moneta, Mary and Roland, Grace, Ivy Metal, Lou and. Lita, Jing and James, Bani and Cynthia, Donna and Nilo, Laila and Willy, Mitchel and Noel, Dolly and Eldie, Ate Loida, Beng and Ren, the Patiences, Ria, Rolly and Tess, Richard and Joyce, the Candelarias, the*

Refugias, Norma and Ronnie, Mervyl, Ricky and Beth, Tess and Efren, Joy and Duane, the Baruts, Cheryl and Tom

We give thanks to God for those who are able to continue sharing with us in the ministry, even in the midst of a pandemic: Arnold and Rose, Naomi M., Paul & Estelle, Lolit, Esther, Aida and Gaby, Eurica and Jun, Ate Betty and Kuya Mike, P. Norman, Evelyn, Freddy and Emmy, Gina and Rey, Del and Carol, Jeff and Laura, Kerry and Cherry, Rod and Elinor, Edwin and Malu, Denny and Jenny, Shawn and Iris, Jack and Rowena, Susie and Ross, Mer and Belen, Rudy and Dolly, Susan, Alma, Charisma, Nancy and Bill, Cecille and Richard, Lin, CEAC, Millview Alliance Church, Halleluiah Fellowship Baptist Church, our "Uncle and Auntie," and family who continue to cheer, encourage and support us in many ways.

We thank God for all our friends and family, most especially for their support in prayers and for sharing with us the ministry challenges and opportunities. We appreciate you all, and we pray for you daily.

"Nothing can separate us from the love of God" (Romans 8:38-39). His Words are full of promises, principles, and prophecies to cling to. He will take us to heaven one day.

QUESTIONS TO PONDER

1. *I was looking for love ever since I was young, friends and family were used by God to meet that need but it is the Love of God that fill all the space of my life or the vacuum) in my heart even in difficult times and trials. It is His love that fill us to overflowing. How do you understand the love of God? Share an example of God's hug and kiss in your life.*

2. *Knowing the width, the height and depth of God's love bring us to an adventure that is extraordinary, unexplainable bringing us to abundant life and joy that is full. What does John 10:10 means to you?*

3. *Ephesians 3:16-21, describes God's love from this passage.*

~ CHAPTER 17 ~
COMMUNICATING WITH GOD

oes God speak and listen to us? I remember when our children were babies. I would talk to them, and they responded by smiling and cooing when I smiled and talked nicely to them. If I were angry, they would cry. Later on, they started to make sounds, afterwards words, then a sentence. What a joy talking with them, it brought delight in my heart, the reward of childbearing. The Bible tells us that God delights in us as we spend time communicating with Him. Communicating is both talking and listening to God. Talking to Him would be telling our needs, desires, problems, interceding for others, inquiring from Him, singing to Him, worshipping Him. Listening would be spending time meditating on His Words, soaking in His Presence, waiting in stillness for Him to speak in your spirit. (Rhema, God's words spoken personally to you). We also communicate to Him non-verbally through our feelings and attitudes.

As I went deeper in my relationship with God, He became my all in all. He is not only my God, but my Father in heaven, my Lord, my King, my Best Friend, my Saviour, Deliverer, my Great Provider (Jehovah Jireh), Great Healer (Jehovah Rapha, Balm of Gilead), my Peace (Jehovah Shalom), my Righteousness (Jehovah Tsidkenu), the God who is Always with me (Jehovah Shammah, Emmanuel), my everything. So, there are lots of levels in my relationship with God and they are all significant. I communicate with Him in all these levels, however, there are three (3) levels that I usually do daily:

1. *as my Abba Father / me as His child,*
2. *as my Bridegroom-my Lover /me as His bride, and (3) as my Master /me as His Army, His Soldier.*

The Bride of Christ

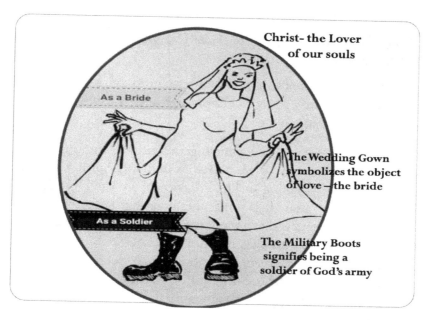

Illustrated by Henrick Vasquez, Animator

<u>As His child</u>, I cry out for help, I have petitions. I ask for the needs of others and for myself. In this level, prayer is a platform of petition. <u>As His Bride</u>, I hunger and thirst for Him—to be intimate with Him, singing Him praises, thanking Him, soaking in His Presence, delighting in Him. This is the best level of communicating with God. It is worshiping God that revives not only my spirit and soul but also my body, it gives me joy.

<u>As His Army (soldier)</u>, I reign with Him in the heavenly realm–taking dominion over spirits of darkness through His leading. We reign in the battle. Everyone who seeks to walk in authority/dominion must walk in prayer. This is the level where you bind the enemy, loose God's blessings, and declare God's Words in power. This is spiritual warfare.

Growing in prayer, I was taught to pray TO the Father, in the NAME of JESUS and in the POWER of the HOLY SPIRIT.

1. I need to pray in the Spirit. Praying in tongues takes me out of myself and brings me in the realm of the spirit. My prayer comes from the Holy Spirit and not from myself. The Holy Spirit helps me as I pray. I just trust Him of what I am uttering.

2. I also need to pray in the Word of God. I declare and confess the Word of God.

3. Praying in the will of God is also important to me. Knowing His will through His words, through His promptings is very effective. It gives you the faith that you need.

At the Upper Room, we come together usually without structured prayer requests. As we start, we pray that the Holy Spirit will guide us what to pray. After soaking in His Presence, there the Holy Spirit just leads us to what to pray. It is sometimes amazing, because God would lead us to prayer requests that are not usually prayed for in church prayer meeting like: prisoners and jailers, film makers, etc. One time, God led us to pray for God to intervene in shooting at the schools. The next day there was an attempted school shooting, but God intervened. One time we prayed for a leading government official making fun of God. The next few months he was taken out from office.

Prayer empowers us to see the spiritual realm. Prayer is God's authorized system of communion and fellowshipping with God. It is a spiritual intimacy. This is the holy of holies in the temple. This is where you hear God in your spirit. This is where revelation comes, and direction given. This is where God meets you in your need—it is through this intimacy where God touches you—His beloved. This is the place of encounter (spirit to spirit).

Soaking is like putting a sponge in a basin of water 'til the sponge is fully soaked. Soaking with God is allowing yourself to be drenched in by the Living Water, the River of Life—to be in His Presence. Julie True, who produces music on soaking says: Soaking is a time to quiet the soul, but to be awakened in the spirit to hear the heart of God in that moment and to interact with Him in a personal way.... [It] is a time of connecting spirit to spirit and heart to heart with the one who loves us like no other and who created us to have relationship with Him. It is an interactive experience with God that has no expectations or limitations."8

Soaking in the spirit is a time of total freedom in the spirit—a time to be saturated by the Presence of God. It's a time to breathe Him in and soak Him into every cell of our being. It's a time to be still and know that He is God. It is a time to stop all striving and to lay our burdens at the feet of Jesus. It's a time to receive fresh healing in our bodies and souls and to fix our eyes on Jesus. It's a time to rest on Him and to know His peace that passes understanding. It is a time to hear His whispers of love for us and to allow our time for that love to completely saturate us. It is a time to be still and know that He is God.

Music that is birthed in the Presence of God without having been previously composed is called spontaneous song. I have experienced this many times. In the preceding chapters, I wrote about our experience in our training in United Arab Emirates. The Holy Spirit brought us into His Presence by allowing me to sing a spontaneous song for about twenty to thirty minutes and there was healing, revelations, and many more.

Soaking in, worshipping God, meditating His words, interacting with Him, being still knowing that He is God. This develops your intimacy with God bringing you into His Presence and receiving fresh revelation and experiencing His touch.

There are times that I inquire from Him about something I do not understand, like one time, I was looking for something important, but I could not find it. I prayed that He would show me where it is. Just as I went out from the washroom, there was an instruction that I received but it was not vocally given, it was in my spirit instructing me to turn left, look at the corner and there I found it. I have never heard God in an audible voice—I have always heard Him in my spirit. Whatever He tells me it never contradicts the Bible. Like when I was questioned if I am still in faith because of the gift of tongues, I didn't understand why they questioned me about it. I was not teaching how to speak in tongues or forcing others to have it. It was only on very rare occasions that it was made public and when it manifested, the moving of the Holy Spirit was evident. So, with this, I almost gave up my faith, I began to doubt my relationship with God—but God spoke to my heart through a C&MA missionary quoting me I Cor.1. The gift of tongues is one of the spiritual

---

8   Julie True, https://isoak.julietrue.com/about-soaking/.

gifts. It is still evident today. I was revived–I went deeper in my encounters with God. God speaks to our spirit in so many ways–through the messages we hear, through events surrounding us, through God's people and even in our silence. In listening to God, we need to have a pure heart to be able to discern His voice for there are so many deceptive voices—your flesh and spirit that are geared to your desires and own understanding, the voice of the world, the voice of Satan, the voice of footholds or strongholds, etc. I found in my life that if my heart is not pure (like when I am irritated with somebody or have ill feelings or like when I am offended and have not forgiven, even when I am complaining and grumbling), I cannot hear well what God is telling me. These negative feelings block my spirit to hear what God is saying. When there is unconfessed sin in my life, it is also hard to hear what God is saying to me.

In Numbers 12:1-15 we see here Moses, Miriam and Aaron (Moses' siblings) communing with God. It began with just a complaint against Moses marrying his Cushite wife. "Has the Lord spoken only through Moses? Hasn't He also spoken through us?" And the Lord heard this. He then instructed them to go to the Tent of Meeting, God came down in a pillar of cloud at the entrance of the tent and He spoke to them (verses 6-8). Did God speak to them in an audible voice or His spirit to their spirit? The text did not say that God spoke audibly, He only appeared in a pillar of cloud and God spoke to their spirits.

When Christians would say "God spoke to me" some probably will not understand these words. "God spoke to me" is somewhat one of the most misunderstood sentences among God's people. For some, out of ignorance that God speaks to us in our spirit, some who would hear "God spoke to me" will judge the one who said it. He is judged as having no knowledge of Theology or judged as proud "who are you that God will speak to" and they become angry. I was taught to be careful in speaking this phrase "God spoke to me" or "God told me." Some people who hear this sometimes argue with me and tell me that "there's no more extra revelation, meaning God doesn't speak any more these days like He spoke with the prophets or priests or to the people of Israel long time ago. He now just speaks through the Bible or through creation. What creation, only the things on earth? Isn't it that man is also a creation, so God can use people to speak to us? But any words that we hear or speak should be in line with the Scriptures, and with the nature and character of God. For example, will God tell me not to have fellowship with another brother or sister especially when there is no valid reason like he/she is not a good model, etc.? That would not be in line with the character of God and His words. Or will God tell you to do something that is opposed to the Bible or His Words? NO.

We hear many voices:

- *The voice of God- The Holy Spirit*
- *The voice of the enemy*
- *The voice of self (desire, etc.)*
- *The voice of the world*

We need to discern the voice of God. How can we differentiate the voice of God and the voice of the enemy? I have been taught that:

1. *God's voice gently leads you—but the enemy drives you.*
2. *God's voice convicts–the enemy condemns and brings guilt*
3. *God's voice woos–the enemy tugs hard.*
4. *God does not use fear–the enemy uses fear.*

The voice of the enemy opposes the Word of God. An example of this is the occurance of suicidal thoughts, etc.

The voice of self brings out the desires of the flesh and the reasoning of the mind.

The voice of the world brings out wrong desires, wrong beliefs, the temptations of life.

For example, concerning the voice of self- (Reasoning): On one of my trips to Japan to conduct a seminar on Family life–two of the speakers told me that they will wait for me before they get out from the customs in the airport. They had to wait for me because it was their first time to go to Japan. So, when I arrived at the airport and got my luggage, I looked for them in the area where we agreed to meet, but they were not there. I checked if their plane had arrived already and, sure, their plane had arrived. I did not know what to do, whether to get out from customs or wait for them still. There was a still small voice that prompted me to get out already, but I reasoned out that it was not what we agreed upon. But soon it was almost an hour later, so I went out. Again, another voice said, "Go and turn left" but I reasoned out. I think they will be waiting on the right side because that is where the moneychanger is. So, I turned to the right, but they were not there. Finally, I turned to the left side and there they were waiting. We need FAITH in communicating with God. Without faith our prayer is just like nothing. Faith is the victory that overcomes the world. The Subject of Faith is always Jesus Christ the hope of glory. We need to obey God's promptings and not reason out. He knows better than us.

John 10:14 says–Jesus is the good Shepherd and His sheep know His voice.

In a troubled world that we live in we hear many voices, so we need to pray for discernment. I remember one time, when we were in New Zealand, we stayed in Maungaturoto, and was invited by a farmer, named Eddie Blasey who owns lots of sheep. We went to where the sheep were going and when Eddie called them–all of them went around him. When Joy tried to call them, the sheep did not go to him because the sheep didn't know his voice. Sometimes when we hear the instructions of God we reason out when it seems out of the ordinary, like Joshua, it must have been confusing to him when God told him to go around the walled city of Jericho parading themselves to their enemy's military with music. That is a no-no strategy, but Joshua did not reason out, he trusted God, so he followed what God told him to do. At the end, the walls of Jericho were broken. Who broke it?

It was the unseen Lord's army.

There were times that I reasoned out to the Lord and so what happened? I failed. I am relearning and relearning to obey God's Words even if it seems out of the natural.

Secret Place

The world we live in was created perfectly but because of the rebellion of Satan to God, he deceived the first people on earth Adam and Eve to disobey God bringing chaos on earth. The world became a place of disorder and trouble making which is difficult to live in. We live in a cursed world brought by sin. There is fear paralyzing individuals to act, mistrust, accuse, and be angry and bitter thus destroying relationships. There are temptations to do forbidden things like stealing people's goods and properties, sexual abuse with innocent children and people through the internet, having forbidden sex through pornography, sexual assault and unlawful relationships. People either become the predators or the victims. There are economic and geographical upheavals, poverty, sickness, tragedies, trials, difficulties, loneliness, persecutions, confusions, and many more.

Where do we go for help? Where do you go when you are in pain?

What do you do when you are confused and do not know what to do?

What do you do when you feel hopeless, when you are tempted to run and end your life? What do you do when you are afraid and intimidated? What do you do when you feel rejected and unloved? What do you do when worry and anxiety come? What do you do when you are tired? What do you do when you are discouraged? What do you do when you are put to shame or feel guilty? RUN TO THE SECRET PLACE!

The secret place is a refuge, a hiding place, a place of help and comfort, a place of rescue, a place of hope and love, a place of strength, a place of direction, a school of faith, endurance, patience and hope. This is what God has been reminding me always to Run to the secret place. The secret place is PRAYER. There you communicate with God. You will find the Heavenly Father loving you, Jesus giving you Grace to cope and overcome and the Holy Spirit directing you what to do and enabling you to do what is right. Prayer is powerful. I often hear that when one prays, the Almighty God works. Run to God in prayer.

QUESTIONS TO PONDER

1. *What is prayer ? How should we pray?*

2. *What new things we learned from this chapter about communicating with God?*

3. *What is soaking in the spirit?*

4. *What is the "secret place?" How important is Faith to prayer? How do I relate with God in prayer.*

---

4 True, Julie, Soaking Worship Music

~ CHAPTER 18 ~

DO I KNOW GOD?

Do I know God? Do I need to know Him? Why should I know Him? What is the importance of knowing Him personally and intimately?

Ask these questions to yourself as you go on:

- *Do I know Him in His power and in His glory?*
- *Do I know Him as the Sovereign Being in control of everything?*
- *Do I know Him as Saviour, Provider, Helper, Healer, and My Peace?*
- *Do I know Him as King?*
- *Am I thrilled with His Words?*
- *Do I worship Him intimately bringing joy to my heart?*

There is a song I love to sing, popularized by C. Barny Robertson talking about the greatness and strength of God. There is nothing He cannot do.

Another one I love sings about God being worthy to receive glory and honour and power. It reminds me that all things were created by Him for His pleasure.

Revelation 4:11 "You are worthy, our Lord and God, to receive glory and honour and power, for you created all things, and by your will they were created and have their being."

The Bible from the book of Genesis to Revelation talks about God as the Creator. All creation did not come by accident—there is a higher power, One that is not created. He is the First, He is above all and that is

LOURDES "LULU" MANDING TIRA

the Almighty God—our Creator. He created you and me, all humanity. He is the first and the last. He has no beginning; He has no end. He is eternal, omnipotent (all powerful), omnipresent (present everywhere), and immutable (He doesn't change). Is there anyone who can make a living being? Is there anyone who can make a creature without sperm of a man and egg of a woman uniting together? Is there anybody who can make a living plant or flower without seed? No one can make such things except the Creator God.

Who can make the sun and the stars shine? Who gives wisdom to men?

Who can destroy the work of the enemy?

It would then be foolishness on my part to make a creature god and worship this god-like images. This is what the Israelites did on their way to the Promised Land where they took their gold earrings and shaped them into a cow and worshiped it.

We communicate with God anytime even when we are at work. One time I did counselling with a married couple who lost their spark for romance in their marriage. They were just living together but not even sleeping in the same room anymore. They had gone into counselling, but it was getting worse. So, when I travelled to their country, they hosted me and allowed me to stay in the master's bedroom where they used to sleep together before. At the end of my scheduled ministry, I did the counselling with them. They were really putting down and blaming each other, I couldn't do anything but to stop them and prayed for God to intervene and speak to us. God is so good, He intervened and guided me during the counselling. He gave me discernment and boldness. At the end, the couple was convicted, they asked forgiveness from each other and hugged each other tightly. That was their first embrace after about a year. The man repented from flirting with another woman and the wife repented from taking offense from her husband's flirting. It was the voice of God who directed me and gave me sensitive ears to His voice. It was the Holy Spirit who communicated to me what questions to ask to the couple and it was the Holy Spirit who also communicated to them with power. I am so glad that God is just around us, so near that you can talk to and listen to Him anytime. I thank Him for His delight and joy in communicating to us.

Why am I writing this portion? Is there a possibility that we humans, if we do not know God, can become foolish: worshiping a creature like a cow and not the Creator God or inventing things and worshiping them as god? Or can people choose a man and make him god? Yes, I was like that before coming to know the true God, the One who created me. I even walked from the door to the altar of that big church in Quiapo, kissing those statues of saints. I kept my laminated rosary day and night every day. I knelt in every place whenever I saw the picture of Joseph, Mary and Jesus hanging on the wall of almost every home in my town Dingras.

As I grew up, I was looking for love. Although my family —my parents and siblings showed love to me, I still felt unsatisfied and rejected. There was a vacuum in my heart that needed to be filled. I tried being religious, devoted to the faith of my parents. I had prayed novena; I prayed the rosary. I had a boyfriend–but it did not help me until I was introduced to Jesus Christ—the Incarnated God, whom all the Godhead–the Father, the Son, the Holy Spirit dwell in bodily form. I accepted the Truth–He alone can satisfy my need of love. He alone can help me to bloom in this difficult world we live in. He alone can empower me to bloom in a fallen, depraved world.

The moment I believed the Truth as He is the Truth, the Life, the Way, I responded to His invitation of being personally related to Him by accepting Jesus Christ as my Lord and Saviour. Since then, I began a great adventure of knowing Him, experiencing His enabling in my life, experiencing His strength in my weakness, hope during difficulties and hopeless times as in sickness or tragedy, love when I felt rejected, forgiveness when I fall into the crossroad or am confused, joy in the midst of sorrow, divine health in the midst of sickness and victory over battles of life.

Daniel 11:32b says "but the people who know their God will firmly resist him (the enemy).

When you know God, you will know what to do and have courage to do it. Daniel and his friends experienced an opposition through a system anciently known as Babylonianism – that is doing something out of God's will. They wanted to make a name for themselves. Daniel and his friends who were Jews were taken as captives to Babylon. The king put them in the training school to become wise men–being fed with rich foods, wine, etc. Knowing God, they asked that they will not be served with those foods which were served as offerings to pagan gods. Rather they requested to be fed with veggies that would make them healthier. The result was good.

As Daniel was blessed by God, he faced another opposition from the system—that is in Daniel 6:1-28 (v8-9 a decree was issued that anyone who prays to any god or human being during the next thirty days, except to king Darius, shall be thrown into the lions' den.) But Daniel knew God, he was not afraid. He continued to pray to God three times a day, so the system put him into the den of lions. But God protected Daniel and sent angel to protect him, the lions, though they were hungry did not harm him. As a result, king Darius issue a decree that in every part of his kingdom people must fear and reverence the God of Daniel for He is the living God, and

He endures forever. (v.26-27)

In Daniel 3, Shadrach, Meshach and Abednego knew God the Creator. But the Babylonian system required them to bow and worship the statue king Nebuchadnezzar made. But because God is the only God that needs to be worshipped, they did not follow. As a result of not following the system, they had to be thrown into a blazing furnace. So, Shadrach, Meshach and Abednego were thrown into the blazing furnace. Because the king was so angry, he ordered the furnace to be heated 7x hotter, so hot that even those who threw them in were burned. But in amazement, the king saw four instead of three men walking unharmed and unburned in the fire.

God the Creator was with them.

Because Shadrach, Meshach and Abednego have known God they knew what to do and the Almighty God rescued them. As a result, king Nebuchadnezzar made a decree that the people will not say any bad or negative words about the God of Shadrach, Meshach and Abednego—the Creator God. Babylonianism still works today. The system is still there, and it is hotter, but it is comforting to realize that when we know God we will be protected, and Babylon will fall as prophesied in Revelation 18. As the Covid-19 escalates resulting in global problems, the Babylonian system is also escalating. We need to know God while there is time.

There were trials and tragedies in my life that I have written in the earlier chapters. Two of them were like being in the fire, it was so painful. First when I was questioned of my faith because of my intimacy with Jesus that resulted to specific spiritual gifts and the second, when I was betrayed by a friend. But knowing God in those times, helped me on what to do. I continued trusting Him for His vindication and I thanked God for His love and deliverance. I am glad that I had overcame the Babylonian system. I am still alive today, proclaiming the Truth that there is Only One God, and He is the Creator God, the foundation of life. He wants all of

His creation—all nations to know Him like Daniel, Shadrach, Meshach and Abednego. He wants us to overcome the difficulties of life and to bloom where we are planted.

How do we know God?

1. *Through the beautiful world He created*

2. *Through the Word of God—the Bible (2 Timothy 3:14-17)*

3. *Through His Covenant Names (Exodus 3:14-15)*

4. *Through JESUS CHRIST (Romans 10:13; Colossians 1:15/ 2:9-11/3:17; Hebrews 1:1-3; and Isaiah 9:6)*

5. *Through EXPERIENCE (Job 42:1-6)*

We need to know God through all of these, not only one source, but all the five sources of knowledge in knowing Him.

For those who are earnestly seeking for love, God is the answer.

He will fill that void inside of you like what He did to mine. He is the only one who can fix our lives. He is the only one who can help us bloom to where we are planted, to help us live to the fullest even in this difficult time of pandemic.

Knowing God directs us, gives us wisdom on what to do and leads us to a quality of life that trouble cannot overcome.

QUESTIONS TO PONDER

1. *Answer the questions in the introduction page of this chapter.*

2. *May it be the cry of our heart to know the True God, the God above all, our Creator who is above all not only in knowledge but experiencing Him in His presence, love, mercy and power.*

3. *How do we know God?*

~ CHAPTER 19 ~

THE POWER OF THE SPOKEN WORD

Flying from Edmonton to Vancouver via Air Canada, then from Vancouver to Tokyo via Japan Airlines, then from Tokyo to Manila via Philippine Airlines–that is a long-haul flight plus all the stopovers. It was tiring, sitting mostly at the time. So, when I arrived in our hotel room, I looked at the big mirror and saw myself haggard and I exclaimed, "Ohhhh, I am ugly." I changed my position in front of the mirror and looked at all angles just to see myself look better but the message to me was "I am ugly" and it made me unhappy. My disposition was negative. But then the gentle whisper of my God reached my spirit saying to me, "You are beautiful. I have created you in my likeness. You are My Child. Beauty comes from the inside." With those words, I smiled and spoke to myself "I am beautiful. Thank you, Lord."

After that, my disposition was changed to positive. I was encouraged and began to prepare myself to meet Joy after his meeting. When I looked at the mirror again, something happened; I saw myself as God sees me: beautiful Lulu, blooming in the Lord. Wow. That was not magic; it was the power of God– The power of God to see His glory in His creation, to see His beauty in me and not to see the lies of the enemy. The enemy tells us that we are ugly, we are not worthy, or we are nothing. But when we sow the seed of God's Word by speaking it out, the spirit realm becomes visible to us and allows us to see the truth. How come the way·I saw myself changed and my disposition changed and then whispered a spontaneous song of praise? That is the power of

God that is harvesting the seed of the spoken word. There is power in the spoken word.

I travelled long haul to attend an international conference with my husband, and so since he was the convener, he travelled earlier than me. What if I meet him with a negative disposition, not happy because of feeling ugly, and so with meeting different people from all parts of the globe and meeting my friends with a negative disposition? Would it be a happier reunion?

The world we live in is full of negative words spoken by many. Some conversation that takes place brings the opposite to blessing. Instead of blessing the children as they go, we give so much instruction, become mad at them, and tell them they are foolish. Why can't we say, "God bless you and keep you safe, and smart and obedient."

Like in marriages, we do not see more of the positive sides, we tend to see more of the negative sides or the flaws and hear words like, "You do not cook well; you drive me crazy; you are stupid," and "I am not good" or hear words that admire others and compare them to you putting you not worthy of appreciation. Those words stir discouragement and paralyze a spouse to give his or her best. The word of God says in Proverbs "The tongue has the power of life and death, and those who love it will eat its fruit (Proverbs 18:21 -NIV). What do we say about our situations, health, our finances, our marriages, our spouses, our work or job, situations, our co-workers, our children, our church, our government, or events surrounding us? It is easier to see the negative, so we complain or grumble.

Let me cite an example: I was going somewhere and because I was advised not to bring my iPad, I did not take it along with me. But when I reached our meeting place, they asked for it. I apologized for not bringing it, but I was reprimanded. I just kept quiet. But then one person kept on grumbling about it to my face, and I was not able to guard my heart. I was hurt and I cried. The Lord spoke to my spirit, telling me to give a sacrifice of praise even though it hurts me. That is what I did. I praised the Lord and told them I am very sorry, please forgive me. The grumbling stopped.

PRAISE is an antidote to complaints and to a grumbling spirit.

One of the fruits of the Holy Spirit is patience or endurance, and when we praise God and thank Him, patience will follow. Similarly, with the other fruits like joy, gentleness, and kindness, then peace, goodness and humility follow. Sowing good seeds is very important. When we sow positive words, especially the Word of God, we are sowing the seeds, so we will harvest good produce; but when we sow negative words, we will also reap a negative or bad harvest. We always reap what we have sown.

The exodus of the Israelites to the Promised Land is an example of how positive or negative words matter. Flying to Tel Aviv, Israel from Cairo, Egypt via Lufthansa Airlines takes only few minutes. You take off, go up in the air and for few minutes you descend and land at the airport. Your stay in the airport is longer than your flight. So, Israel the Promised Land is so close to Egypt. Why did it take about 40 years for the Israelites to arrive in the Promised Land?

One particular story of their exodus tells of when the leaders of the twelve tribes were asked to spy if the Promised Land was good (Numbers 13) After their survey, Joshua and Caleb gave a good report but the leaders of the ten tribes complained and spoke negative things about the land. They gave a bad report. They said that there were giants who live there; the Israelites are compared to like grasshoppers to them. This brought discouragement to the Israelites, in spite of the good report of Caleb and Joshua. The negative report when spoken discouraged them and paralyzed them to act on the good report of Joshua and Caleb (*Numbers 13-14*). As a result, God told them in Numbers 14:26-35 NIV –

"How long will this wicked community grumble against me? I have heard the complaints of these grumbling Israelites. 28 So tell them, 'As surely as I live, declares the Lord, I will do to you the very thing I heard you say;29 In this wilderness your bodies will fall—every one of you twenty years old or more who was counted in the census and who has grumbled against me. 30 Not one of you will enter the land I swore with uplifted hand to make your home, except Caleb son of Jephunneh and Joshua son of Nun. 31 As for your children that you said would be taken as plunder, I will bring them in to enjoy the land you have rejected. 32 But as for you, your bodies will fall in this wilderness. 33 Your children will be shepherds here for forty years, suffering for your unfaithfulness, until the last of your bodies lies in the wilderness. 34 For forty years—one year for each of the forty days you explored the land—you will suffer for your sins and know what it is like to have me against you; 35 I, the LORD, have spoken, and I will surely do these things to this whole wicked community, which has banded together against me. They will meet their end in this wilderness; here they will die."

This is one of the reasons why it took them too long to reach the Promised Land. And only Caleb and Joshua and their tribes plus the younger generations of the other 10 tribes of Israel were able to reach the Promised Land. Also, in another account of their grumbling, snakes came out in the dessert and bit many of them.

Job 22:28 says: Decree a thing and it will be established unto thee and the light shalt shine upon thy ways. (KJV)

You will also declare a thing and it will be established for you. So, light will shine on your way. (NKJV)

In short, what you decide will be done and light will shine on your way. Knowing the will of God through His words, we sow the seed, which is the Word of God through speaking it out. What you decide on will be done, and light will shine on your ways. (NIV) I wish I had known this earlier in my life. We need to declare positive words. We need to declare God's Words over our difficult or impossible situations. To decree is to decide the outcome of the matter (in accordance with God's Words) before it comes to pass. We need to speak God's Words over our difficult situations and circumstances to shift or change them. When we declare His Words, God will release the power or the anointing that will miraculously change our situations. Grumbling is putting a curse, so if we grumble or complain against ourselves, or others, we are cursing ourselves or others.

(I Cor. 10:10 NIV) -And do not grumble, as some of them did — and were killed by the destroying angel;

(James 5:9 NIV) – Don't grumble against one another, brothers and sisters, or you will be judged. The Judge is standing at the door;

(John 6:43 (NIV) " Stop grumbling among yourselves, "Jesus answered;

(1 Peter 4:9 NIV) Offer hospitality to one another without grumbling.

These verses admonish us not to grumble against each other.

What do you declare daily? Do you declare that God's purpose will be done? Declare that you are a child of God, a salt of the earth, light of the earth. We need to declare that we are children of God, so we are beautiful. We are smart because He has given us the Holy Spirit. Do you declare your kingdom authority? We children of God should declare our righteousness.

We need to declare that we are God's children and so we are His heirs with Jesus Christ. We have certain privileges, rights and freedom as children of God. We declare and decree that we are victorious even over Covid-19. We declare that the old things have passed away. We declare protection from the enemy from his attacks. We declare that we arise and shine radiant in the glory of God. We declare our marriage to be glorifying to God. We declare and decree success. We declare and confess our dreams for God to be done, that God will be exalted. We declare Life and Blessings. We declare healing. We lose financial freedom and spiritual freedom.

I have been a Christian for many years, but it was only in my later years that I began practicing this in my life, speaking the Words of God to myself and to others. I began to declare the Words of God. Before practicing this, I was saying to myself (even though nobody was saying it to me) that I am ugly. If someone told me like my husband would tell me before that I am beautiful, I would react negatively by saying; "Do not joke with me." I tended to receive appreciation as a joke before. This contributed to self-pity, to low self-esteem, and to a feeling of rejection and not being liked. But then, I learned the power of the spoken word, especially speaking the Word of God to myself and to others. God transformed me to be a confident woman, not intimidated anymore, not shrinking anymore with difficulties, but moving on with the boldness of God.

When I hear something negative such as, "You are foolish" I would speak and declare to myself, "In the Name of Jesus, I refuse that. I am not foolish. I have wisdom because the Holy Spirit is in me. He gives me wisdom." Or when I feel something like I feel ill, I do not confess that I am sick rather I pray to God and claim healing then confess that "Through the stripes or wounds of Jesus, I am healed." There I find relief and do not feel sick anymore. I can get up and start the day with worship thanking God for His enabling.

If the enemy puts in my mind that I am not loved; instead of meditating on the lie of the enemy, I speak to myself; "I am loved. God loves me. My family loves me and even my friends love me." The enemy puts lies in our mind about ourselves, about others, and about situations we see and when we believe it, we speak it out and it becomes a curse. We allowed ourselves to be used by the enemy against us and against others and against the situations we see. The word we speak becomes like death suppressing our soul, spirit and body. Declaring or speaking the Words of God to ourselves and to others is sowing the seeds of God's Words and we will reap it.

In the morning when I go out and meet people either in the grocery or elsewhere, I want to hear, "Oh, it is a great day today. God bless you." rather than "It is a bad day today, you are already late, you will be in trouble." God will work on the positive words by making it a good day for me. God uses that person to bless me that day. The negative words spoken are the words of the enemy using that person to let the enemy work to make it a bad day for you speaking of trouble on that day.

We dare not take for granted the Words we speak. It is either life or death. We travelled a lot with Joy. Sometimes it is so scary while in flight and you passed air pockets making the flight so bumpy. In those situations, I would remember what Jesus showed me in a vision when I was afraid of flying one time. I saw Jesus in a vision with all the planes around Him and He was watching them including the plane we were boarded. That relieved me. Since then, I have had the guts to fly. So now, going back to turbulence, I also remember Jesus when He and His disciples met a storm saying to the big waves: "Peace! Be still!" and the gusting wind stopped, that is why when I am in a flight and there's turbulence, I speak and say "Turbulence, peace, be still." Praise God, the turbulence stops. It doesn't matter when people hear me pray, they are afraid too and they are praying too. In speaking the Words of God, we need to have faith, that it is His Words and so it is His will. For example, it is always God's will to heal us whether physically or emotionally unless He tells you specifically that He is allowing you to be sick for such a specific reason. It is not what you think but you are sure enough that He told you to be sick and He has reason for it. I trust the Word. I wish that you will prosper (in all areas) even in health (3 John 1:2). In Isaiah 53:5 "by his wounds we are healed." God's provision is the same thing. We do not declare poverty or not having ways but declare that God is our Jehovah Jireh—our Provider, our Great Shepherd we will never be in want.

The Word of God contains His promises, principles to follow and prophesies to look forward to and to trust Him, let us speak them out.

By our mouth, we need to release God's blessings and not the devil's curses. We live in a difficult and troubled world with too much emphasis on negativity. We need to shift our negative environment, our difficult times, and our negative emotions by speaking out the Words of God:

For example:
I am blessed.
You are blessed.
You are beautiful.
I am empowered.
I am healed by the stripes of Jesus.
I am loved.
I am not intimidated.
I am not afraid.
I go by the power of the Holy Spirit.
I can do it through Christ who strengthens me.
I will be okay.
God will answer our prayers.
You will be protected.
I declare and decree that your needs will be met.

I confess that:
I have the mind of Christ.
I have the thoughts, purposes and the feelings of God.
I am not only a reader of God's Word but a doer and not a forgetful, heedless hearer.

Rejection, fear, discouragement, depression, self-pity, envy, jealousy, lust of the flesh, lust of the eyes and pride of life have no power over me in Jesus Name!

I cast down every imagination and lying and deceptive spirits.

I walk in the Spirit and speak to myself hymns, psalms, and spiritual songs, singing spontaneously praising and giving thanks to God for His reign over me.

In closing–speaking the truth, the Word of God when spoken and confessed to people and ourselves are seeds that are sown and it will reap good harvest, words that are positive and encouraging to ourselves and to others have the power to give life but, speaking the lies of the enemy and the negative words that discourage leads to curses and death.

QUESTIONS TO PONDER

1. *Any word that we speak has power to gives life or death, so we need to be careful of what we say. (Proverbs 18:21)); what should we say or declare to our lives and to others?*

2. *What is positive and negative words?*

3. *Does confessing who Jesus to us and who we are in Christ activate the fulfillment of the destiny God planned for us?*

4. *What do we learn from the complains of Aaron and Miriam to Moses their brother and the grumblings of the Hebrew people during their Exodus to the Promised land?*

~ CHAPTER 20 ~

HOSTING THE HOLY SPIRIT

B eing involved with MoveIn, a missionary organization catering
to the needs of new immigrants coming to a new place. Joy and
I decided to move into an apartment where new immigrants live.
The MoveIn staff move to apartments where these new immigrants start
to live until they become established, that is the time they move out. So
last May 2019, we moved to an apartment block and put our house for
sale. We believed that God would send us a buyer if it was His will. 1st
month, 2nd month then on the 10th month, still our house was on sale.
So, we were wondering why? There have been interested buyers but then
they were either not approved by the bank or they suddenly changed
their minds. We prayed about what to do.

It was that time that we had developed some friendship with
those from the apartment. The apartment in which we moved was a
"new home" for immigrants particularly East Indians from all over
India, Africa, etc. I was hesitant to move there the first time because
just getting to the apartment—you smell curry. But while I was praying,
the Lord spoke to my spirit saying, "You have prayed before that I will
not let you go to India. I did not bring you there. I am just sending you
now to a "little India" community." So, we moved there, but then the
house was not selling and then the Covid-19 was expanding to all parts
of the world including Canada. Then came the government order like
"locked-in" and social distancing. How can we have social distancing in
a small, shared laundry room in the apartment block?

Myrna and Dante, our friends and ministry partners advised us to
go back to our house. They said, "Your house is a blessing from the Lord,

go and enjoy it." We realized, yes, our house has been a blessing from the Lord. It was bought when it was not our plan to buy a house–but the former owners Gina and Rey gave it to us for a very modest price. The house is also a blessing as our basement had been used as "Gilgal" or place for servants of God who were in Edmonton for some reasons. So, after a year we decided to go back to our house that was unsold. The house was a blessing especially this time of Covid-19 pandemic–where social distancing can be more observed. Our children and grandchildren could still come and have fellowship at the backyard. There was no place in the apartment for fellowship. Four to ten people could still come to the house for prayer and Bible study with proper distancing. So, we moved back.

Just as we were organizing our stuff, our kind ministry Head Ron asked if we would like to host a missionary couple from Malaysia for their "two weeks quarantine" before they can join their dad who is now elderly. Sure, we said. We decided to continue our Gilgal ministry–offering free "home away from home" for needy missionaries, pastors as they travel here in Edmonton. We always make sure to provide them breakfast before they go out for whatever they need to do. We make sure that we have fellowship with them when they come back after. So, we prepared our basement. Our company staff came and placed a living set and dresser (as we have given away those stuffs we had before). But as we prepared for Bob and Marie, I was bothered by what I was hearing like guests in quarantine should not be allowed to go out or walk around. Then how can they get fresh air for two weeks, it looks like they are in prison. How can we have fellowship with them?

So, I confirmed with the Health Services what I was hearing. They confirmed "Yes" and asked me many questions until they told me– "You are restricted in hosting. You need to follow your doctor's advice." We were restricted to host because we are also elderly and under special care of special doctors or specialists. So, instead, I suggested that Bob and Marie be placed in a hotel where there is better ventilation, better than the basement. Praise God, they were reserved in a hotel with a kitchenette and a balcony. That will be more delightful and comfortable for 14 days of isolation. So why am I telling you this? Just having a guest is different from hosting a guest. I think that having a guest in our home without fellowshipping with them is weird and inappropriate. Staying in the basement for 14 days would be uncomfortable without good ventilation– like a big window opened. I need to bring delight to my guests, not just have them in my house.

It is even hard for a husband and wife (even though they are not social distancing) just to be present in a home but because of busyness they have no time to appreciate or delight each other, that's hard. What am I trying to imply? We have the Holy Spirit indwelling in us since we accepted Jesus to be our Lord and Saviour –but hosting Him is different.

The Holy Spirit is the Almighty God fulfilling His Promise in Ezekiel 36:27 "I will put My Spirit within you." The person of the Holy Spirit is actually the Person of God and is the One who is most qualified to reveal Himself. The more you know God–study His attributes, encounter His nature and review His characteristics, the more you receive deeper revelation of who the one living inside you truly is. Remember, God the Father, God the Son, and God the Spirit are One. This is the mission of the Holy Spirit within us– to represent Jesus accurately in both WORD and DEMONSTRATION which brings great glory to our Father in Heaven. The Presence of God is the Person of the Holy Spirit. The Presence is actually the person of God, the Holy Spirit.

The Holy Spirit is the 3rd person of the Triune God. Hosting Him is hosting the Triune God. When we received Jesus as our Lord and Saviour— we received the Triune God.

Isaiah 9:6 says "For to us a child is born, to us a son is given, and the government will be on his shoulders. And he will be called Wonderful Counsellor, Mighty God, Everlasting Father, Prince of Peace."

Having the Holy Spirit is having the Triune God.

Colossians 1:15-20 says that the fullness of the God Head–Jesus is the image of the invisible God, the first born of all creation.

When I received Jesus as my Lord and Saviour, the fullness of the Triune God came to reside in me through the Holy Spirit. Jesus now resides in me through the Holy Spirit. The Holy Spirit is the Spirit of the Father and the Spirit of the Lord Jesus. Now, He indwells in every child of God. As His child, I need to host Him. I just do not like him sitting there in the "living room" of my life. I want to sit at His feet listening to Him through His words, talking to Him through prayer, fellowshipping with Him and just enjoy His Presence intimately. Not only that, being His host, I need to make Him happy while He indwells in me—by doing or obeying what He wants me to do. He will not be happy if I make fun of His words or do not believe Him or doubt Him. Jesus is the living Word, the Bread of Life, I trust every Word that comes out of His mouth.

Will Jesus be happy if I tell others that some of His words or works ceased to operate like miracles and healing do not exist anymore, or like the gifts of the Holy Spirit as in speaking in tongues, and the gift of interpretation? Will He be happy if I believe that the five-fold ministry gifts are already reduced to only three—pastoring, evangelism and teaching, no more prophetic and apostolic ministry gifts? Will He be delighted if He hears one speaking negative words or bad words? Will He be happy if I am too busy serving others but have no time to listen to Him and be intimate with Him? Will He be delighted when I know so much of His words, but my character doesn't show His likeness?

Hosting God is honouring Him. It is consciously being careful not to offend or grieve Him with my attitudes. Hosting Him is an adventure. The deeper the intimacy with God, the greater is the joy of living even in a difficult world. Remember the River in Ezekiel 47. Is it possible for us to house the most glorious treasure imaginable and yet not host His Presence well? The matter of SALVATION is settled through the regenerative work of the Holy Spirit, EMPOWERMENT is another topic. We can be saved and on our way to Heaven without enjoying the benefits of salvation which involves bringing Heaven to earth. Going to Heaven benefits me while bringing Heaven to earth benefits the world around me.6

We do not only share the salvation of God so they will get to heaven if they respond as I did (we call this EVANGELISM) but also provide them with a VISION for today helping them to walk with the power of the Spirit resting upon them. This is DISCIPLESHIP. Teach them how to navigate in the spiritual realm—through His Words, prayer, walking in the power of the Holy Spirit, fighting the enemy, walking in victory, etc. This means that the ONE who set us up for eternity has been given control and influence over our lives to such degree that every arena is impacted by His Presence. This is DISCIPLESHIP and SANCTIFICATION—the influence of the ONE dwelling within now coming upon us and transforming every part of us to more accurately represent the image of Jesus Christ.7 Hosting Him is listening to His instruction for you personally, like one example that happened in Abu Dhabi during the training there–He instructed me what to do in Kuwait.

Without spending time to soak in His Presence, I do not hear much of His instructions to me personally, even if He is indwelling in me. If I have a problem or an inquiry, or something I need to discuss with Him, I need to soak in His Presence. I have fellowship with Him. Jesus made it possible for us to host the fullness of God on earth through His Spirit. We partner with God to accomplish His purpose on earth. While He is sovereign, He has nevertheless established a system where His purposes would be accomplished here on earth through a unique partnership birthed out of intimacy and friendship. As intimates, we catch a glimpse of what the Master is doing. As servants we joyfully participate with Him in bringing His Kingdom work to power. I always marvel on the work of the Holy Spirit. Listening to Kathryn Khulman's messages always makes me hungry and thirsty for God.

It is the Holy Spirit who uniquely empowers God's friends to accomplish His work. Beyond empowerment the Presence is not just God enabling us to do something–it is Him working with us His current pulsing through our hands, our feet and for our lips. He empowers, yes but He also works through us.8

We, His children need to learn to host the Holy Spirit, not only indwelling in us but overflowing that He fills us completely. As I have experienced, there are two keys to hosting the Holy Spirit:

1. Not to grieve Him (causing Him to be sad)
2. Not to quench Him (to stop His flow on me)

I have experienced these when I learned to delight in Him. Not doubting Him but trusting and obeying God are a must to host the Holy Spirit. We need to be willing always to say Yes to Him even if it means out of the natural. We should respect His move and not to reject or judge that it is a move of the enemy. The Holy Spirit looks for people whom He can rest on, not just on as an unseen guest. He desires to move in our midst, so let us be a good steward of the Father's promised Holy Spirit.

Power and authority introduce us to the nature of the Holy Spirit with a primary focus on hosting His Presence. Authority comes with the commission (Matthew 28:19-20) but Power comes from the encounter (Acts 2).9

QUESTIONS TO PONDER

1. *Hosting involves welcoming, entertaining that includes fellowshipping and interacting - have you ever experienced being hosted well or hosted unpleasantly?*

2. *When we received Jesus as our Lord, God in His Spirit is now indwelling in us, do you recognize Him as the "unseen Guest" of your life? How are you hosting Him? Are you hosting Him well?*

3. *What are the two keys to host the Holy Spirit?*

4. *What are the rewards of hosting Him well?*

---

5 Johnson, Bill, Hosting The Presence Every Day: 365 Days to Unveiling Heaven's Agenda to Your Life, January 4 and 5 Reading
6 Ibid, June 30 Reading
7 Ibid, June 29 Reading
8 Ibid, October 29 and 30 Reading

CHAPTER 21

THE ENEMY

This book you are reading is about the love and faithfulness of God. In this chapter, I will recount the victory of God over the work of the enemy in our lives. Some say that we should not be talking about the enemy. That is really true, but we do not have to be ignorant about Satan and his wiles. Ephesians 6:12, Ephesians 1:19-21, Ephesians 2:4-6 say we are in a war. But we are reigning with Christ in the heaven lies. Satan is the enemy, and he hides and pretends that he doesn't exist. He hides even in the things we value and give more time to them—these are called idols. Being ignorant of the enemy and his tactics will prevent us to overcome him, to overcome the negatives of life that we face every day. Unless man learns to fight him, man will become a loser and suffer and will not enjoy life to the fullest. I have experienced this in my life. I knew there is an enemy, but I had not learned to fight him at that time. I was always on the defensive side, until the break-through came. I learned to fight offensively. I thank God for revealing to me how to do it. You will see more on this in the next chapter entitled Breakthrough.

The world has been created good but because of sin, the world has become a troubled filled with difficulties. We experience setbacks every day. They come, even without warning: like STRESS (physical or emotional), worry and anxiety, sickness, financial problems, marriage or family crises, problems at work, tragedy etc. But because God loves the world so much (the nations), Jesus came to destroy the work of the enemy (I John 3:8).

Whether we believe it or not, the truth is we have an enemy around us but hiding either in people we meet every day or in things we use, the animals we face or even in such tradition, culture, belief systems, things we see on the screen, the food and drinks we consume, the decorations in our home or in the places we visit, etc. I am writing in this chapter about the enemy and some encounter with him in which God gave me/ us the victory.

From my study of Demonology, the "enemy" was originally one of the archangels (Isaiah 14: 12 -15 and Ezekiel 28:12-15). He was perfect. He was called Lucifer and led one third of the angels. But then he sinned against God. His heart became proud. He wanted to be like God in power and authority. He wanted to be above the clouds of God and be in the summit, so he was thrown into the pit. Since then, he was referred to as Satan, ruling the kingdom of darkness. The Bible talks about him. He is the unseen enemy, the thief that steals, destroys and kills humans (John 10:10a). He is also referred to as the tempter (Matthew 4:3); the ruler of demons (1John 5:18); deceiver and liar, red dragon, etc. Satan or the devil seduces humans to disobey God by telling them that what God tells is a lie. Indirectly Satan is saying, God does not want us to enjoy life, so go for it so we can enjoy life. But that is a lie, a deception. He tempts humans through the eyes, the flesh, and pride of life. To understand more of this chapter, you need to read Chapter 22 of this book. People ask why God created Satan. Satan was not created as Satan; he was created as an angel leading 1/3 of the angels or the worshiping angels. He was called Lucifer–light of dawn. Satan became a perversion of Lucifer. (Isaiah 14:12-15)

The first truth talks about God and His love to humanity. He created man in his image and likeness and given them dominion on earth. They were perfect and had no knowledge of evil. They were commanded to subdue the earth as there are some elements that would need to be brought into subjection to the divine order that the Creator had originally established. It suffered under the influence of the rebellious one, Satan and his agenda to destroy, tarnish and maim all that was beautiful and good. There was a darkness present that was alien to a planet fashioned for perfection. The rebellion of Satan brought a scar into what was otherwise a perfect creation. Disorder had tarnished God's creation. It was now light against darkness, order versus chaos and glory against that which is inferior, lacking, and hollow. Satan needs to be defeated.9

God told Adam and Eve not to eat the fruit of the knowledge of good and evil, because if they eat of it, they will surely die, meaning they will be separated from God (spiritual death) and die physically. Wanting the dominion given to man, Satan went and deceived them telling them that if they eat the fruit of the tree of the knowledge of good and evil, they will not die as God said to them, but they will be like God knowing good and evil. So, believing the lie of Satan, they ate it. That cost the fall of humanity. Man gave the keys of earthly authority over to Satan when Adam and Eve rebelled. (In Eden, humanity handed the keys of authority over to the enemy through disobedience, which is called sin. All disobedience to God is SIN. The effect of that disobedience is universal, even the world we live in is affected, so now we live in a FALLEN or TROUBLED WORLD as we read in Genesis 3. Not only that, humanity was embondaged to Satan and hell-bound, with no more fellowship with God as before in the Garden of Eden.

The fall separated them from God, which prevented them from seeing the glory of God and enjoying God's love, peace and blessings. God is not happy about this, so because God loves people so much, He sent Jesus to redeem us from sin and destroy the works of the enemy.

Jesus came to destroy the work of the enemy. He was prophesied to destroy the enemy (Genesis 3:15), so even in the infancy of Jesus, Satan tried to destroy him by using Herod the Great. Satan did not want Jesus to die on the cross, so people would not be redeemed and be back to a personal relationship with God. Satan wanted men to belong to him and suffer with him in the kingdom of darkness. Satan doesn't want man to know that LIFE is found in Jesus, that JESUS is the answer to all of our longings. He is the Saviour of creation.

God loves all people including me. His plan is to prosper us and not to harm us but to give a future and a hope. (Jeremiah 29:1-15.) But the enemy tries to distract and destroy this plan. That is why it is important not to be ignorant of who Satan is and his scheme. We need to learn how to operate and walk in God's direction in obedience and faith. I will just write of some encounters with the enemy and how God intervened. I trust that you will learn from this.

I have written in the preceding chapters how the enemy tried to steal and to destroy me. Even from my childhood when I was sick, my parents did a ritual and gave me a nickname associated with that ritual to improve my health. But it was in vain. (Later as I grew deeper in my relationship with God, He instructed me to mortify or put to death those things that do not glorify God, and one of those was that ritual my parents made and the name they gave me on that ritual ceremony). I had to renounce that, even my going to quack doctors who seemed to have extra power in healing. You remember the carabao or water buffalo, and the horse that tried to hurt me? How about the pimp, the cobra, the parked vehicle that almost hit me, and the accident that killed our third child and left me not being able to walk for three months? There were more instances.

We need to know how the spirit of darkness operates. Sometimes people do not know that they are already at the devil's net. For example: Having a tattoo of a snake on their bodies, using symbols of the enemy in our jewellery, clothing, decorations at home like an inverted cross which they use as sign of peace, dragons, snakes, idols and gods or goddesses like Asherah, Greek gods and goddesses, the million Indian deities, the saint's statues, Polynesian deities, evil faces, signs of death like skull or skeleton, anting-anting or charms, and sacred objects that are not of God and many more. Watching movies or games that would transfer the evil spirit as one watches or reads or participating in games like playing the Tarot cards, spirit of the glass, palm and horoscope reading.

Other doors of the enemy to come and control humanity are immorality, destructive attitudes and behaviours like anger, wrath; greed; pride, grumbling, hatred, controlling fear, perfectionism, racism, bitterness, unforgiveness, unbelief, vengeance, materialism, laziness, envy, pleasing man more than God, covetousness, self-righteousness, and self-pity. Others are destructive actions and habits like, repeatedly returning to a death wish, suicide attempts, abortion, dirty language and swearing, hurtful and negative words, dirty jokes, lying, stealing, having ungodly soul mates, abusive behaviours, rebellion, addiction–to alcohol, drugs, food, smoking, use of credit cards, excessive use of techno toys (as in computer, iPad, cell phone texting), too much TV watching of unhealthy scenarios (like soap operas), gambling, and idolatry.

The spirits of darkness also come into the door of one's life through impurity like pornography, fornication, adultery. Humanity opens the doors of their lives through involvement with dark spiritual practices, etc. We need to know where we should be involving ourselves even as just an observer.

"There are two equal and opposite errors into which our race can fall into the devil: 1) is to disbelieve in their existence. 2) to believe and to feel an excessive and unhealthy interest in them. They themselves (the devil) are equally pleased by both error and hail a materialist or a magician wish with the same delight."9

When I did not yet know Jesus, I was introduced to the practice of "the spirit of the glass" (somewhat like the use of a Ouija board). I was just an observer, but it was a strange experience eventhough I was just an observer. The glass controlled by the players would walk through the letters of the alphabet forming the answer to the question asked of the "spirits of the dead" called upon. You would wonder how the different hands go together in one direction. Who led the hands? It is the spirit of darkness. From then on, I experienced mental telepathy. For example, I would sense that there was something burning in a particular location, etc. So, from then on, I did not participate in such games again, and I asked forgiveness from the Lord for participating even just as an observer.

There was one time that Joy and Ianne had a conflict and he told her, "We will not attend your graduation." I was caught in between. I really wanted them to reconcile and attend her graduation. I brought this problem to the Lord. One afternoon as I was praying in the church, the Lord showed me a vision of a snake rug coiled. So, when we got home, I asked Ianne, "Do you have something new that I have not seen yet?" She answered "Yes, mom I just received it as a graduation gift." I asked her to show it to me. It was a CD by a famous musician who testified that his power comes from Satan, and the cover was the vision I saw, a snake coiling inside a rug costume. I instructed her to throw it away. When she threw it away, they just reconciled, and we were able to go and celebrate her graduation.

Another example was a visit to one observer in our training in Japan. At the closing of the training, VG arrived inviting the church leaders and I to their home for a meal. We decided to go the next day. When we arrived, she was at the door gate of their new house welcoming us. She then carried Butch while in fact VG is smaller in height than Butch. Oh, she seemed to be with extra strength. When we came into the house, we passed the room in front with an altar of three large Buddha statues. Then we went inside the living room where she was watching a rock show on a very big TV screen. We wondered why there's no food on the table, but later we saw VG preparing to cook rice. At that moment, one of us saw her as if she couldn't hold her head anymore, so I ran to her. We were five visitors, so we carried her to the couch. Oh, she was so heavy--like a big stone. I prayed and rebuked the enemy and somehow, we felt the other side of the house go up then suddenly go down causing so many footsteps going out of the house. The house where we went had many spirits of darkness. VG was a Filipina married to a wealthy Japanese man. VG was given lots of opportunities to follow Jesus and live to the fullest, but she died young in her sleep. A spirit of death blocked that blessing of living to the fullest. How I wished she learned to fight the enemy and walk with her Creator in victory.

For me, the enemy wanted to block the destiny God prepared for me. He used the carabao, the horse, the vehicle, the pimp, the accident and even distress and discouragement and fear that made me suicidal that could have resulted in a premature death. Praise God, I am walking in victory now. I am not ignorant or intimidated anymore of the enemy. I know God my Creator; His great love and faithfulness will keep me safe. I know the enemy and his tactics. Believing his lies is partnering with him. I fight offensively. He is defeated.

What motivates people to do such things? There is an element causing people to react like that. We live in a fallen world. Because of the fall of man, they were separated from God. Yes, they have the bio life but living dead and in bondage of the enemy creating false beliefs, footholds and confusion.

I was full of fears until I learned more of the enemy and his tactics. Even with the snake toys that were hanging at the dollar stores, I was so afraid to pass them on aisle with toy snakes, so I would avoid that aisle. I was always intimidated with people especially those who were angry and those who were authoritative. On one ministry trip to the Philippines, I stayed in the house where a cobra was found crawling outside our bedroom wall before starting ministry in Edmonton. The house had been re-modelled and more secure. When I went back to the Philippines after a few years, I could not sleep because it was too hot. But as I tried to sleep, my mind was battling whether I would open the window as it was too hot. But then I thought what if there were a snake that would come in through the window? So, I decided to close the windows, but then it was too hot.

So, knowing the tactic of the enemy, I stood up and rebuked the enemy. "In the Name of Jesus, I bind you serpent spirit. You are not coming to my room. I declare my safety. God is watching over me. I charge you ministering angels to be on your post to guard me while I sleep. I declare that I am going to sleep well tonight." That night, I was able to sleep. The mind is the battlefield. The enemy injects lies in our mind and if we believe it–then it affects our emotion and moods negatively causing us to act negatively.

There is what we call <u>transfer of spirit</u>, so we need to be careful of what we watch on the screen or what we read and be careful not to be influenced by people who are negative in spirit.

For example, one beautiful lady just loves watching Filipino soap opera. She would tape them when she goes to work so she can watch after work. One famous soap opera series was a story of two sisters. The other sister seems to be successful in her career and love life while the other one was the opposite; so, as a result the other sister seemed to be after her sister's success and love life. The story led her to take her sister's boyfriend, and profession by manipulation. This was a TV series. What happened in real life? What happened to the beautiful lady I am telling you about? There was a <u>transfer of spirit</u>. The beautiful lady had an affair with the beloved of her sister.

That is a transfer of spirit. We are at war with spirits of darkness–the enemy. Let us be careful of what we watch, read, what we eat or drink, what we say. Is it life and blessing or death and curse? Life and death are in the power of the tongue, we need to be careful of what we say even to ourselves--let us be careful not to be used by Satan by speaking his words (negative words that became curses) like "you are stupid" or I am like this, etc." Let us use our mouth to speak God's words to others like "you are good." Don't say negative words like "you are bad." The enemy can even use our tongue to curse ourselves, by speaking negatively about ourselves.

We have an enemy, Satan, but our King Jesus still declares that all authority in heaven and on earth has been given to Him (Matthew 28:18). Nobody can be compared to Him. Isaiah 40:25 "To whom will you compare me? Or who is my equal?" says the Holy One. Although Satan stole authority from Adam and Eve by deception, Jesus' resurrection reinstated His and humanity's authority over the earth. Jesus has been given all authority, but Satan still tries to disrupt God's purposes for people. Satan has an army with demons, principalities, powers and world rulers to work to carry out the ungodly scheme of separation and condemnation. Our role is to fight these corrupting influences–not by engaging in warfare with our neighbours, spouses, or co-workers but through bringing God's goodness, love and truth into every situation.

With Jesus' declaration of all authority belonging to Him – He is sending us with an assurance to go and extend His kingdom in all hearts because He is always with us. He has delegated us His children to have dominion over them. This dominion given to us came into effect when we are walking with the Holy Spirit trusting and obeying Him. God told us not to be afraid nor be dismayed at this hurdle, for the battle is not ours but God's (2 Chronicles 20:15 And he said, "Hearken ye, all Judah, and ye inhabitants of Jerusalem, and thou king Jehoshaphat, Thus saith the Lord unto you, Be not afraid nor dismayed by reason of this great multitude; for the battle is not yours, but God's." (KJV)

We need to pray for discernment and be sensitive to His voice. Obey even if you do not understand. Let me cite an example: As we were driving in Canada from the U.S.–we came upon a so-called "enchanted park." We thought it would be nice to go and pray there. But as we approached the park I felt in my spirit "don't get inside" but one of us said, "We will just go there and pray." So, we went and prayed inside. As we were inside, I heard a voice in my spirit saying, "Your child." I was pregnant at that time with our third child. I never knew the repercussions of going there, but the day before the accident where our Charis Faith died in my womb, (I carried her dead for 9 days before I gave birth to her)–I was groaning in prayer "to preserve my life." I did not realize that we would have an accident the next day. I should have prayed for our child too. When I was in the process of inner healing and deliverance, I saw in my vision one of those Disney characters that was in the forest which I saw in that enchanted park. The enemy tried to destroy me–but God intervened. He comforted me for the loss of our child, because she is now in heaven enjoying God our Maker.

The enemy is a deceiver and a liar. Let me cite an example. A group of believers wanted to have an outreach Bible study, so in their first outreach meeting they invited me to be the teacher. One of those who came to the outreach was Mat whom they were eyeing to be the Bible study teacher. Praise God, after the Bible study five women prayed to receive Jesus as their Saviour and Lord. When most of the attendees left, I asked Mat to give his testimony on when and how he accepted Jesus, so he did. As he was testifying my spirit was like a wall, negating what he was saying. He knew the scripture, but I could not receive it. My spirit was saying NO. So, I stopped him and asked him "Is Jesus your Lord and Saviour?" There he could not answer–so I prayed and rebuked the blinding and deceiving spirit. He knew a lot of Bible passages but did not have a personal relationship with God. It was good we found that out before he was given responsibility to lead the outreach Bible study.

We need to have a discerning spirit. Even though we live in a physical world, we are surrounded with spiritual beings that we cannot see–spiritual beings from the heavenly kingdom and spiritual beings from the kingdom of darkness that oppose and destroy the destiny that God prepared for us. The enemy blinds us or confuses us so that we will be out in darkness. But the spirits from the heavenly kingdom show us the true and right path to fulfil God's destiny–a future and a hope and not to harm us. A life to the fullest called eternal life.

One movie that I watched entitled, "Aquaman," helped me to understand the spiritual world that we cannot see with our naked eyes. Our children treated us to see this movie and so I asked the Lord to show me what I can learn from the movie. This is what I've learned. "We are both in the physical and spirit world, but we only see the physical, we cannot see spiritual beings and activities unless God opens our eyes."

QUESTIONS TO PONDER

1. *Who was given earthly dominion and authority originally?*

2. *Who is the enemy? How did he become the ruler of darkness? Was he given originally earthly authority? Who gave earthly authority to him, God or Adam the first man?*

3. *Why do we have a fallen and troubled world ? What happened to creation after Adam and Eve disobeyed God by eating the fruit of the tree of knowing good and evil?*

4. *What are the strategies and tactics of the enemy? What are open doors for the enemy to come in people's lives? Are you convicted on one of those? Take time to search your life? Renounce any ritual that you participated and ask for forgiveness.*

---

9 Johnson, Bill, The Presence Every Day: 365 Days to Unveiling Heaven's Agenda to Your Life, Destiny Image Publishers Inc. February 16 Reading
10 de Silva, Dawna, Prayers, Declarations and Strategies for Shifting Atmosphere: 90 Days to Victorious Spiritual Warfare, p. 36

~ CHAPTER 22 ~

SPIRITUAL WARFARE

From the movie "War Room," we first see a busy couple: The husband is starting to be attracted to another lady. Affection between the husband and wife is reducing. Then, the threat of divorce came. This was how the enemy–the spirit of darkness works. Satan comes to steal, to kill, and to destroy. He steals affection, controlling them with irritation or anger even in small things like blaming and fear. Then Satan stole their marriage. It's not only that, as a result the victims of became so depressed that life was destroyed either by suicide or insanity. They were not able to fulfil the destiny God planned for each of them. Satan had stolen and obstructed their destiny.

I learned that there is a spirit of darkness called a "controlling spirit" that is assigned to every couple to destroy their marriages. But there is a solution, the "War Room." It is a place to battle the enemy–through reigning with Christ in the heavenlies. We the children of God are raised with Christ and seated with Him in the heavenlies. Sitting with Him in the heavenlies is reigning with Him over the ungodly elements, over the diabolical kingdom. It is sitting with authority and identifying with Him or letting the Spirit of God control you and not identifying with the enemy, not letting them control your emotion with negative feelings like fear or anger.

The War Room story ended with an old woman, a child of God, introducing the wife to God and His great love. She told her about the "war room" where she battles with the enemy. So, the wife made her own war room and started battling the enemy who is trying to destroy her marriage. So, at the end, in the war room, the enemy is defeated. Affection between the couple was restored and did not end in divorce.

Spiritual Conflict is a reality. The kingdom of light is fighting the kingdom of darkness. The kingdom of light is the kingdom of God, the Divine. The kingdom of darkness is the kingdom of Satan. It is called the diabolical kingdom. Francis Frangipane wrote, "Some of us may never actually initiate spiritual warfare but all of us must face the fact that the devil has initiated a war against us God has provided victory in this battle, but we need to take possession of God's Word and arm ourselves like mighty warrior carrying the weapons of our warfare that are not carnal but mighty. We should not be ignorant of the enemy; we must keep our eyes focused on God and the truth of the Scripture.

Originally, the purpose of God for humanity is to rule over the earth, over creation–but sin entered when Adam and Eve disobeyed God's command on not to eat the fruit of the tree of the knowledge of good and evil. They gave in to the lies and deception of Satan–the enemy. Man fell and the world became a fallen world. Creation has been affected with pollution; sickness and diseases; natural disasters like earthquakes, floods, tsunami, etc.; poverty; afflicting spirits causing anger, depression, fear, weird thoughts, demonic influence, guilt, condemnation, etc. We cannot avoid this warfare; we are in a battle daily.

How do we deal with the enemy? Will we just allow him to cause havoc?

I heard some revelations on how some military works in some countries. In one of my "study tours" our tour guide told us that a tribe or a country would send one of their children to live in the enemy's tribe or country. They let him live there until he becomes one of them. He is encouraged to excel in military training and be one of the top people until he reached the top position in the military. Then the country would use him to control their military, but instead of defeating his true country, he would make a way to defend them.

Why do we need to know and outsmart the enemy? Why should we know his tactics? We should not underestimate the enemy. He has power too, but of course God is more powerful, and we His children have been given His delegated authority. We have dominion over the enemy, since we received Jesus as our Lord and Saviour that dominion over the earth was restored to us His children. We have the Truth — God's Word is the great weapon against the lies and deception of the enemy. Satan is a liar, a deceiver, but he has no authority or rule over us unless we agree with him. If we agree with his lies and deception—there he can control us. If Adam and Eve did not believe and agree with Satan's lies about eating the fruit of the knowledge of good and evil that will make them like God, then humanity should not have fallen.

Spiritual Warfare is fighting against principalities—through prayer, through reigning with Christ in the heavenlies, through standing on our identity in Him and walking in humility and obedience in the Holy Spirit. We need to remain focused in the Blueprint of God—His Words, like putting in the whole armour of God, walking in holiness and not in sin.

We need to know our enemy and what are his tactics to be able to shoot them. Our enemy is Satan and his fallen angels (spirits of darkness). Remember, he was not created as Satan, he was created as Lucifer, one of the archangels but he rebelled against God by exalting himself above God, so he was thrown into the pit and his name was changed to Satan. Satan is the perversion of Lucifer, the angel that carried light. Satan is powerful but God is all powerful. Satan is limited but God has no limit. God's dominion is over all. He is sovereign.

I was first taught in Spiritual Warfare, through the Intercessors International in one of their seminars on Prayer in Texas. It was there that I learned more on prayer, hearing from God and spiritual warfare. Who is our enemy? Satan leads the kingdom of darkness, the diabolical kingdom. He is the accuser of the brethren, the father of lies, tempter, deceiver, angel of darkness, the dragon, the serpent, the infidel, the destroyer, premature killer, avenger, ruler of demons, evil one, god of this troubled world, prince of the bottomless pit. What are Satan's tactics and how does his kingdom work??

- *Makes people ignorant of who he is and his tactics*
- *Promotes lies and deception*
- *Brings guilt, fear, tells you that you are blaming him for people's sin or tell you that you are not supposed to talk about him.*
- *Blames men and circumstances*
- *Lays claim to the principalities*
- *Causes depression*
- *Reminds of guilt, stimulates your obsessions*
- *Deepens Loneliness*

- *Heightens Fear*
- *Makes Discouragement worse*
- *Stimulates Negative talking, bad words, gossip*
- *Increases Temptation—lust of the flesh, lust of the eyes and pride of life*
- *Accusation causes bad feelings, telling you are nothing and useless.*

How

- *He uses one's mind and raises doubts*
- *Creates fear*
- *Use one's words to speak negative words (life and death are in the power of tongue- Proverbs 18:21).*

Our strategy must be to fight him in the spiritual realm because they are spirits that belong to the small kingdom of darkness. We should not be afraid or be intimidated. We should fight offensively.

- *We use the authority of Jesus*
- *Be sensitive to attacks like accidents and sickness.*
- *We need to recognize the place of battle in us: our spirit, soul and body.*

Man is spirit, soul and body. Satan hits these 3 areas. Sometimes he hits the spirit with doubt; other times he hits the body with sickness or disease or accident; most of the times he hits the mind with fear, confusion, anxiety, lies and mental torments. The devil's primary attack is over our mind, to raise questions, to influence you to doubt the Bible and God's faithfulness and promises. We need to recognize the voice, we need to differentiate if it is a voice from God, from the enemy or from ourselves.

Spiritual things must be spiritually discerned—not figured out by human reasoning (1 Corinthians 2:14-16.) If Satan can control you, you will not grow to maturity and enjoy life to the fullest. As the movie "War Room" suggests, we need to take our part actively as army of God. We need to fight the enemy daily in the war room. We are not fighting only for ourselves, or for our loved ones and others, but mainly for the will of God to be done, and for His kingdom to come because the enemy opposes the kingdom of God. He opposes God's good plans and blessings in our lives. He opposes the agenda of God. Spiritual warfare is not just taking over the enemy. It is reigning with Christ in the heavenlies, Spiritual warfare most of all is discovering God's sovereignty, supremacy, power, and the majesty of the Lord Jesus Christ. <u>He reigns.</u>

Every kingdom has an arsenal. The kingdom of God has an arsenal where we can find spiritual weapons.

THE BELIEVER'S ARSENAL OF SPIRITUAL WEAPONS:

Two Pillars:

1. *Faith and Obedience – pillar of victory*
2. *Prayer and Intercessions – pillar of communication and power*

Weapons of Warfare:

1. *The Name of Jesus – our Authority*
2. *The Blood of Jesus – our Covering*
3. *Agreement – our Bonding*
4. *Binding and Loosing – our Keys (forbidding the enemy and permitting God to work)*
5. *Fasting – our Cutting Edge*
6. *Praise – our Banner (worship, prophetic and scriptural declaration, acts of love and intercession. We need to learn how to "bind and loose."*
7. *The Word and our Testimony – our Foundation*

Names of God – our Covenant
Elohim- God/Father
El Shaddai- Almighty God
El Elyon- God Most High
Adonai- our Ruler
Jehovah Rapha- our Healer
Jehovah Nissi- our Victory
Jehovah M'Kaddesh-our Sanctifier
Jehovah Shalom- our Peace
Jehovah Tsidkenu- our Righteousness
Jehovah Shammah- God who always with us
Jehovah Rohi- God who sees us
Lord over all

King of kings
Lord of lords
Redeemer
Saviour
Everlasting God
Deliverer
Mediator
Quickening Spirit

What is our authority? The Name of Jesus, this is our badge, our uniform. If a traffic policeman cannot control the traffic unless he wears his uniform and badge it is also true with us, without the delegated authority of Jesus, we cannot fully function.

There is power in the **Name of Jesus.** I once heard a testimony of a lady. As she was fitting a dress in the fitting room of a department store, a man rushed into the fitting room pointing a gun toward her. The lady with authority said: "In the Name of Jesus, get behind me Satan." The man was speechless; he turned and left the lady. That is the power of the name of Jesus, even dogs will bow to that name of Jesus as I experienced with the three bulldogs.

The blood of Jesus is very powerful. It is our covering, a wall of protection around us. The blood did not only cover our sins but even to the present the blood is still saving us, protecting us from the evil one, even from deadly pestilence like the Covid-19. We need to learn to pray and plead to the Father for the blood of Jesus to cover us. We need to learn to draw a blood line around us to protect us.

Agreement is important in prayer. Satan can use division to obstruct our prayer and make us ineffective in spiritual warfare. Even intercessors or groups gathered for prayer should be of one accord of good fellowship. Prayers are not effective when there are others who oppose the prayer request. In Spiritual Warfare we all need to be in one accord praying in the will of God.

For example: If you are praying for a sick person, but that sick person doubts that God can heal him, then there is no agreement. The same thing applies when binding an enemy; all should believe and not oppose.

In Spiritual Warfare we need to use the keys of binding and loosing (Matthew 16:19 NIV "I will give you the keys of the kingdom of heaven; whatever you bind on earth will be bound in heaven, and whatever you loose on earth will be loosed in heaven.") Early in my Christian life even as a pastor's wife, I have not really learned to bind the enemy and loose the power of God. But as I went deeper in my relationship with God, I also learned to reign with Christ through binding and loosing. Binding is using the Name of Jesus in the power of the Holy Spirit. For example: "In the Name of Jesus and by the power of the Holy Spirit, I take authority over the blinding spirit, I loose truth to illumine this person. Binding is forbidding the work of the enemy and loosing is permitting the work and power of God."

I have always prayed not to have suicidal thoughts after experiencing an attempted suicide until I learned to reign over the spirit of suicide by binding it. Loosing is also compared to declaration, declaring the Word of the Lord with power. For example, I pray, "In the name of Jesus, I declare victory and deliverance over the enemy today. I am protected; I am covered with the blood of Jesus." Or, "In the name of Jesus, I declare healing in the midst of sickness." Or, "I declare financial breakthrough in the midst of financial bondage." Or, "I declare blessings of God in the midst of curses."

Fasting is one of the spiritual disciplines. (Mark 9:29/Matthew 17:21 – This kind can come out only by prayer and fasting.) Fasting is intentionally denying the flesh in order to gain a response from the spirit. It is renouncing the natural to invoke the supernatural. Fasting is also for intimacy with God--not praise from men. I have observed in the ministry that when I speak or preach, when I spend time in prayer and fasting the anointing of God or the presence of God is manifested.

Praise, prophetic utterance and declaration are also powerful weapons of warfare. Praising God has power. It intimidates the enemy causing them to flee. I heard a testimony of a servant of God while at a camp. As the campers were singing, he saw black spirits surrounding the campers, but as they praised God in songs the black spirits surrounding them were changed to white uniformed spirits. When the Israelites ended their 7 days marching around Jericho to route their enemy, they made music and shouted praises and then the Jericho wall fell with the help of angelic host from heaven. That is what praises do. Hebrews 13:15 - Through Jesus, therefore, let us continually offer to God a sacrifice of praise–the fruit of lips that openly profess his name.

Word of God and Testimony. The Word of God is the truth. We need to put on the belt of truth in spiritual warfare. There are lies of the enemy which will confuse or torment believers. We need to claim the

Word just as Jesus used the Word of God when he was tempted by Satan (Matthew 4:1-11). When our testimony testifies the power of God, the character and beauty, the love of God is glorified, and the enemy is intimidated. Our testimony is like praise—it is very powerful. Our good testimony takes away the legal right of the enemy over us so we can fight in victory. When we respond with the fruit of the Holy Spirit to assault and attack the people used by the enemy to assault or accuse us, they will see God instead in us so they will stop.

Let me cite some examples of Spiritual Warfare: One time, I was in Hawaii and preparing for my message that morning. I saw in the room where I slept a picture of Tiki. Tiki is a Hawaiian character sold for souvenirs to tourists, it is a Polynesian statue or picture representing an ancient Hawaiian deity. So, when I went down, I told my brother, "You should throw that idol even if you are not worshiping it. Having or keeping a symbol of the enemy can be a door to your life for him to enter." After saying that, I sat and worked on the computer. My hands slowly started to shake and then my whole body was shaking that I could not control. I managed to go to the room and called my brother. They put two wool blankets around me, but I was still shaking strongly. So, my brother told my sister to call an ambulance, I said "No, the enemy doesn't want me to preach, let us just pray and bind the enemy." That is what we did, and I stopped shaking, we rushed to the church on time for me to preach with God's power.

A similar thing happened one time in Toronto. After being involved at the Annual MoveIn International Conference with Joy, I prepared myself for a preaching assignment in one of the churches there. Just after the conference, I felt ill. I prayed that the next day, a Saturday, I would feel better, but I felt more ill. Again, I prayed and expected to get better the next day, which was Sunday—but I felt worse. I was so weak and dizzy that it was hard for me to stand. My host, Ate Betty told me that we will call the pastor and tell him that I cannot preach. But I believed in the power of God. I said, "I can do it by God's enabling." So, while I groped along the wall to help me walk, I was declaring "God is powerful." When I arrived at the church, Magda, the pastor's wife gave me a glass of water because according to her I was already so pale. I just sat down during the service, but when it was time for me to preach, I stood up, reached the pulpit, and preached with God's anointing. After the preaching, I was okay and was able to eat. The saints were blessed. Praise God, He showed His sovereignty and power.

Nothing is impossible with God. He reigns! Spiritual warfare is discovering God's sovereignty and power, it is reigning with Christ in the heavenlies. In spite of chaos, trials, suffering and pain—God empowers us to live above these.

As I wrote the concluding portion of this chapter, I felt the enemy's attack and interruptions through insomnia, and other illnesses. On July 3, 2020, my husband had had a haemorrhagic stroke (bleeding in the brain).

It was hard as I saw his pain and suffering especially when the doctor said, "If he goes into a coma, we will not resuscitate him anymore, we will just let him go." I cried unto the Lord–He is sovereign, He is all powerful, He is merciful, He is loving and faithful. He knows what He is doing. I hold on to His Words, to His promises. I also had a power encounter with the enemy–accusing me, blaming me like "you should have...so this would not have happened. These are all lies of the enemy, I was so guilty but Praise God for my son who walked with me doing "soul care," the guilt was overcome, and I had peace. After more than a week, the bleeding in my husband's brain stopped, he was stabilized. He was taken out of the ICU Critical Unit later, still suffering, but healing was in progress. For me, it is a joy to have Christ– The Life, in our lives. Jesus is the hope of glory. What a freedom to be free from guilt, and from the lies of the enemy-the accuser. I am blessed with so many promises of God particularly Jeremiah 33:6-26

The enemy tried to destroy us, but God worked it out for our good (Romans 8:28). God gave us Jeremiah 33:1-6–using the trial to renovate us instead. Renovation consists of removing stain, rust and parts that are not working then replacing it with new paint and new parts. So, in this trial, He's been using it to release us from pain and hurts in the past from negative emotions like anger or pride. God is using this trial to restore us to a better Joy and Lulu, to strengthen our faith; reconnecting us to people we need to reconnect with and to widen our relationships. Spiritual Warfare is reigning with Christ over negative circumstances of life over the enemy. I see the hand of the Lord answering our prayers for purity to become more effective as His children-giving glory to God the Most High. I see God doing "renovation" of our lives. Renovating a house or something includes removing the dirt, the stains, the rust, the old paint. Since we are human, it takes pain from us as the dirt of our spirit, soul and body (toxins of guilt, frustrations, shortcomings, sins, unhealthy habits like eating unhealthy delicious foods like ice cream, pop, etc.) are being removed. By God's grace we look forward to a new Joy and a new Lulu, better looking in spirit, soul and body and God will be glorified. Joy and us, his family will come out as gold "renovated" in body, soul and spirit. This is life to the fullest.

In closing this chapter on Spiritual Warfare, we need to be reminded that life to the fullest is reigning in spiritual warfare. It is discovering again and again the love of God, approaching to the Father in the name of the Lord Jesus Christ and in the power of the Holy Spirit. We have to have a deep relationship with God. We have to do actions to go deeper in our relationship with Him.

Dawna de Silva wrote in her book Prayers, Declarations and Strategies for Shifting Atmosphere, we have to nourish our spirit. After salvation, we received God's Holy Spirit which means the enslaved spirit we were born with gets switched out with God. Our spirit--people's spiritual bodies get <u>possessed by God</u>.14 The devil cannot win against God's Spirit, so he spends his time attacking our minds and bodies. If he can get us to ignore/malnourish our spirit, it does not matter how "spirit filled" we think we are, life without the Holy Spirit is spiritual death and where spiritual death resides, so does darkness living under the influence of lies (even if one is saved) cripples our ability to live victoriously. A Christian can still be "saved" but living under an oppressed mind-set

Dennis, Lora, Santi, Isa, Zen, Tony, Bishop visiting Joy at the Glenrose Rehabilitation Hospital, September 2020

causes them to be separated from the very Spirit who can pull them out of the harassment.

Feeding our spirit is key to protecting ourselves in times of spiritual battle. If our bodies or minds are weak, the Holy Spirit can make us strong. Nourishing our spirit and staying close to God is key to develop our strength. Praying, studying God's words, fellowshipping with other strong believers and developing our intimacy with God—help in nourishing our spirit.

Remember, we have dominion over the enemy and the Holy Spirit indwells in us. He is our Power. God provided us the weapon of warfare that is mighty and powerful over the strongholds. God is with us.

QUESTIONS TO PONDER

1. *What is spiritual warfare? Whether we believe it or not we have an enemy to fight everyday, we do not need only to to be in the defensive side but but actively involved in the offensive side. How are you dealing with the enemy ?*

2. *As believers we are given dominion (to take control) on earth with God's direction, what is our authority?*

3. *What are the believer's arsenal of spiritual weapons?*

4. *What is the key to protect ourselves in times of spiritual battle?*

---

11 12 de Silva, Dawna Prayers, Declarations and Strategies for Shifting Atmosphere p. 1

10 13 Alves, Elizabeth, The Mighty Warrior: A Guide to Effective Prayer, Canopy Press, 1992, pp. 49-55

11 14 de Silva, Dawna, Prayers, Declarations and Strategies for Shifting Atmosphere. pp. 16-17

~ CHAPTER 23 ~

BREAKTHROUGH

In the winning of a battle, the enemy surrenders and the winning soldiers would cry out hurray, our enemies are defeated. We won. In a battle, we need a breakthrough. In my experience with warfare, I have always observed my God, my Saviour, My Captain to be faithful and in action in fighting for us. How did I ever have breakthrough in my life?

- *If it is not for the mercy of God, I do not know where I would be today.*
- *He is my deliverer, my shield and buckler, my hiding place.*

I am going to write about some things that opened my eyes and gave me breakthroughs.

I have told you earlier that I was full of fears: fear of irritating or making a person upset or angry, fear of making a mistake, fear of the unknown, sickness, evil spirits, fear of flying, and many more. I was always intimidated with people. I felt that I was not liked and rejected. I had low self-esteem that made me suicidal, even when I was already in ministry. But God has always been faithful to intervene. Praise God, He gave me a BREAKTHROUGH from all of these.

I have told you of the surprise scholarship to study. I was so upbeat as I studied His Words. It was so alive. It was amazing to me and quickened me to do action for God.

Studying who God is, His power, His three persons, His great love and faithfulness, His forgiveness and His sovereignty, my identity with Him, His delegated authority, His anointing etc. made me stronger in my faith. That study included also a course on demonology and angels which made me more keen to the spirit world and Spiritual Warfare and Prayer that made me understand the power of God through His Spirit dwelling in His children.

After this study, I experienced the enemy shifting me.

As we prepared for a very big conference, we had setbacks as a family. Sometimes, in the middle of the night I would have a horrible dream, and, in that dream, I am rebuking the enemy. These dreams became a series of dreams that awakened me almost every night, and I would be crying to the Lord. There was one time that three of us in the family were attacked with pain at the same time while we were at different places. When I was attacked with pain, I called Ianne and as we talked, she was suffering from pain too, then Tonyvic called in a few seconds while Ianne and I were talking, he too was in pain. Upon sharing this experience to a prayer partner, she told me that the unseen enemy attacked us as a family. It is difficult to tell all the details here, but God fought for us. We had overcome the attack, and the conference was a success. After the conference the enemy tried to strike back. I was walking down the street with two others. I suddenly felt so down that it brought me into the middle of the street facing a running vehicle. That running car was able to swerve in the other side. Then a big truck followed. I then faced it but then my hands rose up that the driver suddenly stepped on the brakes. I am so short that a truck driver could not see me unless I raised my hands. Just one step, and I should had been hit.

After that incident that could have killed me, I was so ashamed of what

I did. I knew that it was a sin to be suicidal. So, in humility, I asked the Lord's forgiveness and asked why it happened. Then a TRUTH was revealed to me. The Lord told me; "It happened so you will know that evil is real, and you need to fight. SUICIDE is NOT JUST AN EMOTION; it is due to a spirit. It is the same with other negative emotions like anger, fear, depression, feelings of rejection, feelings of hopelessness, guilt etc. They are not just emotions; they are spirits that trigger the feelings. You overcome these feelings by rebuking and binding the spirit that triggers anger, which is spirit of anger or the spirit of fear that triggers you to fear. You do not only pray, "Lord help me not to be afraid." You must also bind the spirit of fear, for you have been given delegated authority as in Jesus' name. You have to bind the spirit of suicide that has been attacking you. The enemy wants to destroy you and your testimony. That was a breakthrough for me in defeating fear, damaging thoughts, etc. These negative spirits are demonic spirits.

I also learned that if there is somebody that I am praying with who has a bad attitude, like she is always angry, I did not only pray that her attitude will change but I also bound the spirit of anger. Then her attitude started to change. I also realized that people were asking for the salvation of their loved ones. For example, they would give a prayer request like; "Please pray that the Lord will save my husband." Why pray like that when Jesus died already for their husband. He is just waiting for them to accept the gift of salvation. I have learned that we need to pray for their salvation but also bind the enemy blinding them, so they are unable to see God's love and salvation. We need to renounce false beliefs, the spirit of unbelief, the foothold or stronghold in their lives, etc. After binding the spirits of darkness, we loose the corresponding virtues such as truth against lies, love against hatred, boldness over the spirit of fear. When we are walking in humility, love and in holiness, God will empower us to walk in victory over the enemy. He gives us discernment.

I remember an incident about thirty years ago, even I was not keen on this stuff. I went to the USA to attend a college graduation with my sister and mom. We are all petite ladies. It was a celebration. On our way home, our relative was sitting in front of me, while my other sister was driving. It was a three-hour drive home. The road was higher than both of the roadsides. Suddenly, after half an hour as we drove on the highway, our relative opened the door. I had to hold his shoulders and shouted, "In the Name of Jesus, you stop." There, he closed the door of the car. After half an hour, he did it again and I did the same. He did the third time and I rebuked him to stop. But on the 4th time, he did, I rebuked him saying; "In the Name of Jesus, you spirit of suicide, get out of him right now." It was the specific spirit that I rebuked and that was the last time he did it. When we arrived home, I thought he was going to hurt me because he came to me in the room, but he knelt before me asking for forgiveness. I had to ask for forgiveness too because I shouted at him, but he told me, "Oh, it is okay, I did a stupid thing, I needed your rebuke. It was when I rebuke the spirit of suicide that our relative returned to his right mind. Our relative at that time was taking anti-depressant medicine to calm him.

Many intellectual people would reason out that an emotion or attitude is not spirit inflicted, but we need to remember that the enemy is a liar, a deceiver too, he can stir one's emotion then hide in it. The enemy hid in the serpent when he went to tempt Eve. The spirit of betrayal hid in Judas Iscariot when he betrayed Jesus.

I am thankful for the breakthroughs. I am not intimidated anymore or afraid or suicidal.

We can declare:

By faith, I use spiritual weapons. I put on the whole armour of God. I am strong in the Lord.

Through my God, I am more than a conqueror through Christ.

I am anointed.

In the name of Jesus, I vigorously oppose, resist and arrest powers, principalities, spirits of darkness and spiritual wickedness in high places and forbid them to operate against me and my family. I declare you defeated and destroyed.

No weapon formed against me shall rise.

I am an over comer.

Father, I plead for the blood of Jesus, Your Son, our Redeemer to cover me and my family. I draw a blood line around us. I confess that we are delivered from deadly pestilence like Covid-19. I have a breakthrough today.

QUESTIONS TO PONDER

1. *God's revealing to me after my last suicidal attempt " that suicide is not just an emotion but a spirit of darkness or a demon called spirit of suicide that triggers one to be suicidal " was my breakthrough over being suicidal, over my negative emotions and over my response to fear, anger, lies, deception, difficult people etc . It opened more my knowledge on the spiritual realm, about spiritual warfare and reigning with Jesus in the heavenlies. This brought renewal to my mind that brought me to a recognition that we are God's workmanship to bring the negative atmosphere to a positive atmosphere. What does Ephesians 6:10 - 18 says?*

2. *Instead of partnering with negative influences, we need to partner with the Holy Spirit by letting Him control us and not allowing the spirits of darkness to control our emotions . How? Give an example of what I shared.*

3. *Bind any spirit that you know has been controlling you like suicide or fear or anger and loose the spirit of sound mind, spirit of boldness and spirit of love.*

4. *Thank God for His protection and deliverance.*

CHAPTER 24

MY IDENTITY

Living in Canada for about 40 years, I have already embraced Canadian Citizenship that made me desire to be a law abiding citizen. So now I am identified with Canada even though I have brown skin with black hair. One that interests me as a Canadian is the Royal Family of the United Kingdom. I like reading about them, especially their ministry in the social and cultural life of The Commonwealth Nations.

Being a Canadian, I found particular interest in following the life and work of the future king of the Commonwealth, Prince William, the Duke of Cambridge, and of his wife, Catherine Middleton, the Duchess of Cambridge. Catherine was born a "commoner," but Prince William was in love with her and in time proposed marriage to Catherine. Catherine responded to that love, and she said "Yes" to Prince William. So, they got married and Catherine ceased to be a commoner, becoming a member of the royal family. She is now identified as royalty even though she is not of royal blood. She belongs to a royalty where people would look up to them. She joined the royalty as representative of the Commonwealth, serving and loving her people. She no longer identifies herself as a commoner, but a princess and one day, if things go as tradition plans, a queen. To be able to act as royalty, Catherine, had undergone trainings and practices.

I see myself like Catherine in her new identity. I am identified as an earthly dweller but when I received Jesus as my Lord and Saviour, I became also a citizen of heaven. My stay here on earth is just temporary, I am here on earth as an ambassador representing heaven–doing the work of a royalty of the highest kingdom, the kingdom of God. Who Am I? I have been born physically through my earthly parents Tony and Fremia Manding and have been born spiritually through receiving Jesus Christ as my Lord and Saviour. With these, I have two identities: My earthly identity here on earth and my heavenly identity. I live in two realms, the earthly realm and the heavenly realm.

Diagram

Heavenly Identity	Earthly Identity
Spiritual Realm	Earthly Realm
Invisible	Visible

I am living and navigating–
In the spiritual realm through my spirit and soul

I am living and navigating–
On earth through my body and soul

Earthly Identity

I am a sister of 6 living siblings. I am a Filipino Canadian living in Canada. I was a student and a nurse, a pastor's wife and a missionary.

Heavenly Identity

When I accepted Jesus as my Saviour and Lord–I became a child of God. Like Kate, I am no longer just a commoner on earth but now I belong to the highest kingdom—the Kingdom of God-the Maker of heaven and earth, the Almighty God who has no beginning and end, the Eternal God, the loving God, the Great I Am. I am a child of God. I belong to the royal kingdom of Heaven since God is the creator, the Sovereign Ruler of the highest kingdom—the heavenly kingdom, I am identified with Him. I am positionally related to Him, through accepting Jesus as my Lord and Saviour. The fullness of the Godhead is in Jesus. Since Jesus is the King of kings, I am a royalty, a princess. Having Jesus is having the Triune God– The Father, the Son and the Holy Spirit. I am what the Bible says about me. I am not what people say about me contradicting what the Word of God says. All these are lies. It is the Word of God that is the Truth. I am made righteous by what Jesus did on the cross. His blood washed my sins away. I am no longer guilty; I am a saint not a sinner anymore. I died with Christ and rose up, seated with Him in the heavenly realm. I reign with Him in the heavenlies. I have authority over the spirits of darkness; I am not afraid or intimidated by them. God has delegated His authority to His children. I am a soldier of God, an over-comer.

I am identified with Christ—the King of kings, the Lord of lords. My identity with Christ commissioned me with delegated authority to have <u>dominion</u> here on earth, to subdue the wicked elements. We have dominion. We are reigning with Christ in the heavenlies, over principalities and rulers in the heavenlies. This dominion comes into <u>effect</u> as we walk in trust and obedience to God, walking with His Spirit. Intimacy with God brings <u>power</u> to live to the fullest, power to change the negative atmosphere of darkness, power to shift this negative atmosphere into the positive atmosphere of light, peace joy and order.

Just like me, however, I knew I am identified with Christ, but I was not practicing who I am in Christ. I knew I am a child of God, but I was not practicing who I am. I knew Jesus is the King of kings, He is the Lord—but I was not practicing my royalty. I felt I was nobody. I had low self-esteem. I was not walking as a princess with dignity and confidence. I felt like a loser and not a winner. I was always afraid even of toy snakes, and of people with authority. I always wanted to evaporate; I had suicidal attempts, even as a pastor's wife. I was always intimidated with people, with events in life. When I was intimidated, I would shrink back and be scared to make a move. Sometimes, I just accepted what people said of me before but knowing my identity I need to practice who I am <u>now</u> and not what I was before. I need to live as a saint, to live as an ambassador (a representative of heaven, to live as a princess with honour and authority living in the will of God). If I hear such negative words and it is a lie I'll say, "In the name of Jesus, I refuse that. I know who I am. I am not intimidated anymore. I rebuke you spirit of lies and deception."

I observed that I know my identity in Christ before since I accepted Jesus as my Lord and Saviour, but I did not practice who I am. The child of God must live as a child of the King of kings, walking in holiness and in authority, living life to the fullest, and living with the beauty of God in us in character and in power. Knowing our identity in Christ is not only mind-knowing—it is acting on who I am in Christ.

The Word of God says that I am no longer a sinner but a saint, so I should walk in holiness, that is how a saint lives, no longer walking as a sinner. The Word of God says He restored me back His delegated authority or dominion over the earth so I should walk as an active army of God—changing the negative atmosphere or the difficult world by declaring the Word of God, His victory over them, His reign, His kingdom. I should not walk as a loser but as a winner, as a victor over the trials and tragedy of life in this troubled world I need to bloom in the place where God planted me, whatever the difficulties are. I need to shine. I remember how I carried myself before, I would walk with my head bowing down so one person would tell his friend, "Here comes the woman with her head going first then her feet"—meaning with my head bowed down so the head was more forward than the feet. I was walking with low self-esteem, intimidated, without confidence. Now, thank God, I have been learning to walk as royalty, as an ambassador of heaven with confidence and authority from God. I am not intimidated anymore. I speak when I need to speak. I know and practice my identity in Jesus Christ.

Sometimes in ignorance, the children of God tends to identify more with their earthly identity. They forgot their heavenly identity. All of humanity's earthly identity will be gone but the heavenly identity of the children of God will be with them forever. Their spirits will be in heaven with God the Creator, the only God. All other gods are idols. I have learned that when a person is born again (meaning one has repented for their sins and accepted Jesus Christ as their Lord and Saviour) the first thing to change is their spirit. Their "old person" dies, and they are reborn of the Spirit of God. They now live in two realms—earthly and heavenly realm. They now have two identities, not only earthly identity but also a heavenly identity.

As I've written earlier in this chapter, the new identity must also learn to navigate in the spiritual realm. A person's new identity is a heavenly identity. This person navigates in the spiritual realm by spending time in the Word of God.

As a person grows in the word and by faith, the spirit begins to mature. This I have been experiencing since I received the Lord Jesus Christ into my life.

Our spiritual relationship with God will grow in proportion to our faith.

The new quality that permeates us is our new nature and identity. We have a new spirit. Then our soul changes by the renewing of our mind brought by the Word of God. I have also written in an earlier chapter that people are a spirit with a soul and a body. The soul is made up of the <u>mind, emotion</u> and <u>will</u>. What the mind dictates, emotion will follow–that results in the action of the will either negatively or positively. Without changing our will and emotions we will not be able to get our flesh under control. The more we transform our nature, the closer we become to the identity of Christ. To live in our heavenly identity, we need to put on the "new man" meaning to live in our new identity and put off the "old man" (the old nature which desires things that are not of God like: worldliness, hatred, anger, greed, fear, bitterness, worry and a lot more.) To live in our heavenly identity, we must give God full reign as we are the dwelling place of the Holy Spirit. We must go deeper in our relationship with God so that we can walk in agreement with Him.

The "old man' is dead at the cross and was buried with Christ. Therefore, we must completely disassociate ourselves from him. By receiving Jesus, we are seated with Him in heavenly places. We have a delegated authority from Christ. He is in us, the hope of glory. Our delegated authority is the badge of our office and the Holy Spirit moving is the power behind the authority. We as children of God are ambassadors of Christ (II Corinthians 5:20) and we come in the power and authority of the kingdom we represent. We must walk and talk in line with the Word of God to enforce that authority.

We have a delegated authority. To delegate means to commit and entrust as an agent. We are God's agents commissioned to carry out his mission on earth. To be effective in this dominion which God had delegated to us, we must avoid distractions of the enemy because distraction can cause our priorities to end up casualties. Satan, our enemy has lots of strategies to distract us. The major areas of distractions the enemy uses are food and drinks, entertainment, weariness and negative emotions like fear, discouragement, oppression, pride, anger and unforgiveness. These distractions can steal our time and priorities and can get us out from under the grace of God and His protection. Once out from the covering of the Word one cannot effectively operate in our God given delegated authority. <u>The keys to power and authority are prayer, the Word of God and walking in trust and obedience.</u>

By having a full revelation of who we are in Christ and what He has done for us, we can deal with the enemy every time from a position of authority and with power. God's ultimate desire is to completely reign in us– spirit, soul and body. God cannot fully inhabit our minds unless they are completely renewed. We must implant the nature of Christ by completely transforming our mind through the Word of God. Our thought life is the key to our destiny. We need to yield to God and His Word. The decision we made must be in line with the responsibility and revelations according to the Word of God. We must know our identity in Christ and live with it – meaning practice it. The Word of God says I am loved–so I need to believe and act on it. The Word of God says I am empowered to be His child– so I must live like a royalty, a winner not a loser, with confidence in my heavenly Father and not be intimidated by the enemy.

Who are we?

We are the children of God.

We need to declare and confess that we are His children.

We walk by the Word of righteousness because His Word is in our mouths and in our hearts.

We can declare and confess that we rule and reign in life as the righteousness of God in Christ. We can confess that the Father of glory grants us spirit of wisdom and revelation of insight into mysteries and secrets in the deep and intimate knowledge of Him by having the eyes of our hearts flooded with light. We declare that we are seated in heavenly places with Christ far above all demonic forces.

Our significance is God–not because of what we can do, but because of what He did and deposited in us—the Holy Spirit. We should not focus on our own significance; it will only lead to discouragement and limitation.

Our validation only comes through Jesus Christ.

Declaration:

I know who I am in Christ. I am what the Word of God says.

I will never waver; I know the Word of God and have the Holy Spirit who leads me in the will of God by leading me to the Word of God.

I know my rights and privileges, I lay claim to them.

I resist the devil. I stop the thief!

I bind the spirit of darkness and I loose the power of God.

I am an undertaker; I will rule and reign in life.

I will take charge of my life by allowing the will of God.

What I believe I will undertake until heaven's best is living in me.

I will do what Jesus wants me to do.

I will say what Jesus wants me to say.
When people see me, they will see Jesus in me.
Thank you, God, for giving me heaven's best.
I am identified with Jesus Christ.
I am empowered as His child.
I've been born in the spirit.
I am bought with the blood of Jesus.
The Spirit of God lives in me therefore, I have the mind of Christ and Wisdom of God lives in me by the Holy Spirit.
I have God-given abilities to be in agreement with God's vision to prosper and succeed in life
God's destiny for me will be fulfilled.
I have made a decision to be educated and trained by God's Word; to think His thoughts, to speak His words and to walk in His path.
I believe that He will be exalted and glorified in my life.

What I hear about me that is contrary to the Word of God are lies. Anything that is not in line with the Word of God is a lie or deception. The enemy is an accuser, and he can use the mouths of others and my own mouth to accuse me. I will not give in to his lies. The truth is the Word of God. I will declare God's Word and not the word of the enemy. I am identified with Jesus. I belong to the kingdom of God. I am a citizen of heaven– that is my eternal place.

I see more of God's power working on the events surrounding me than the circumstances. When negative circumstances come, I go to Him and entrust the circumstances to Him. Then I will have His peace. God indwells me and I am hosting Him with love and desperation for Him to be glorified. I will always identify with Christ, and not with the enemy.

We as children of God need to understand our identity as children of God, as "new creation." We need to know answers to questions like:

1. What is our heavenly perspective? How do we see our stand in God? (Ephesians 4:22-23) We are "new men" and so we need to put off the "old men" and put on the "new men." The old man is dead with Christ and buried with Christ and now we are new and raised with Christ in heaven. What are the realities that we should know as new men?

2. If we are more of a citizen of heaven, then how do we draw from our heavenly account? Invest in heaven–Build your faith. If we do not know faith, we have nothing to deposit and so we have nothing to

withdraw. (Matthew 6:33-But seek first his kingdom and his righteousness and all these things will be given to you as well.) If we do not have faith in the present, we do not have hope in the future. Faith comes by hearing the Word of God.

3. What is our heavenly identity, our dominion or delegated authority? We children of God are commissioned to change the negative atmosphere on earth caused by rulers and principalities in the heavenlies- the spirits of darkness. We learn to bind the enemy and to loose what is needed. We are encouraged to declare and decree the Word of God; to confess the will of God. We should not partner with the spirits of darkness. We need to bless instead of curse (speaking negatively of people and others). We are ambassadors of Christ, so we need to displace all negative mindsets such as pride with humility; fear with boldness; hatred with love; sickness with health; hopelessness with hope.

I believe that God has a purpose in my life, so He changed my identity. From the pit of darkness, He brought me into the Light to be identified with Him the highest authority whose dominion is overall the earth and heaven. I feel like Queen Esther who was an ordinary Jewish girl mentored by Mordecai. From a village girl, she won the heart of the king. Before she was selected to be the next queen, she did not know the protocol of royalty like table manners, always smiling, using the appropriate clothes and accessories or jewellery. She did detoxification and then anointing with oil and fragrance. She was then favoured and became Queen Esther of Babylon even though she was not originally of that kingdom. She became an authority. Wow, what a new identification! Just like Esther I embraced my new identity, a princess of the highest kingdom. I am enjoying my relationship with God, reigning with Jesus in the heavenlies. I am enjoying a quality of life even in the midst of problems on earth, like the pandemic, economic problems, chaos, and others. Like me, God also wants you to be identified with Him, to be royalty. Taste and see what is to be identified with Him.

In conclusion, knowing our identity, we always need to remember that we are identified with God our creator, the Almighty God. Nothing is impossible with Him. This identity is coupled with dominion/authority. We are commissioned to rule—Genesis 1:27; Matthew 28:18-20. But this dominion comes with power through the Holy Spirit when we have intimacy with God and when we trust and obey Him.

QUESTIONS TO PONDER

1. *If you had received Jesus as your Lord and Saviour, then you are His child (John 1:12) you are identified with Him. You have earthly identity and heavenly identity, do you recognize it? Are you practicing as a royalty of heaven or still living the way you live in the past, more of a commoner here on earth, a loser and not a winner over circumstances of life and over the enemy?*

2. *To be effective in the authority that God entrusted to us we must avoid distractions of the enemy, because these distractions (mainly food and drinks, entertainment, weariness and negative emotions) can steal our time our priorities and can get us from under the grace of God and His protection. What are the keys to power and authority?*

3. *Declaring who Jesus Christ in our lives and who we are in Christ is very helpful in practicing our royal identity, do this as you finish this chapter and daily. Declare in your life: pp182-183.*

4. *Are there priorities in your life that need to be in place?*

~ CHAPTER 25 ~

ENJOYING THE POSITIVES (+) AND DEALING WITH THE NEGATIVES (-) OF LIFE

Positive is symbolized by plus (+) sign while negative is symbolized by minus sign (-) sign. When I am enjoying the positives, I am gaining more of the good things in life. But if I do not deal the negatives of life, I am losing some of the positives of life. If I do not deal the negatives, the positives in my life are subtracted.

What are the negatives of life and positives of life?

Negatives of life are suffering, troubles, difficulties, sickness and illness, tragedy, negative emotions like ill feelings, anger and bitterness, loneliness, fear, depression, low self-esteem, self-pity, anxiety and worry, feelings of rejection or not being liked, emptiness, feelings of not having enough, frustration, pride and arrogance; bad attitudes like laziness, procrastination, complaining and grumbling, being judgemental and gossipy, self-righteousness, presumptuousness, condemning, being critical, disobedience etc.; wanting for more (greediness), materialism or worldliness, addictions, any problem (physically emotionally, mentally, spiritually, relationally, or educationally), and problems with others and the events surrounding us.

Positives of life are our basic needs including: food, shelter, good relationships (spouse and family, friends), benefits, health, triumph and victory, fulfilment, finances, immaterial needs (joy, peace, love, patience, kindness, goodness, humility, etc.), strength and power to live, a good job, good surroundings, provisions, education, money, gifts, and many others.

I am in my golden years as I write this book. For more than 50 years of life, there were negatives of life that I have learned to deal with; otherwise, I should have been dead a long time ago. First is negative emotion. I was afraid of many things like an angry person, whether my mom or dad or my teacher or anybody who is angry.

When I saw an angry person before, I would get nervous. One time, in my elementary school time, I just told my teacher that the spelling on the blackboard was wrong. He got angry with me, and I trembled till my extremities became stiff. They had to bring me to the health teacher who massaged my stiff extremities. I suffered with this emotional problem of fear for a long time in my life. It was only when I had a breakthrough (you read this on my chapter of Breakthrough) that I had victory over it.

Fear of an angry person multiplied to many negative thoughts that led me to negative feelings like "Oh, I am not loved, or I am dumb, I made a mistake again." Such thoughts led me to be nervous and have self-pity and self-deprecation and then I became suicidal. I would then look for a room all by myself, and cry to the Lord, my Saviour. In the midst of anguish, God comes so lovingly that He would open my spiritual senses to feel His love and I would be comforted and that makes me smile again. If I failed to go to the Lord, there was no relief.

I remember I failed to go to the Lord about three times and that resulted to an attempt of suicide. But praise God! He saved me from destruction and premature death. The last suicidal act was the time that He taught me how to successfully overcome fear and negative emotions including being suicidal. It was in this last suicidal incident that God opened my eyes. "Being suicidal is not only a negative emotion, but also a spirit of suicide" The moment you become suicidal, you need to recognize it and rebuke it in the name of Jesus. "In the Name of Jesus, I take authority over the spirit of suicide. Be destroyed by the power of God." It was this time that I remembered an incident that I rebuked a relative who tried to get out from our car running on the highway. I rebuked him saying, "In the name of Jesus, you stop." He did this three times and I rebuked him three times. On the fourth time he did it, I rebuked him saying this; "In the name of Jesus, you spirit of suicide, get out of him right now." That was the last time he did it. He came back to his right mind and asked forgiveness for being stupid. That was how he described himself—stupid.

Negative emotions like anger, fear, wrath, and depression, are caused by oppressing or tormenting spirits. There are such spirits called spirit of anger or spirit of fear. The moment they come to us we need to rebuke and bind them. Do not just pray that God will take away your fear. You need to rebuke the spirit of fear, do not allow that spirit to control you. This is how I am overcoming negative emotions. If they come, I even say, "I am not intimidated, get away from me." Deal with every negative thing by the power of God in you. What is God telling you with your problem? Go to Him through His words and through prayers. Ask him what to do and He will instruct you. Do not let negative things be left undealt with, deal with it; otherwise, they will control you and make you miserable.

Remember your identity. Always identify with God, always partner with the Holy Spirit. Do not identify with the spirit of darkness if you see fear coming—do not partner with the spirit of fear by becoming afraid. You should rebuke it and confess "I am not partnering with you spirit of fear, I am not intimidated, I am partnering with the Holy Spirit." I have always experienced the goodness of God in all the problems I have encountered in life. You have witnessed that through the chapters of this book.

Now what do we do with the positives of life?

Let us remember John 10:10. The enemy comes to steal our positives, so we have to be on guard. We need to learn to enjoy the positives of life like relationships. If we give little attention and take them for granted, soon, they will be stolen from us by the enemy. This is how affection in marriages are stolen especially these days. Even no-fault divorce is already allowed.

Nobody is perfect. We need to learn how to maintain balance. Balance in relationship should be dealt with forgiveness and love. Balance in our material and financial blessings should be dealt with wisdom— the ability to distinguish needs and wants; to distinguish enough and not enough; the ability to share what we have and the ability to invest in the life of others not only ourselves.

Joy and I are not wealthy, but God has always provided our needs and we learn to live in what we have.

When a situation comes like somebody needs help, we are always open to share our resources and our time whether it is out of our way or not. Here are some examples. One time we were awakened by a distressed wife at 4am. So, we called one of our church leaders to come and babysit our kids and went to that distressed wife. There is joy in helping even if it takes your time and sleep sometimes. One church member needed a plane ticket to take her exam in Toronto from Edmonton, again we got her a ticket by donating some of our air miles points. One was hungry, we took him for a meal and gave him groceries. We do not have a big vegetable garden, but we share some of our produce from the garden.

When we are invited for an occasion like birthdays or weddings, we make sure we have a gift to the celebrant. In ministry functions like conferences, we share our resources. These are all investing in heaven, and we have the joy and willingness to do it. God sees what we do, and He surprises us with rewards in gifts like: people putting us into a hotel for our wedding anniversary, letting us stay in their homes when we are away from home, giving us a free meal or surprise cash. I remember a saying which says: "The loneliest man is one who lives for himself alone and one who is not generous.

I know a couple of our friends: Mike and Nen, when coming to Canada donated their house and lot in the Philippines for a congregation to meet. That house became a church. They prayed too that in Canada they would have a house with a large room for worship service. They were not working at that time, but God miraculously worked on their approval to get their dream house to accommodate worship service on Sundays. As I wrote this chapter, Mike and Nen have owned several houses in Canada, helped each of their three children with their families to have their own homes, as well as a rental home too. They are a great help to us at this difficult time in our lives when Joy was in the hospital and afterwards. They are always ready to help, even though they are busy they make a way to help. The same is true with Richard and Cecille, Rhajan and Lydia, Lota, Helen and others.

The Balonas in Japan also exemplify a very generous devoted family. They are tent makers. Their home is open to missionaries like me, to students at the Christian school, new immigrants, Bible Studies, etc. Food is so expensive in Japan, but they love sharing their home without fee. In return, God blessed them with good and smart kids and God miraculously provided scholarships for them in the U.S.A.

What about talents and spiritual gifts? Use talents, abilities and spiritual gifts for the glory of God. I have been told that one of my gifts is teaching or speaking. When God gives me opportunities, I always say "Yes," even if I have been given short notice. I even knock on doors for opportunities to speak, to teach, to preach, etc. We enjoy our neighbours. When we got back to our own house that was not sold, oh our neighbours were happy to have us back. We communicated with them and befriended them. We invited them to our home, and they too did the same. While Joy was in the hospital, some of them came to offer help to mow the lawns and gave get well soon cards and flowers.

We have always enjoyed our spiritual family and friends. We are close to them, and they are close to us. We share to them especially our time. They too are big help to us like the Filipino ZAMIE Bible Study group and our Millview church. Our pastors are big encouragement to us.

One of the positives of life that I do not take for granted is my family. On earth my husband will always be the first, then my children and grandchildren.

This is our family acting silly which is something enjoyable. 2012

Enjoying the family includes:

1. *Doing rules and responsibilities*
2. *Blessing the family with edifying communication and worship.*
3. *Developing intimacy and forgiveness (family bonding).*
4. *Always resolving conflict.*
5. *Managing finances.*

For all our supporters, we will always be thankful to God–for all their supports, encouragement and help.

QUESTIONS TO PONDER

1. *What are the positives in life? How should we enjoy them?*
2. *What are the negatives in life? How should we deal with them?*
3. *What particular positives in your life that you are not enjoying?*
4. *What is the Lord telling you? What do you need to declare?*
5. *Are there some particular negatives in your life that need to be dealt with? What is the Lord telling you? What do you need to renounce and repent of?*

~ CHAPTER 26 ~

THE RIVER OF LIFE

Back in my childhood I was afraid of the river. But when I was about 6 years old, my mom, my sisters and I crossed the river on foot, which is near our house. Crossing to the other side of the river, it was my sister Lydia who held my hands, but the current was so strong it got carried me away from her.

From the shallow part I went deeper and deeper until my feet could not reach the bottom anymore. I was forced to learn how to swim to survive. I forced my feet to move so I could go out to the surface to breathe like a dog. I did that until I reached the shallow part again where my mother was already waiting for me. I don't know how I survived. I was not a swimmer at that time. I do not know how long I was in the deep part of the river. Again, I believe there must have been an angel pushing me to the surface of the river in order for me to breathe. This incident encouraged me to learn how to swim until I became a good swimmer. Every day, from the cliff I would dive into the water and enjoy it especially going deep, deeper, deepest to the riverbed and I would find duck eggs which had been laid in the river. There we would cook them for breakfast.

I have learned that unless you know how to swim–you will not be encouraged to go deep down in the river. Unless you go deep you will not enjoy the river fully. This is true in life. Unless you know God person-ally– the producer of life, through Jesus who is the Life, you will not know life in its true sense. Jesus is the living water. The Holy Spirit who is the Spirit of God, He is also called the Spirit of the Father, the Spirit of Jesus—is the River of Life. In the first pages, I wrote that I received Jesus because I did not want to go to hell. I was afraid that God would punish me and judge me and bring me to hell. But after receiving Him, that fear became a godly fear, which is <u>Reverence</u>–Honour and Respect to who He is. Going deeper in my relationship with Him, I began to long for Him, for His presence and I began to be in love with Him.

So having Jesus, the Life–we need to go deeper in our relationship with Him in order to enjoy Him. Enjoying Him is enjoying life to the fullest even in a troubled world where we live. The earth is a <u>war zone</u>, the battlefield between the Kingdom of God and the kingdom of darkness, battle between the divine kingdom and the demonic kingdom. Going deeper in the Holy Spirit enables you to live life to the fullest in the middle of such war.

The enemy comes to kill, steal and destroy our joy, time, blessings, affection, marriages, and success; but Jesus said, "I came to destroy the works of the enemy." When I go deeper in the River of Life, peace that passes understanding comes in the midst of trials, joy comes in the midst of sorrow, hope comes in the midst of impossible situations, courage comes in the midst of fear and boldness comes in the midst of intimidation. *But the fruit of the Holy Spirit is love, joy, peace, forbearance, kindness, goodness, faithfulness, gentleness and self-control (Galatians 5:22-23) comes when the enemy attacks with the acts of the flesh which are: sexual immorality; impurity and debauchery; idolatry and witchcraft; hatred, discord, jealousy, fits of rage, selfish ambition, dissensions, factions and envy; drunkenness, orgies, and the like (Galatians 5:20-21).*

We cannot enjoy life to the fullest unless we go deep in our relationship with God. The ankle-deep relationship should go deeper to knee deep, then to waist deep, to shoulder deep and when we are completely submerged, the Holy Spirit completely reigns. This empowers you to live and enjoy life to the fullest. Intimacy with God is the secret of living life to the fullest. We, who have accepted Jesus as Saviour and Lord, are called to fellowship with

Him (I Corinthians 1:9). God who has called you into fellowship with His Son Jesus Christ as Lord is "faithful." We are called to enjoy His presence, His blessings. He is the River of Life! Let us dive into 'til He completely take control of us. That is living life to the fullest.

QUESTIONS TO PONDER

1. *Jesus is the Living Water, He too, in His Spirit is the River of Life*
2. *Going back to Ezekiel 47:1-12, how should we go deeper to the River of Life*
3. *Meaning - how should we go deeper in our relationship with God?*
4. *What is the key to intimacy with God?*
5. *Practice it daily and your joy will be full.*

~ CHAPTER 27 ~

VERY IMPORTANT

CREATION OF MAN, THE FALL OF MAN AND GOD'S LOVE

I have learned that there are four principles we need to know in order to understand God's love and salvation. These are three important truths and one important thing to do (based on Campus Crusade for Christ's Knowing God Personally Evangelistic Tract and the Bible):

1.) The truth about God and His love

John 3:16 For God so loved the world that he gave his one and only Son, that whoever believes in him shall not perish but have eternal life.

When God created humanity, He created man in His own image and His likeness. He gave them dominion over the earth and blessed them.

Genesis 1: 26-30

26. *Then God said, "Let us make mankind in our image, in our likeness, so that they may rule over the fish in the sea and the birds in the sky, over the livestock and all the wild animals, and over all the creatures that move along the ground."*

27. *So God created mankind in his own image, in the image of God he created them; male and female he created them.*

28. *God blessed them and said to them, "Be fruitful and increase in number; fill the earth and subdue it. Rule over the fish in the sea and the birds in the sky and over every living creature that moves on the ground."*

29. Then God said, "I give you every seed-bearing plant on the face of the whole earth and every tree that has fruit with seed in it. They will be yours for food.

30. And to all the beasts of the earth and all the birds in the sky and all the creatures that move along the ground – everything that has the breath of life in it – I give every green plant for food." And it was so.

Genesis 2: 7 Then the Lord God formed a man from the dust of the ground and breathed into his nostrils the breath of life, and the man became a living being.

Diagram 1
Man created in the image of God (Genesis 1:26-27) God is a Spirit and so man is a spirit. Man relates to God in his spirit

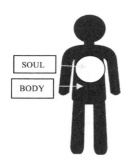

Diagram 2
God made a case for the spirit of man out from the dust of the ground – a body. He made the body and God breathed into man's nostril the breath of life and man became a living being. Man is a spirit with a soul and a body. In other translation "being" is soul.

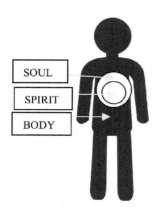

Diagram 3
Man was created in the image and likeness of God. He has the character of God; he has the intellect and will to be able to decide for himself and can relate well with others. The creation responded to their needs. There was harmony of nature, between them and the living animals and there was relationship between the first men, Adam and Eve, with God in their spirit. They saw and had fellowship with God; they saw the glory of God. They did not know evil; all they knew was good. All their needs were met. The trees bore lots of fruits. They did

not have to fertilize the ground – all were in harmony with nature. They were given authority to have dominion or to rule the earth and the living animals (birds, fish, beasts, etc.)

The soul consists of the Mind (thoughts & intellect), the Heart (emotion) and Will (action). The soul shows the likeness of God. It is the PERSONALITY. It shows the character of God like love, kindness, goodness, humility, joy, patience, gentleness and many more.

Man is not a robot. God has given man a <u>will</u> to choose for himself. God will not impose on you. He gives instructions and commands but allows you to decide for yourself on what to do. Will you obey Him or not? It's up to you.

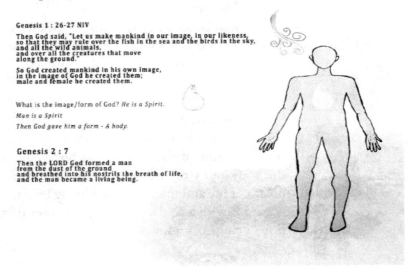

Genesis 1 : 26-27 NIV

Then God said, "Let us make mankind in our image, in our likeness, so that they may rule over the fish in the sea and the birds in the sky, and all the wild animals, and over all the creatures that move along the ground."

So God created mankind in his own image, in the image of God he created them; male and female he created them.

What is the image/form of God? He is a Spirit.

Man is a Spirit

Then God gave him a form - A body.

Genesis 2 : 7

Then the LORD God formed a man from the dust of the ground and breathed into his nostrils the breath of life, and the man became a living being.

(Illustrated by Nikita Sushma)

In the creation God entrusted the earth and the living things to man represented by the first man and woman created on earth–Adam and Eve. They were to rule over all the earth. They began their rule at the Garden of Eden (Genesis 1:26). Through their service, the earth would reflect the glory of God. Since the creation of the world, the almighty power of God has been clearly seen. In Genesis 2:15-17 a command was given to them, to give them opportunity to trust God and obey Him as the bearer of God's image and likeness–but if they disobey Him, they will die and become a broken or polluted image.

What happened next? How come we don't experience that kind of life, that Adam and Eve had in the beginning? Why did life become a struggle, a series of ups and downs, have and have not, frustrations, trials, difficulties, failures, sickness, death, negativity, polluted mind, wickedness, evil, etc. How come the ability to see God's glory was lost?

2.) The second truth we need to know and understand is that man sinned and fell short of the glory of God.

Genesis 2: 15-17

15 The Lord God took the man and put him in the Garden of Eden to work it and take care of it. 16 And the Lord God commanded the man, "You are free to eat from any tree in the garden; 17 but you must not eat from the tree of the knowledge of good and evil, for when you eat from it you will certainly die."

Genesis 3

3. *Now the serpent was more crafty than any of the wild animals the Lord God had made. He said to the woman, "Did God really say, 'You must not eat from any tree in the garden'?"*

4. *The woman said to the serpent, "We may eat fruit from the trees in the garden, 3 but God did say, 'You must not eat fruit from the tree that is in the middle of the garden, and you must not touch it, or you will die.'"*

5. *"You will not certainly die," the serpent said to the woman. 5 "For God knows that when you eat from it your eyes will be opened, and you will be like God, knowing good and evil."*

6. *When the woman saw that the fruit of the tree was good for food and pleasing to the eye, and also desirable for gaining wisdom, she took some and ate it. She also gave some to her husband, who was with her, and he ate it. 7 Then the eyes of both of them were opened, and they realized they were naked; so they sewed fig leaves together and made coverings for themselves.*

7. *Then the man and his wife heard the sound of the Lord God as he was walking in the garden in the cool of the day, and they hid from the Lord God among the trees of the garden. 9 But the Lord God called to the man, "Where are you?"*

8. *He answered, "I heard you in the garden, and I was afraid because I was naked; so I hid."*

9. *And he said, "Who told you that you were naked? Have you eaten from the tree that I commanded you not to eat from?"*

10. *The man said, "The woman you put here with me-she gave me some fruit from the tree, and I ate it."*

11. *Then the Lord God said to the woman, "What is this you have done?" The woman said, "The serpent deceived me, and I ate."*

12. *So the Lord God said to the serpent, "Because you have done this, "Cursed are you above all livestock and all wild animals! You will crawl on your belly and you will eat dust all the days of your life.*

13. *And I will put enmity between you and the woman, and between your offspring and hers; he will crush your head, and you will strike his heel."*

14. *To the woman he said, "I will greatly increase your pains in childbearing; with pain you will give birth to children. Your desire will be for your husband, and he will rule over you."*

15. *To Adam he said, "Because you listened to your wife and ate from the tree about which I commanded you, 'You must not eat of it,' "Cursed is the ground because of you; through painful toll you will eat of it all the days of your life.*

16. *It will produce thorns and thistles for you, and you will eat the plants of the field.*

17. *By the sweat of your brow you will eat your food until you return to the ground, since from it you were taken; for dust you are and to dust you will return."*

18. *Adam named his wife Eve, because she would become the mother of all the living.*

19. *The Lord God made garments of skin for Adam and his wife and clothe them. 22 And the Lord God said, "The man has now become like one of us, knowing good and evil. He must not be allowed to reach out his hand and take also from the tree of life and eat, and live forever." 23 So the Lord God banished him from the Garden of Eden to work the ground from which he had been taken. 24 After he drove the man out, he placed on the east side of the Garden of Eden cherubim and a flaming sword flashing back and forth to guard the way to the tree of life.*

So, the first created man and woman, Adam and Eve, were tempted and deceived by Satan. He told Eve – it's not true that you will die if you eat of the fruit of the tree of knowledge of good and evil, rather your eyes will be opened, and you will be like God. You will know good and evil.

Because they wanted to be like God, knowing good and evil, they succumbed to that temptation and disobeyed God. Soon, their eyes were opened and the ability to see God's glory was lost. Instead, they saw their nakedness, they became malicious, and then hid from God. This is the fall of man. The spirit that God gave them died (separated from God). The human spirit became a vacuum, to which the self is drawn to (self-centeredness). Man became spiritually dead after the fall. They are separated from God; they became living dead. Their eyes were opened, and their minds became polluted resulting to confusion and negative emotions and attitudes. This fall of man is what we call the universal sin.

Believing the lies of the enemy, Adam without recognizing it, succumbed to the enemy and gave the key to rule the earth–that is why in Ephesians 6:10 it says we are not fighting against flesh and blood but with principalities in the heavenlies. It was not God who gave the key, Satan got the key by deception.

Romans 3:23 for all have sinned and fall short of the glory of God

Romans 6:23 For the wages of sin is death, but the gift of God is eternal life in Christ Jesus our Lord.

So, what happened to man?
Diagram 4
Man after the fall

So, what happened to man?

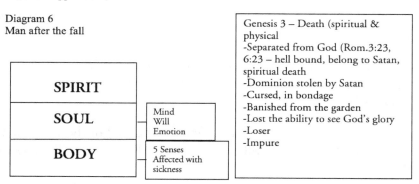

Diagram 6
Man after the fall

Genesis 3 – Death (spiritual & physical
-Separated from God (Rom.3:23, 6:23 – hell bound, belong to Satan, spiritual death
-Dominion stolen by Satan
-Cursed, in bondage
-Banished from the garden
-Lost the ability to see God's glory
-Loser
-Impure

SPIRIT

SOUL — Mind / Will / Emotion

BODY — 5 Senses / Affected with sickness

Because of sin, which is disobedience to God, men were separated from God. Death was the result of sin. The living spirit died but the body remained until physical death comes, and the body returns to the ground. Spiritual death is separation from God. Man lost the ability to see God's glory (Romans 3:23, Romans 6:23) Man's spirit is no longer heaven bound but hell bound. Man lost his dominion over the earth, over the fish, over the animals, and others. It was usurped by Satan through his lies and deception. Adam and Eve gave in to his temptation. By the disobedience of Adam and Eve, they handed to Satan the key to authority that was given to them over the earth. By Satan's lies, Adam and Eve ate the fruit of the knowledge of good and evil that God told them not to eat. They succumbed to the temptation and disobeyed God. Man sinned and fell short of the glory of God. This is the Universal Sin. Because of the fall, man's spirit was separated from God. Man's soul and body became polluted—giving way to suffering, confusion and physical death. He can no longer enjoy God's love and fellowship. Because of the fall, men became hell bound. When men die physically, the body return to dust, but the soul goes to the pit called hell where they will suffer day and night.

The likeness of God in man was corrupted, polluted. Their mind is no longer pure but mixed with impurity (impure thoughts – resulting to negative emotions, negative attitudes, and negative actions). Because of disobedience – man fell, he can no longer enjoy the love of God and His presence. Man, then became in bondage to the enemy, the power of darkness. They no longer belong to God. Men became sinners and he cannot fellowship with the holy God. They have physical life, but they are dead spiritually. This explains the reason why we live in a troubled world.

The third truth is Jesus Christ – He alone can restore us to the Father. He is the only way, only truth and only life. He is the Gift of God the Father to us.

> *Genesis 3:15 And I will put enmity between you and the woman, and between your offspring and hers; He will crush your head, and you will strike his heel."*

This is the first prophecy about Jesus – the seed of the woman. To Satan He said "He (Jesus) will crush your head and you will strike his heel."

This is the victory of Jesus over His crucifixion and death

> *1 Corinthians 15:3-6*
>
> *3 For what I received I passed on to you as of first importance: that Christ died for our sins according to the Scriptures, 4 that he was*

buried, that he was raised on the third day according to the Scriptures, 5 and that he appeared to Peter, and then to the Twelve. 6 After that, he appeared to more than five hundred of the brothers at the same time, most of whom are still living, though some have fallen asleep.

Because of God's love, He sent Jesus His son to become flesh and be sacrificed for us for the remission of our sins. He suffered under Pontius Pilate, was crucified on the cross and His blood poured out. He died, was buried, but on the third day He arose. Jesus had overcome Satan as prophesied in Genesis 3:15. Jesus made the way for our salvation. He is the only way – the GIFT of GOD the FATHER. Without Jesus, there is no salvation. What does it profit a man if he shall gain the whole world but lose his own soul? (Matthew 16:26).

In Eden, man handed the keys of authority over to the devil through sin. At the cross Christ reclaimed those lost keys so He could give them back to man. When man received Jesus as Lord and Saviour this authority is given back to him. [9]

The born-again believer. There is one important thing we need to do.

<u>Individually</u>, we should receive the gift of God the Father, who is Jesus Christ. Salvation is an individual response. If we do not recognize this truth and do not receive Jesus Christ, then we will not have the gift of eternal life.

John 1:12 Yet to all who received him, to those who believed in his name, he gave the right to become children of God

We need to receive Jesus as our Saviour and Lord. We need to believe Him and repent from our sins. Receiving Him as Lord means you let Him reign in your life through obedience. <u>Dethrone yourself in your life and let Christ sit at the throne of your life.</u>

I began that new relationship with Him – through prayer, meditating on his Words, and fellowshipping with other children of God.

Let me cite an example of what happened to a person after he prayed to receive Jesus as Lord and Saviour and repented of his sins. One day, we received a call from a certain British person that we had never met. Chris had been a tourist and one of the countries he included to see

---

9   Johnson, Bill Hosting the Presence Everyday: 365 Days to Unveiling Heaven's Agenda for Your Life, Destiny Image Publishers, Inc., Shippensburg, PA, 2014, Sept. 18 Reading,

Illustration: Receiving Jesus—the Gift of God the Father through prayer

is the Philippines. He is an educated man, a university graduate in the United Kingdom. But he was trying to find the meaning of his life. Joy found out later that Chris is the son of one of the volunteers whom he met in M.V Logos. After the call, Joy went to see Chris and his fellow British tourist, Tony. He treated them for a meal. The next day, we had visitors, Chris and Tony with their backpacks–meaning they want to stay with us.

So, we welcomed them as our guests. We found out that Chris, in spite of being educated in a famous university, was looking <u>for more</u> in his life. At that time, he had long hair. Tony, on the other hand was looking for something to satisfy him, so at that time he was trying Eastern religion. The following morning after breakfast, dad Victor shared to them about Jesus–the Truth, the Way and the Life. The Spirit of God moved in Chris' heart. He responded by praying, receiving Jesus as his Lord and Saviour. After praying he asked permission to make a long-distance call to his mom saying, "Mom, I am here at Joy's house. I just decided to receive Jesus as my Lord and Saviour." He was so happy and so was his mom. His next move was another long-distance call to Australia calling an insurance company. "Hello, I am Chris and from the UK, I have reported that I lost my camera and was claiming some amount. I am very sorry that is not true, I lied. Please forgive me." That was a true transformation!

Chris found life. He was then involved in reaching out to the lost internationally. After his visit he went back to the Philippines to reach out to the Filipinos in gratitude to God and to the Filipinos for it was

Filipinos who reached out to him. As I write this book, he and his family continue to be international leaders reaching out to people who need meaning in their lives, to live to the fullest. For Tony, he continued with his eastern religion, and we have never heard from him since.

I wrote this chapter and entitled it <u>Very Important</u> so we can understand better what life is. <u>What is life to the fullest?</u> What is the key so you can understand better what is going on in you? Do you recognize why you were created? What is the purpose of your life? For those who have life, this chapter is very important so you can share the most important things we need to do. Knowing this will make you better in reaching out to the lost.

QUESTIONS TO PONDER

1. *What are the three important truths that we need to know? How is man created? What are the three components of man? What is the significance of will given to man?*

2. *What happened to man after the fall? What is the effect of the fall?(p. 200)*

3. *What was God's response to the fall of man?*

4. *What should be our response to the three very important truths? Have you made this respond?*

CHAPTER 28

PORTRAITS OF MAN

Man's **Original** IMAGE Created by God

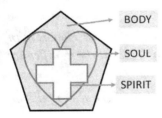

Gen. 1:27 – Created in the image of God.
-Given dominion over the birds, fish, etc.
-Harmonious relationship (see God's glory
-Blessed
-Provided for
-Have fellowship with God
- Only know what is good

Man has **Fallen** into SIN

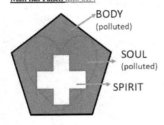

Genesis 3 – Death (spiritual & physical
-Separated from God (Rom.3:23, 6:23 – hell bound,
belong to Satan
-Dominion stolen by Satan
-Cursed
-Banished from the garden
-Lost the ability to see God's glory

Man **Born Again** through Christ

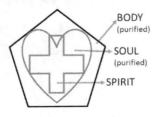

Goal of Evangelism - WIN (The WHY of Reaching
Out)
-Christ came into your life
-Redeemed/Justified
-Becomes a new creation, born in the spirit/spirit being
alive
-Dominion given back to him
-Fellowship with God
-Heaven bound/citizen of heaven
-Eternal life – John 5:24
-Sins forgiven- Gal 1:14
-Blessed, you begin a great adventure for which God
created you

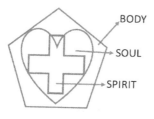

BODY

SOUL

SPIRIT

<u>Goal of Discipleship</u> – BUILD (The WHY of building up)
-Growth in Christ - Maturity
-Over comer, Winner/Success
-Life to the fullest (Abundant)
-Empowered by the Holy Spirit
-Reigning with Christ, Power in ministry
-Intimate with God

SUMMARY:
Subject:

Lessons learned from the Portraits of Man

Man is a spirit with a soul and a body—we call this the trichotomy of man.

Summarizing what I have been learning from the Bible, from different mentors like Neil Anderson (Seven Steps to Freedom), and other great men of faith and experiences:

1. Man is a spirit with a soul encased in a body.

- *Spiritual life (zoa) is the spirit and the soul in union with God.*
- *Physical life (bios) is the soul and the spirit in union with our body.*

2. Significance (purpose)!

- *Gen.1:28 - safety and security*
- *Gen.1:29f - belongingness*
- *Gen. 2:18f - harmony and dominion characterize man before the fall.*

3. The effects of the fall are the following:

- *separation from God (dead spirit)*
- *slavery to sin (sinful nature)*
- *cursed*
- *the image of God in us is marred or polluted*
- *negativism*

- *hell bound*
- *conflict or war within*
- *authority (dominion) lost*
- *rejection—therefore, need to belong*
- *guilt and shame- therefore, need of self-worth*
- *weak and helpless- therefore, need of strength and self-control*
- *lost the ability to see God's glory*
- *lost the ability to see the spiritual realm*

4. Life is recovered in Christ. It is only by accepting Jesus Christ as Saviour and Lord that we have life. Redemption only comes through Jesus by His finished work at Calvary. John 3:16 describes eternal or everlasting life. The redeemed life results in:

- *spirit became alive again*
- *authority was restored*
- *sanctification/transformation through the Word of God*
- *intimacy with God*
- *faith*
- *heaven bound*
- *identified with Christ*
- *the Holy Spirit was given to indwell in us*
- *made right with God*
- *character and beauty of Jesus manifested as we change from glory to glory*
- *We are new creatures. Upon accepting Christ, we become the dwelling place of God (temple of the Holy Spirit who empowers us to live the Christian life- I Cor. 3:16).*
- *Being redeemed is not just getting something; it is being someone. We should live in our identity.*
- *It is not what the Christian does that determines identity. It is who we are in Christ and how we perceive ourselves that determines what we do.*

- *1 Peter 2:9-10 Chosen race, a royal priesthood, holy nation, a people for God's own possession, that we may declare the praises of Him.*

Think of what God has done for you and me.
5. Feed on the Bible/Scripture

- *We have to renew our mind. Romans 12:1-2 by meditating the Word of God and put it to practice (obedience).*

- *Faith becomes the 6th sense. Faith is seeing with spiritual eyes, hearing with spiritual ears, touching with spiritual touch etc.*

- *Words spoken to us, or words spoken by us to others and even to ourselves affect others and us. It is meditated in the mind then to the heart that affects our emotions. It affects our responses or attitudes then our will.*

- *So, when our words are <u>positive</u> it becomes a blessing that brings life— life to our spirit, to our soul and to our body. But if it is <u>negative,</u> it becomes a curse that brings death.*

- *Life and death are in the power of the tongue (Prov. 18.21)*

- *Declare a thing in Christ's Name and it shall be established unto thee (Job 22:28)*

- *Confess the word of God not the word of the enemy. Confess what is positive by faith/confess your faith not your fear. Do not be critical.*

6. Whether we like it or not, we have an enemy that tries to steal, destroy or kill us every day.
Learn to fight the enemy and his strategies. Do not underestimate Satan and his cohorts. Do not believe him, he is a great deceiver and put many lies in our mind.
Guard yourself with the Words of God and prayer. Learn to live in victory over this war by:
Eph. 6:10-18

- *Praise*

- *Prayer*

- *Walking in the Spirit*

- *Spiritual Warfare*

7. Have a life of TRUST & OBEDIENCE to God and His Words. Walk with the Holy Spirit every day

- *Aim high to the 4th or the best portrait of man, which is the victorious, intimate life with God giving Him glory. Learn to reign with Jesus Christ.*

QUESTIONS TO PONDER

1. *Which portrait are you?*

2. *If you are not sure if you had received Jesus already would you like to move to portrait #3 by repenting for your sins and accepting Jesus as your Lord and Saviour? Pray the prayer I prayed when I accepted Jesus in chapter 4 or in chapter 30.*

3. *Take note of the summary afterwards, to move to portrait #4.*

~ CHAPTER 29 ~

UNDERSTANDING LIFE TO THE FULLEST

WHAT DOES IT MEAN TO RECEIVE JESUS CHRIST AS OUR SAVIOUR AND LORD? Receiving Jesus Christ as Saviour is putting our faith in Jesus Christ, that He alone is the only way to heaven, no other way, either through religion, or church, or good deeds. Jesus was sent by God to restore man to God. Colossians 1:1920 says: 19 For God was pleased to have all his fullness dwell in him, 20 and through him to reconcile to himself all things, whether things on earth or things in heaven, by making peace through his blood, shed on the cross.

Jesus is God in the flesh. He needed to be incarnated (to become human) so by His life given to us; He became the perfect sacrifice for us to be restored to God. So, believing that He is the ONLY ONE who can save us, I repented of all my sins and accepted Him as my SAVIOUR. Receiving Him as <u>Saviour</u> is not enough, we need to receive Him as <u>Lord of our lives</u>. That means you let Him reign over you. He is God, He is loving and faithful. He knows what is best for us. In one of his messages, Chris Oyakhilome said, "He being the Lord of your life means you exist for Him. He is the one in charge of your life. The good thing about this is— we do not have to worry or be afraid of what He will do because He loves us so much and so He knows what is best for us. The lordship of Jesus Christ is the lordship of love. It means submitting ourselves to the loving power of God. So, when Jesus became the lord of your life, love will dominate your life. There is no selfishness or power struggle. Whatever you need, He will meet that need. He is more concerned for your happiness, peace, joy, your well-being, and all your needs. He knows your future – letting Him be lord of your life brings you to a journey of abundant life, life to the fullest."

My Illustration: Life where the Lord Jesus sits at the throne of Life is symbolized by the heart below:

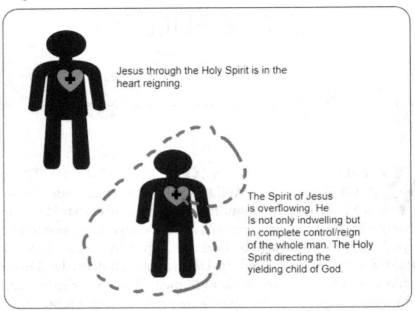

Jesus through the Holy Spirit is in the heart reigning.

The Spirit of Jesus is overflowing. He Is not only indwelling but in complete control/reign of the whole man. The Holy Spirit directing the yielding child of God.

WHAT DOES IT MEAN TO BE BORN AGAIN? When one receives Jesus Christ as Lord and Saviour, a spiritual birth has happened mysteriously. He is born of the Word of God and the Spirit of God. That is how one has the life, nature and character of God in his spirit. It is a completely new life. I did not understand well what this meant until I learned and experienced God through His Spirit and His words. Christianity is God working in man. The divine life of Jesus is imparted to believers. The human becomes his dwelling. You are born again, not in the physical sense, but born again in the spirit.

The dictionary defines Bio as life. All living organisms have life. A living organism has the capacity to grow, metabolize, respond to stimuli and reproduce. So, all humans have life. But what is this LIFE that I am talking about? It is God the Creator who orchestrated and produced life. In reality, because of the fall we became living dead, since we were separated from God. It is only when we received the life who is Jesus that we are restored to God and a new life begins in us. We have Jesus in his Spirit indwelling in us.

What then is ETERNAL LIFE that is found when one accepts JESUS as SAVIOUR and LORD? What does it mean to have ETERNAL LIFE?

Eternal Life: When one accepts Jesus in his life as Saviour and Lord – Jesus in his Spirit begins to dwell in the person. He begins to transform the life of that person as he communes with Him through prayer and His word (the Bible). Jesus is both divine and human. He was born from a woman, conceived by the Holy Spirit. He was sent from above. In Him is the fullness of the Godhead.

Colossians 2:9-10 9 For in Christ all the fullness of the Deity lives in bodily form, 10 and you have been given fullness in Christ, who is the head over every power and authority.

The totality of divinity resides in Jesus Christ, <u>if you look at Jesus, He is a man, but the Bible says that he Himself is God. Fullness here means complete, no lack or shortage.</u>

Eternal life is having Jesus in one's life (I John 5:12; John 5:24). Eternal life is a personal relationship with God. So then being born again is having Jesus in one's life. Having Jesus is having eternal life. Eternal life is not ONLY after physical death. It is not only going to heaven after death. It begins when one receives Jesus as Lord and Saviour. Eternal life then is a quality of life. This is the God type of life, the Holy Spirit is with man. It is the character of God found in people who have Jesus reigning in their lives—victorious, a triumphant overcomer, with power from God, at peace even in the midst of adversities, compassionate, an encourager, with wisdom, having joy, patient, a doer of good things not bad things. There is love in the midst of hatred, joy in the midst of problems, provision in the midst of economic upheaval, forgiveness in the midst of people hurting you. Eternal life is freedom, freedom over the influence of the negatives of life. Eternal life, then, is the life Jesus spoke of in John 10:10 CEB "The thief enters only to steal, kill, and destroy. I came so that they could have life — indeed, so that they could live life to the fullest."

Eternal life is living to the fullest. This is life abundant. It is freedom from bondage of the enemy, victory over the negativity of life. It is having Jesus in my life. I'm living in His reign. He is all my sufficiency. Abundant life is having everything I need materially (clothing, food, etc.) and immaterially (love, joy, peace, patience, gentleness, humility, wisdom, and victory over trials). It is becoming a winner and not a loser. It is a life with Jesus in control, meeting all my needs and empowering me to live a victorious and joyful life, despite any problem here on earth. It is being blessed and becoming a blessing to others. It is a Christ-centred life over self-centeredness. It is being divinely devoted. It is enjoying life with God as your everything, your peace, your joy, your fulfilment.

> *Note: Once we accept Jesus as our Lord and Saviour, we begin an adventure of eternal life. The more we become intimate with Christ we experience more and more life to the fullest. This does not come automatically. Just as we learn to navigate in the physical realm like learning how to smile, to eat, to walk, to speak, to read — we need to learn to navigate also in the spiritual realm like renewing our mind through the Scriptures, learning how to pray, learning to soak in his presence, learning to do warfare in the spirit world to overcome them, etc. You will understand more of this as you read my story.*

The born-again believer lives in two realms — the earthly realm and the spirit realm. The born-again believer does not only live by sight using his physical senses, but he also lives in the spirit realm by using and training his spiritual senses through faith. The born-again believer has gained another sense added to his 5 senses. The 6th sense is FAITH, which is seeing with spiritual eyes, hearing with spiritual ears, touching with spiritual touch, smelling and tasting spiritually.

Man is a spirit with a soul encased in a body

I Thessalonians 5:23 May God Himself, the God of peace, sanctify you through and through. May your whole spirit, soul and body be kept blameless at the coming of our Lord Jesus Christ.

After receiving Jesus as Lord and Saviour, as a spiritual baby we need to grow. We pass through the process of growth and development like a physical baby. We need to eat our spiritual food daily, which is the Word of God, the Bible. We need to communicate with God in prayer. We need to grow with our spiritual family, which is our local church and the whole family of God around the world. Wow, being a traveller internationally, I always enjoy being with the family of God wherever I am. I learned that a child of God has two families—my earthly family and my spiritual family.

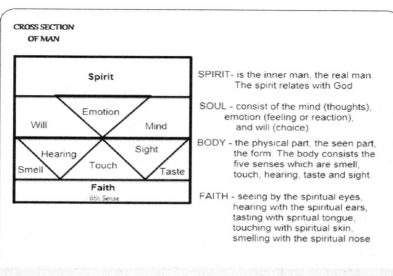

CROSS SECTION
OF MAN

Spirit

Emotion

Will

Mind

Hearing

Sight

Smell

Touch

Taste

Faith
6th Sense

SPIRIT - is the inner man, the real man. The spirit relates with God

SOUL - consist of the mind (thoughts), emotion (feeling or reaction), and will (choice)

BODY - the physical part, the seen part, the form. The body consists the five senses which are smell, touch, hearing, taste and sight.

FAITH - seeing by the spiritual eyes, hearing with the spiritual ears, tasting with spriritual tongue, touching with spiritual skin, smelling with the spiritual nose

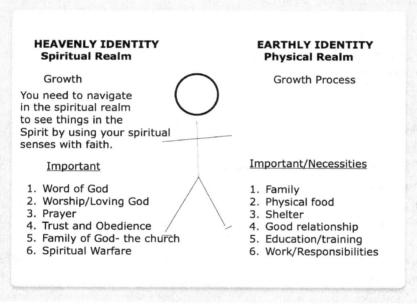

HEAVENLY IDENTITY
Spiritual Realm

Growth

You need to navigate in the spiritual realm to see things in the Spirit by using your spiritual senses with faith.

Important

1. Word of God
2. Worship/Loving God
3. Prayer
4. Trust and Obedience
5. Family of God- the church
6. Spiritual Warfare

EARTHLY IDENTITY
Physical Realm

Growth Process

Important/Necessities

1. Family
2. Physical food
3. Shelter
4. Good relationship
5. Education/training
6. Work/Responsibilities

To grow in the spirit, I learned the need to eat the food of the spirit, which is the Word of God. I learned that I need also to become a good student of the Word of God – not only as a reader or listener but a DOER of the Word and SPEAKER of the Word (to confess, speak and declare). In obedience I started reading the Bible daily. It became a part of my daily routine. I find the word of God so stimulating like watching something and I find it so irresistible to continue watching. Not only that, but my knowledge of God also increased, and I began to see and understand things in the spiritual realm by faith.

Faith is <u>believing God and acting upon His Words</u>. His Words became an instruction to me. The Bible became a "Blue Book" of instructions to me. Like anything that we use, when we buy something there is an instruction from the manufacturer on how to use it. This is also true with us, since God is our Creator and our Maker, there is an instruction book for us, which is the Bible, to guide us how to live the life He gave us. For example, even in the midst of trials God would instruct me through His Words on what to do. Faith is a gift from God (Ephesians 2:8) "However, when our minds are renewed and transformed by the presence of God operating in us, we start to understand how the unseen operates. Faith sees and responds to unseen realities. Faith doesn't come from the mind, it comes from the heart, yet a renewed mind enhances our faith through an understanding of the unseen. Faith actually has a transformative impact to our thinking if we allow it to. What God deposited into our hearts in our salvation remains there but continues to change every area of our lives—particularly the way we think. When the faith that God deposited into my heart began to shape my <u>thought life</u>—this is a sign that my mind is being renewed. "Walking by faith and not by sight is the believer's lifestyle."10 The belief in one's heart is released by faith through the Word. Faith grows as we continue to read, hear and obey.

I was born again not from the womb of my mother but from above. I was born in the Spirit. As a babe in Christ, I was so hungry for food from heaven which is the Word of God. I began to navigate in the spiritual realm by studying the Bible, meditating on it day and night. Joshua 1:8 says *"Do not let this Book of the Law depart from your mouth; meditate on it day and night, so that you may be careful to do everything written in it. Then you will be prosperous and successful."* I began talking to God like a baby who began a relationship with his mother. I sought for God, my Father. Through His Words, I learned more about Him. There is only ONE GOD in Three Persons – the Father (Jehovah), the Son (Jesus Christ), and the Holy Spirit. The Trinity is a mystery. If you have Jesus–you have the Spirit of the Father, the Spirit of Jesus, that is the Holy Spirit. Through the Bible my knowledge of Him increased.

---

10   Johnson, Bill Hosting the Presence Everyday: 365 Days to Unveiling Heaven's Agenda for Your Life, Destiny Image Publishers, Inc., Shippensburg, PA, 2014, January 10 Reading

Then I started experiencing Him, communing with Him, spirit to spirit. I began to understand more who He is; how He loves us so much, His purpose for us, etc. We became to be so close; He became so close to me like a daddy and friend, in fact closer than my biological father and closer than my best friend.

Who is this God that I accepted? What does it mean to be personally related to Him? He is not just a God up there, but He is also my heavenly Father, my Lord, my Saviour, my Helper, my friend, my everything. Isaiah 9:6 says *"For to us a child is born, to us a son is given, and the government will be on his shoulders. And he will be called Wonderful Counsellor, Mighty God, Everlasting Father, Prince of Peace."* Just like other relationships I want to know Him, to enjoy His presence even if I don't see Him with my physical eyes. My prayer has always been this: "I want to know You more God – not just seeing You by faith, but also by experiencing Your touch, Your visitation, Your manifest presence."

Some believe in many gods – we call that polytheistic (meaning many gods). While others believe in only one God – we call this monotheistic. A few people believe that there is no God. We call them atheists. They believe that the world came out of nothing. But how can nothing produce something? In math 0+0 = 0; 0x0 = 0. I needed to know what to believe. Did you ever try to seek the truth about God? Many people believe in a god, but they have not known God personally, and so this results in many beliefs and confusion. We do not only need to learn about God, but we need to experience and have encounters with Him. Or you may know about God, but you do not know Him personally. Most of us know about President Biden of the USA or President Duterte of the Philippines but we don't know them personally.

For me, growing up, I knew about God, the Creator of life, and I feared Him, but things became different when I accepted Jesus our Lord as Saviour of my life. I began to relate to Him personally as my heavenly dad, who answers my prayers. I also know Him as a helper, comforter, guide, healer, the One who gives me peace, and everything. God became real to me. In my sadness–He gives me joy, in my confusion–He directs me, in my trouble–He gives me peace, in my temptation–He empowers me to fight, in my battle–He gives me victory, etc.

Genesis 1:1 In the beginning God created the heavens and the earth.

Genesis 1: 26 Then God said, "Let us make mankind in our image, in our likeness, so that they may rule over the fish in the sea and the birds in the sky, over the livestock and all the wild animals, and over all the creatures that move along the ground." 27 So God created mankind in his own image, in the image of God he created them; male and female he created them.

Mark 12:29 – the Lord our God, the Lord is one.

Luke 1:37- For nothing is impossible with God.

Revelation 4:8- Holy, holy, holy is the Lord God Almighty, who was, and is, and is to come.

Revelation 7:17- For the Lamb at the centre of the throne will be their shepherd; he will lead them to springs of living water, and God will wipe away every tear from their eyes.

Revelation 19:6- Hallelujah! For our Lord God Almighty reigns.

From Genesis to Revelation the Bible talks about God. The Bible begins with God creating the world, humanity and other living creatures. The Bible ends with God still reigning. He is the first, the beginning. Nobody comes first before Him or after Him. God is eternal. He does not end. He is unchangeable, infinite, all powerful, all present, all knowing.

GOD is the Creator. He created us. He created the heavens and the earth. He created the stars, the sun and the moon. He holds all things together; He holds the planets and the stars in their orbits just as He holds all our body cells together. If He is The Creator, then He is the most powerful one. Nobody is above Him, nobody created Him so, why should I believe in the creations of God as gods. Is creation greater than the Creator?

He is ONE GOD in three persons: God the Father, God the Son and God the Holy Spirit. The Triune God was involved in the creation. The Triune God is a mystery. As children of God, we are related to Him as our Father, to Him as our Lord and Saviour and to Him our Counsellor and Teacher.

GOD THE FATHER His name is Eternal Father, the Almighty God, the Great I AM, El Elyon, The Great Jehovah and many more. God the Father is my heavenly Daddy. His love is so great that He sent Himself (through His Son the Lord Jesus Christ) to redeem us. He is the Only One God the Creator. **Isaiah 42:5** "This is what God the Lord says–the Creator of the heaven, who stretches them out, who spreads out the earth with all that springs from it, who gives breath to its people, and life to those who walk on it; **Isaiah 44:24** "This is what the Lord says–your Redeemer, who formed you in the womb; I am the Lord, the Maker of all things, who stretches out the heavens, who spreads out the earth by myself"; **Isaiah 45:18** For this is what the Lord says–he who created the heaven, he is God; he who fashioned and made the earth, he founded it; he did not create it to be empty, but formed it to be inhabited–he says; "I am the Lord, and there is no other." See other verses in the other chapters.

JESUS is the second person of the Triune God- **Isaiah 9:6** For to us a child is born, to us a son is given, and the government will be on his shoulders. And he will be called Wonderful Counsellor, Mighty God, Everlasting Father,

Prince of Peace.); John 1:1 In the beginning was the Word, and Word was with God, and the Word was God. **John 1:14** The Word became flesh and made his dwelling among us. We have seen his glory, the glory of the one and only Son, who came from the Father, full of grace and truth.; **Colossians 1:15-20** 15 The Son is the image of the invisible God, the firstborn over all creation. 16 For in him all things were created: things in heaven and on earth, visible and invisible, whether thrones or powers or rulers or authorities; all things have been created through him and for him. 17 He is before all things, and in him all things hold together. 18 And he is the head of the body, the church; he is the beginning and the firstborn from among the dead, so that in everything he might have the supremacy. 19 For God was pleased to have all his fullness dwell in him, 20 and through him to reconcile to himself all things, whether things on earth or things in heaven, by making peace through his blood, shed on the cross.

The **HOLY SPIRIT** is the third person of the Triune God—He is the Spirit of God the Father, the Spirit of Jesus. **Acts 1:4** On one occasion, while he was eating with them, he gave them this command: "Do not leave Jerusalem, but wait for the gift my Father promised, which you have heard me speak about. **Acts 1:8** But you will receive power when the Holy Spirit comes on you; and you will be my witnesses in Jerusalem, and in all Judea and Samaria, and to the ends of the earth." The Presence of God is the Person of the Holy Spirit. The Presence is actually the Person of God, the Holy Spirit.

God the Father, God the Son, and God the Holy Spirit are One. This is the mission of the Holy Spirit within the Christian—to represent Jesus accurately in both words and actions that bring great glory to the Father in heaven.11

QUESTIONS TO PONDER

1. *What does it means to receive Jesus as your personal Saviour and Lord?*
2. *What is eternal life? What does it means to be born again?*
3. *What is the physical realm and the spiritual realm?*
4. *What is your action point in this chapter? What God is telling you?*

---

11   Ibid, January 4 reading

~ CHAPTER 30 ~
EMBRACING THE TRUTH

The following recounts a dream I had one night, while I was writing this book.

It was in a rural place somewhat dark, but I could see my way. I went somewhere. Going back, I was lost. I tried to find my way. I saw some ladies and I asked them the way going back to where I came from. They were not sure, but they pointed the way that they know. I went to the direction they pointed. I found two ways; one is a hilly place and I found it difficult to go up. The other way is a way that is in a lower plane but rugged; this is the road I took. As I journeyed through it, I saw mud and dirty stuff, so I was careful not to step on those things. Walking through the back of a house passing through the garbage, oh, it was smelly, I saw faeces, decays and other trash. As I walked through them, I was declaring: "In the Name of Jesus, I take dominion over this filth, over the spirits of uncleanness, over the spirit of distractions." and by God's grace I walked through it. Then a lady came out of the house who repeated my declaration, and she was happy to see me, she smiled and waved her hand to me."

Waking up in real life trying to remember the dream; I asked the Lord, what does this dream mean Lord? The Lord reminded me of the journey we have as we live here on earth. Because of the fall of man when Adam and Eve disobeyed God by eating the fruit of knowledge of good and evil, humanity was not only polluted; but also, the world we live in. It is full of troubles. Because humanity has known evil also, the evil deeds will also harm our surroundings making the journey difficult. The dominion God had given to man, was given to Satan by Adam when

Satan lied and deceived Adam and Eve, telling them that if they eat the fruit of the knowledge of good and evil, they will be like God. Their disobedience affected all creation. People were separated from God.

But because God love us so much, He made a way for us to go back to Him by sending Jesus—the Life, the Way and the Truth, to become a sacrifice for us, to carry our sins to the grave. As He walked through Calvary, He suffered humiliation, was bruised for our iniquities—the dirt and ugliness of sins. Yet He arose again, and He ascended to heaven at the right hand of the Father. It is finished; He won over the enemy, giving a way for us to become New Creatures, empowered by His Spirit. Christ is enough. There is power in His sufferings. There is power on the Cross. There is power from the Resurrection. There is power because of His wounds; there is power in His wounded body and in His blood.

JESUS CHRIST IS ENOUGH for all our needs. He is enough for us to enable us to journey over the difficulties of life. He is the POWER through his Spirit in us to bloom in a difficult world, in a troubled world. It is through Jesus' sacrifice that we got back the dominion over the enemy Satan and His cohorts, the principalities here on earth. We who have received Jesus as our Lord and Saviour, have been given back the dominion over the enemy.

This is my testimony: I have been journeying through rugged difficult roads with filth but through the Power of God, His Spirit dwelling in me and containing me like the River of Life; I am blooming. You have read my journey. I have received and embraced the Truth who is Jesus Christ and He set me free: free from greed of wanting more of this world, free from gluttony, from addiction, free from materialism, free from wanting more power, free from the struggle to be loved, free from feelings of rejection, free from looking for love. JESUS is ENOUGH for me. He makes me live to the fullest not lacking even in the midst of uncertainties like now with the Covid-19 pandemic. If the enemy comes to obstruct God's blessings or provision, He empower me to shift the situation, to fight the enemy offensively—that is the power of spiritual warfare. We as children of God are given the dominion over the enemy. You already read of some of our encounters with a God as a family and for me personally.

My sister Lydia was the last one of my siblings to come to know Jesus personally. She was so religious. She was so active in the church; so, with what she knew, she thought that she was going to heaven. So even though I tried to tell her that she needs to know God personally and accept the Truth, she did not bother to do it. But when I left, she herself read the Bible and she found these words in John 8:31b-32. (NIV) *To the Jews who have believed Him, Jesus said, "If you hold to my teaching you are really my disciples. Then you will know the truth, and the truth will SET YOU FREE."* God in His Spirit reached to her heart. That was the time she prayed to receive Jesus as her Saviour and Lord. Today she is walking with the Holy Spirit and one of the pastors of her local church.

Tessie my best friend, prayed to receive Jesus as her Saviour and Lord before we graduated from our course, Bachelor of Science in Nursing. After passing the government exam to become registered nurses she was accepted to work in Florida. After a few months, she was promoted to glory, to be with her Saviour. She died in a car accident. I am glad she received eternal life before she died. To be with Jesus should be our desired destiny not the allure of the world we live in. For after all, what does it profit a man if he shall gain the whole world but lose his own soul *(Mark 8:34-38: 34 Then he called the crowd to him along with his disciples and said: "Whoever wants to be my disciple must deny themselves and tape up their cross and follow me. 35 For whoever wants to save their life will lose it, but whoever loses their life for me and for the gospel will save it. 36 What good is it for someone to gain the whole world, yet forfeit his soul? 37Or what can anyone give in exchange for their soul? 38 If anyone is ashamed of me and my words in this adulterous and sinful generation, the Son of Man will be ashamed of them when he comes in his Father's glory with the holy angels.")*

I trust that through my testimonies you will also accept and embrace Jesus the Truth if you have not done it yet. Pray this prayer with sincerity:

"Thank you, God, for your great love. I realize that I need you to walk with me as I journey through life. Please forgive me for all my sins. This moment, I give my life to you. I receive You Jesus as my Lord and Saviour. I give you the throne of my life, please reign in me. In Jesus Name, Amen."

Talk to Him always. Find your siblings in Christ or your Christian family and learn from them. Read His Words and meditate on them daily. And if you have received Him already as your Lord and Saviour, I pray that you will go deeper in your relationship with Him. Embrace His WORDS– They are the Truth. Study the Bible and meditate on it daily. You will be inspired and encouraged. The Words of God are alive. Jesus is the Living Word. Speak His Words to yourself and to others. Make God your priority and grow deeper in your relationship with Him.

QUESTIONS TO PONDER

1. *You are at the end of the book. What is the Truth that you need to embrace?*

Note:
If you have any questions or positive comments, please write me at this address:

Box 42120 RPO Millbourne
Edmonton, AB
T6K 4C4
Canada

~ CHAPTER 31 ~

EXIT DOOR FROM
THIS TROUBLED WORLD

Many long to get out of this troubled world. Suicide is one of the causes of death especially in young people. They struggle. But is this right?

What happens when one dies physically? When one dies, the human spirit exits the home of his spirit and soul i.e., is his body. As it is written "from dust you were formed and to dust you will return." *(Genesis 3:18.)*. Be reminded that physical and spiritual death came as a result of the first men Adam and Eve's disobedience, by eating the prohibited fruit of the tree of knowledge of good and evil. Their sin led humanity to universal sin. All men became sinners and fall short of the glory of God *(Romans 3:23)*. Even the earth we live in was affected. Man became knowledgeable of both good and evil. So, the world we live in became difficult, it became a troubled world.

From the Pilgrims Progress book, written by John Bunyan in 1678, the main character describes his journey from the City of Destruction to the Celestial City. It is an allegory of a journey from Earth, which has lots of troubles to the celestial city symbolizing Heaven. Living on earth has become a struggle to almost everybody, a survival of the fittest. People learned to survive even in hard work, even taking advantage of one another by lying, robbery in different forms as in stealing money, material needs, stealing affection and spouses, and even friends and relationships. Men became greedy and corrupt, politically and even in the religious arena. There is power struggle everywhere. So, we are all affected with this. It suffocates life and there is a longing to be freed from these struggles.

How can one live life to the fullest in this troubled world? How can one live free from fear in the midst of calamity, in the midst of pandemic? Does one have to take his life to end struggles and suffering? NO, for suicide is a work of the enemy. We do not need to partner with the spirit of suicide; we need to rule over it by binding it. Does one have to exit the door now to be freed from these struggles and suffering? I trust that you have found the answers in the pages of this book.

To repeat my point, the body that is made from dust will return to dust when death comes. My body is not the real me. The real me is my spirit. Physical death is needed to exit this troubled world.

BUT WAIT, when we consider the exit from life, we should know that there is a judgment for all.

Physical death is not the end of life. (Revelation 20:7-14 says: *7 And when the thousand years are expired, Satan shall loosed out of his prison, 8 And shall go out to deceive the nations which are in the four quarters of the earth, Gog and Magog, to gather them together to battle; the number of whom is as the sand of the sea. 9 And they went up on the breadth of the earth, and compassed the camp of the saints about, and the beloved city: and fire came down from God out of heaven, and devoured them. 10 And the devil that deceived them was cast into the lake of fire and brimstone, where the beast and the false prophet are, and shall be tormented day and night for ever and ever. 11 And I saw a great white throne, and him that sat on it, from whose face the earth and the heaven fled away; and there was found no place for them. 12 And I saw the dead, small and great, stand before God; and the books were opened: and another book was opened, which is the book of life: and the dead were judged out of those things which were written in the books, according to their works. 13 And the sea gave up the dead which were in it; and death and hell delivered up the dead which were in them: and they were judged every man according to their works. 14 And death and hell were cast into the lake of fire. This is the second death.*)

So, exiting from this troubled world is the beginning of unending life, either an eternal life with Jesus or an unending suffering in the lake of fire and destruction with Satan. Because I have accepted Jesus as my Lord and Saviour, the real me which is my spirit will join my Creator in the beautiful celestial city of God when I exit this troubled world; whereas those who do not have the Son Jesus will perish to the worst City of Destruction called Hell with Satan and all the powers of darkness.

Why am I ending this book with this chapter? This book doesn't only show how to live life to the fullest in this troubled world but tells how to exit this troubled world to a peaceful place of glorious joyful life without end. Recently, my beloved sister in the Lord, Moneta, exited this troubled world after a battle with sickness. We celebrated her life yesterday. It was a God honouring service. Moneta had lived life to the fullest. She was always laughing and smiling. Many had come to know the Life through her. She was an urban missionary spending every Monday night knocking at doors in the neighbourhood of Edmonton introducing Jesus. She had joined many mission teams to different countries like Taiwan, Japan, Belize and the Philippines. She was always bold to talk about Jesus even in her workplace. Now she is promoted to glory—with Jesus the Life. I miss her but one day I will see her again in the Peaceful City of God. I mourned for her going away but rejoicing because she is now happy, no more tears, no more sickness in heaven. Jesus the Life is there. Moneta prepared for her exit; she got her reservation in the Celestial City. By faith she gave her life to Jesus. She believed in the True Almighty God, the Ruler of Heaven and Earth.

On earth there are lots of temptations to overcome, hurts and pain to endure, doubts, anxieties and fears to triumph over, spirits of darkness to fight and to defeat. BUT God offers strength and help. Because of the effect of sin, particularly to humans, God made a way to redeem humanity, to bring peace on earth and goodwill to men. God had to come down on earth incarnated or become flesh that is Jesus. Jesus is the Answer to this troubled world, He is the answer to the bad will of men. *Luke 2:14- Glory to God in the highest, Peace on earth and Good Will to men.* This is the reason why we have Christmas. Jesus had to be born and suffer for us to bring Peace and Good Will to men. As God needed to be incarnated, people need to be born in the Spirit to become a new creation, to become a child of God. This can only be done, by accepting the Life, the Truth, and the Way, who is Jesus Christ.

Living to the fullest does not only begin when one accepts Jesus Christ

as his Lord and Saviour but continues even when he exits in this troubled world. He is an alien in this world, he is just a passer-by or what the Bible calls an Ambassador for Jesus Christ. We who received Jesus are representing Heaven, promoting it to everyone so they too will enjoy the Creator in His heavenly Kingdom! We have to tell everyone of God's love wanting everyone to have eternal life and enjoy life in the celestial city. When we, the children of God, exit from this troubled world, our true self which is our spirit will join our Maker in the Celestial City of Heaven where there is no more crying or pain (*Revelation 21:1-4*). Many who have had a near death experience saw a vision of heaven and testify that heaven is so beautiful that you cannot compare it to anything. It is Wow! Wow! Wow!—the Paradise of paradise with celestial beings like angels and beautiful people of

God. Before my mom died, God showed me a colourful awesome vision of heaven with my mom worshiping God. This vision comforted me so much in the death of my mom as she had received Jesus many years before she died. A Korean husband testified that when he was in a near death experience, he went to heaven and saw his wife no longer with infirmities but was so beautiful.

I am still in the City of Destruction—the Earth, much more these days as the Covid-19 pandemic continues to infect and affected the lives of millions. To many this is scary and worse than a world war with bombs and guns. I believe these days are the "last days" which the Bible tells of. Matthew 24:4-14 says: *Jesus answered: "Watch out that no one deceives you. 5 For many will come in my name, claiming, `I am the Messiah, ` and will deceive many. 6 You will hear of wars and rumours of wars, but see to it that you are not alarmed. Such things must happen, but the end is still to come. 7Nation will rise against nation, and kingdom against kingdom. There will be famines and earthquakes in various places. 8 All these are the beginning of birth pains. 9Then you will be handed over to be persecuted and put to death, and you will be hated by all nations because of me. 10At that time many will turn away from the faith and will betray and hate each other, 11and many false prophets will appear and deceive many people. 12Because of the increase of wickedness, the love of most will grow cold, 13but the one who stands firm to the end will be saved. 14And this gospel of the kingdom will be preached in the whole world as a testimony to all nations, and then the end will come.*

My heart is steadfast with God even in the midst of trials and difficulties. The Spirit of God is empowering me to live life to the fullest. I am still waiting on the Lord to manifest His complete healing of Joy, my husband. The first two months of his hospitalization, he could not even lift his head or turn to the sides, and he also could not swallow. The bleeding in the brain could not be stopped with surgery and medication because of his pre-existing condition. The doctor said, "If he goes into coma that's it, we will not resuscitate him anymore. You can ask now your children and grandchildren to visit and say goodbye." But now praise God, good memory and speech are restored, he can eat solid food now; he can walk with a cane. Soon and very soon, he will be completely restored and recovered.

I do not know about tomorrow, but I know my Saviour, my Jesus, my Life holds tomorrow, my future, my family's future—so we do not have to be afraid. My family and I have experienced Him so many times and He will continue to protect us, to guide us, to provide our needs, to empower us to live life to the fullest here on earth.

Ecclesiastes says, "There is a time to be born and a time to die. Everything is Vanity, what is important is to fear or revere God. Remember God in your youth, before your sense of sight, hearing, tasting, feeling and touch will be lost, before you die. Seek Him while He may be found.

Taste and see that He is good (Psalms 34:8).

Seek first the kingdom of God and all these things (needs and blessings, help etc.) will follow *Matthew 6:33*

Finally, exiting this troubled world does not mean that all will arrive to the Celestial City of God called Heaven. Only those who receive Jesus as their Lord and Saviour will join the Heavenly Father in heaven. They have a reservation in heaven because their names are written in the book of life. Those who did not receive Him and have not put their faith in Him will perish to eternal destruction, the second death, the lake of fire called Hell.

As I journey to Heaven, I can testify that among all the love and relationships I have ever experienced: like the love of my parents and siblings, love of friends, my husband and children and grandchildren, I can never compare the love of God. It is true that as I go deeper in my relationship with Him, I understand more the width, the height and depth of his love completing my joy. Even in the midst of difficulties and trials, I can sing in victory and hope in God, Christ in me, the hope of glory.

Living on earth, the troubled world is very challenging especially these days as the pandemic on corona virus escalates affecting normalcy of life, but God is holding my hands or carrying me through. He will lead me and protect me and my family too because they too had received Jesus as their Saviour and Lord. Surely goodness and mercy shall follow us all the days of our lives. (Psalms 23) My destiny and my family's destiny are in God, His will in our lives is the Celestial City of God. I trust and pray that when we exit the door here on earth it will be a triumphant exit. We will exit with God holding our hands with the brightness of Heaven and shouting with victory.

I trust that as you end this book, at least you have a grasp of what is to be deeply related to the True God, the Almighty God who made heaven and earth.

I want to end this book with an invitation. Would you like to have a reservation in Heaven? Rev. 20 says that only those whose name is written in the Book of Life are those who will be welcomed because their name is written in the Book of Life. If you're not sure if you have received Jesus the Life you better make sure, as our son, Tony, said and what his seven-year-old son Bishop said, "I want to make sure that I have received Jesus as my Saviour and Lord, so I am praying again to give my life to Jesus and accept Him as my Lord and Saviour."

For those children of God that would like to be friendly with Him, get deeper into the River of Life. He will reveal Himself to you in a special way. He will open the eyes of your heart.

Just persevere.

Before you close this book, let me tell you that BOOKS were written to entertain, to inform, to teach, to give wisdom and direction, to clarify etc. This particular book, Life to the Fullest in a Troubled World, was written with excitement because of the opportunity to tell others about God who loves us so much. It is written with compassion and love to all readers that they may know the Life and live life to the fullest, to overcoming troubles here on earth and to be delivered from the eternal suffering of hell. It is important to make a right decision for us to move forward to SUCCESS. Without making right decision, we will stagnate or even move backward. After reading this book, if you have not received the Life who is Jesus, then decide today to believe and accept Him sincerely in prayer so that you will have eternal life. And for those who have received Jesus as Saviour and Lord, decide to seek Him more through prayer and study of His Words, to overcome this troubled world.

Love and Prayer, Lulu

QUESTIONS TO PONDER

1. *Like Domie that I wrote in the first chapter and Moneta in the last chapter, they found life in the Lord Jesus and they exited in this world ready to meet the Saviour in heaven. They found eternal life and now with Jesus. How about you? Are you ready to meet God. How would you answer God if He ask you, Why should I let you in heaven? Are you sure your name is written in the Book of Life because you have received Jesus as your Lord and Saviour?*

2. *Suicide is not a good way to exit this troubled world, because it is a sin to partner with the spirit of suicide, how would you counsel a person who is suicidal?*

3. *What are the things that trouble you today? Give it all to Jesus and live life to the fullest til the plan of God in your life which "is a future and a hope and not to harm you " be fulfilled and then be promoted to glory in heaven.*

Note: My story will be more touching with a vision the Lord showed me while we were student of Canadian Theological Seminary in the early 80s. The vision was of a crazy woman crying and laughing at the same time. I asked Him who the crazy woman was, and He answered: "You are that woman if you had not known me personally and received Me as your Saviour and Lord." His great love and response touched my heart and from that time, I decided to serve Him always.

INTRODUCING THE AUTHOR

"God, please send someone to help the Filipinos
and Japanese nationals find hope in you"

In 2003, I was about ready to leave Japan for the Philippines but my heart was burdened. I saw countless of Japanese nationals who are lost, finding solace in committing suicide. On the other hand, there were plenty of Filipinos working in different sectors of this host country who were seeking comfort in gambling or momentary joy in illicit relationships in exchange for the comfort of their love ones back in the Philippines.

Ate Lulu (as we fondly call her), a petite woman came as a gentle wind. You hardly notice her until you realized the essentiality of her presence. She was introduced as a retreat speaker.

All of us thought she was still jet-lagged from a long trip from Canada but when she prayed and spoke we sensed the Presence of the Almighty God. From then on she would come to Japan with others speaking hope and love.

Following that year, we saw many Filipinos trained in sharing the love of God and transforming of some Japanese spouses and friends. There were also amazing testimonies of how God used her for some of these trainees spiritual gifts came to fore.

Our relationship (I consider her a mentor and a dear friend) continued as we journey together in Japan, in Canada when I was there and in the Philippines when we do training in evangelism and discipleship. She gives new insights and passion to what others consider as so basic training materials. She is passionate about Jesus and it resonates to the people she gets acquainted with. Her prayer life and her dedication to share the Good News and train people for Christ, despite all odds, is undeniable. She is what we call an AAA person (available anytime anywhere) who openly shares her life's struggles and victories by God's grace.

When I prayed back in 2003 to send someone to reach Filipino and nationals, God send Ate Lulu.

Thank God that even with travel restrictions, because of the Covid 19 pandemic, Ate Lulu still get connected with them through ZOOM and Face Time.

I am glad Ate Lulu decided to write this book. For,those of us who already "read" her life. publishing this book, we pray will also be a blessing to you as it has been to us.

Jocelyn Dino, Journalist
Former OMer, FIN trainer and OMF- Philippines Missionary

PageMaster Store
https://pagemasterpublishing.ca/by/lulu-tira

To order more copies of this book, find books by other
Canadian authors, or make inquiries about publishing your
own book, contact PageMaster at:

PageMaster Publication Services Inc.
11340-120 Street, Edmonton, AB T5G 0W5
books@pagemaster.ca
780-425-9303

catalogue and e-commerce store
PageMasterPublishing.ca/Shop

CPSIA information can be obtained
at www.ICGtesting.com
Printed in the USA
BVHW031748110922
646765BV00014B/451